STRIKING A BALANCE

A Primer in Traditional Asian Values

Michael Brannigan

*The Center for the Study of Ethics
La Roche College*

SEVEN BRIDGES PRESS, LLC

CHATHAM HOUSE PUBLISHERS

NEW YORK · LONDON

To my dear brother Tom,
who gently carries out his path
in the spirit of *wu-wei*

Seven Bridges Press, LLC
135 Fifth Avenue
New York, NY 10010

Copyright © 2000 by Seven Bridges Press, LLC

Publisher: Clay Glad
Managing Editor: Katharine Miller
Production Supervisor: Melissa A. Martin
Composition: Linda Pawelchak/Lori Clinton
Cover Design: Inari Information Services
Printing and Binding: Canterbury Press

Library of Congress Cataloging-in-Publication Data

Brannigan, Michael C.
    Striking a balance : a primer in traditional Asian values /
Michael Brannigan.
        p.   cm.
    ISBN 1-889119-05-9
    1. Ethics—Asia. 2. Religious ethics. I. Title.
BJ125.A78B73   2000
170'.95—dc21
                                                    99-11846
                                                      CIP

Manufactured in the United States of America
10 9 8 7 6 5 4 3 2 1

Contents

Preface

The West's former dominance in global affairs is evidenced by those immigrants who came to America and changed their names. There are countless examples, such as Hilda Lee, one of the first Chinese women in California to work on airplanes, and George Shima, a Japanese farmer whose original name was Kinji Ushijima. When my mother changed her name, Misae, to Mary, it was a way to accommodate her Japanese heritage to her new American world. All this reflected Western culture's defining authority.

Now, things have changed. An increasing number of Asians who live in the West are keeping their original names. Witness the changing names of cities: Bombay has been renamed Mumbai; Saigon has become Ho Chi Minh City; Peking is now Beijing. Witness the names of countries: Burma is now Myanmar. Consider Hong Kong's farewell to British rule in 1997 and China's embrace of Macau in 1999. These are clear signs that the once-governing axis of the West is giving ground to Asian autonomy.

As we enter a new millennium, Asia, a conglomerate of more than thirty countries with a combined population of more than half the world's peoples, will no doubt exert a far-reaching influence upon the rest of the planet. This influence will be profound, affecting global security, economy, and politics. Developments, particularly in countries such as China (predicted by many to become the new superpower), Hong Kong, India, Japan, South Korea, Taiwan, the Philippines, Singapore, Thailand, and Malaysia, will send political, cultural, and economic shock waves throughout the world.

Asia's momentous ascendancy has compelled us all the more to engage in global dialogue. More than at any other time in history, Westerners need to make an earnest effort to understand Asian worldviews. We must try on Asian lenses in order to see reality from Asian perspectives. In order to participate in global dialogue, we need to construct secure bridges of cultural awareness, sensitivity, and understanding that run deeper than a merely superficial interest in Asian imports, such as martial arts, Chinese acupuncture, yoga, Japanese acupressure, Tai Chi, and Korean ginseng.

This book offers a prudent set of tools for constructing this bridge to understanding. Its underlying premise is that we in the West have much to learn from Asian values. For instance, Western cultures stress the importance of individual self-determination. Yet, while we cherish personal independence and individual liberties, we can also stand to learn from Asia's emphasis on family, social interdependence, and the priority of communal well-being over individual self-interests. Indeed, at least in the United States, we are desperately in need of a moral awakening. Perhaps a study of values that have been firmly rooted throughout Asian cultures and that have withstood the test of time and history may help to spark this awakening by urging us to reassess our own values and priorities.

v

Against a backdrop of philosophy, religion, literature, and history, this text introduces us to the long-standing ethical teachings espoused by the five major currents of Asian thought: Hinduism, Buddhism, Zen Buddhism, Taoism, and Confucianism. These currents have indelibly shaped every corner of Asian society and culture. Even in the face of Asia's increasing modernization, these ethical teachings continue to hold their ground.

But, one may reasonably ask, *Is* there such a thing as Asian ethics? In Western philosophy, ethics generally refers to the systematic, disciplined analysis of morality. The great Western philosophers, such as Aristotle, Thomas Aquinas, John Stuart Mill, and Immanuel Kant, have approached ethics in this strict, systematic fashion. As such, the discipline of ethics occupies a large room in the house of philosophy. Asian ethics, however, lacks this rigorous approach. For this reason, some Western philosophers may claim that, strictly speaking, there is no Asian ethics.

The author challenges this notion. Though their values are not analyzed in systematic fashion, the major Asian traditions do provide a serious and critical examination of questions such as, What does it mean to be a good person? How can I cultivate good character? What do we mean by "right" and "wrong"? How can we authentically live with others? What constitutes a just society? Though the moral teachings of these great traditions may lack what we consider to be intellectual rigor, they are nevertheless ultimately rigorous in demanding a total commitment to living a lifestyle that cultivates good character. For, according to these Asian traditions, philosophy is not a compartmentalized academic discipline, but a way of living, and thereby it has a naturally close kinship with religion.

This text certainly reveals some significant differences among the five traditions. At the same time, it hopes to show that their moral teachings and values resound in a common rhythm: Living authentically requires living morally, and this, in turn, requires living in balance. We need to strike a balance in the way we live our lives. For Hindus, this means a balance between material security and spiritual realization. This entails, as yoga emphasizes, a poise of knowledge, action, and devotion. For Buddhists, it means pursuing the Middle Path by avoiding the extremes of asceticism and overindulgence, of deficit and excess. The Buddhist emphasis on the interconnectedness of all things especially underscores the need to stay balanced by respecting individuals, all other beings, and nature. Zen Buddhists stress the need to balance awakening to the perfection of each present moment with responsibility for the consequences of our actions. Taoists urge us to maintain an equilibrium between cultivating both heart and mind, as well as between enhancing spontaneity and discipline. Confucians remind us of the need to balance personal integrity with social demands. They also urge us to measure familial responsibilities with social obligations.

All in all, these paths exhort us to strike a balance between who we are and what we do, between self and other, between individual and community. Cultivating this balance constitutes the fundamental cornerstone for moral activity and a just society.

ACKNOWLEDGMENTS

We all face our Everests at some points in our lives. A genuine measure of who we are lies in how we manage to maintain our center in the face of them. I thank those special people who have embodied for me the invaluable lesson of cultivating this balance. As a start, my parents, Misae and Thomas, continue to be special mentors as they have carved out their own loving harmony of their Japanese and Irish heritages. My sisters, Margaret and Marie, and my brother, Tom, have fashioned for themselves an ongoing balance of energy and poise. The biggest burden borne in the course of writing surely belongs to the writer's spouse. Yet my wife, Brooke, still tolerates my obsessions and gives to me her never-ending support as well as enduring patience and love. This must also run in her family. For her parents, Del and Carl, have never ceased to show us their balance of generosity and understanding. And her brother, Ken, who seems especially drawn to matters Asian, manifests a unique balance of creativity and commitment.

I also thank the faculty and staff at La Roche College, who have helped me through their support and counsel. Professor of Literature Janine Bayer painstakingly reviewed the manuscript and offered her sound advice and steadfast encouragement. Other members of the Humanities Division—Professors Pat O'Brien, Carol Moltz, Rita Yeasted, and Michelle Maher—have always shown their faithful support. Special gratitude goes to the library director, Cole Puvogel, and to his competent and superior staff. Laverne Collins and Darlene Veghts were especially helpful in locating critical source material. Many measures of thanks also go to our dedicated secretaries, Ruth Lide and Marcia Geis, for their splendid help with the manuscrpt. As for any errors in the text, I take full responsibility.

Respectful gratitude goes to the project manager, Linda Pawelchak, for her expert and efficient scrutiny of the text. Finally, special thanks go to my publisher, Ted Bolen, and to his colleagues Clay Glad and Clare Williams. They all share a rare and humane vision regarding the value of scholarship, and they have supported the project from start to finish.

Without all this gracious and valuable support, my own trek to the completion of this project would have been much more difficult.

ONE

Hindu Ethics

As pennants curl in the wind, and the sound from horns fills the air, Arjuna is about to lead his four brothers and their armies into the long-awaited battle against the imposing forces of the Kauravas. After suffering a bitter fourteen-year exile, Arjuna and the Pandavas face their opportunity to finally regain their rightful rule of the kingdom. Yet he is suddenly stung with a gut-wrenching realization: The Kauravas are his cousins. And if he fights, all of them—cousins, dear friends, respected elders—will taste death. On the other hand, if he does not fight, he not only shamefully abdicates his duty as a warrior, but he will also fail to rectify the injustices inflicted upon his immediate family. Utterly despondent, his soul agonizes over what he should do. We now read on as he confesses his confusion to his friend and charioteer, Krishna.

FROM THE BHAGAVAD GITA

20–21.   Arjuna, known by the monkey in his banner,   *# Monkey*
       looked upon Dhṛtarāṣṭra's men in battle order
   —Arrows had already begun to fly—
       lifted his bow
And then spoke to Kṛṣṇa:
       "Unshakable One,
Halt my chariot
       between the two armies,

22.   While I survey
       those pugnacious troops arrayed for battle
With whom I am to wage
       this great war.

---

23. Let me look at those who are assembled here
        and who will fight,
    Who are eager to please in battle
        Dhṛtarāṣṭra's perverse son."

24. Kṛṣṇa heeded
        Arjuna's request.
    He halted the superb chariot
        between the two armies,

25. In front of Bhīṣma, Droṇa,
        and all the princes of the earth,
    And said: "See, Son of Pṛthā,
        the assembled Kurus."

26. In that place Arjuna saw
        fathers, grandfathers,
    Mentors, uncles, brothers,
        sons, grandsons, playmates,

27–28. Fathers-in-law, and close friends
        in both armies.
    Seeing all these kinsmen
        in array, the son of Kuntī
    Was overwhelmed by emotion
        and in despair he said:
    "O Kṛṣṇa, when I see my relatives here
        who have come together and want to fight,

29. I feel paralyzed,
        my mouth becomes dry,
    I tremble within,
        my hair stands on end;

30. The bow Gāṇḍīva slips from my hand,
        my skin feels hot,
    I cannot keep steady,
        my mind whirls.

33. These men here drawn up in battle
        giving their lives and possessions
    Are the ones for whose sake we desired
        kingship, pleasures, happiness.

34. Teachers, fathers, sons,
       grandfathers,
    Uncles, fathers-in-law, grandsons,
       brothers-in-law, and other kinsmen—

36. What joy could we have, Stirrer of Men,
       if we should slay Dhṛtarāṣṭra's party?
    The atrocity would pursue us if we killed
       those men who are aiming their bows at us.

37. We do not have the right to slay
       Dhṛtarāṣṭra's men, our own kin.
    For how could we be happy
       after slaying our relatives?

39. Should we not be wise enough
       to turn back from this evil,
    O Stirrer of Men, as we see before us
       the wickedness of annihilating the entire family?

40. With the disruption of the family,
       the eternal family tradition perishes.
    With the collapse of the tradition
       chaos overtakes the whole race.

44. Surely, Janārdana, men
       who overturn the family traditions
    Will end up in hell.
       This is what we have been taught.

46. I would be happier
       if Dhṛtarāṣṭra's men killed me in the battle,
    While I was unarmed
       and offered no resistance.

47. With these words Arjuna sank down on his seat
       in the midst of the battle.
    He had let go of his bow and arrows.
       Sorrow had overwhelmed him.

Relief sculpture of Arjuna and his forces from the Mahabharata. (Corbis)

This is, without reservation, one of the most memorable passages in all of Indian literature. It is the opening scene in the Bhagavad Gita (Song of the Lord), composed around the fifth century B.C.E., and regarded as the most influential work in Hindu thought.[1] The "Lord" refers to Krishna, who, besides being the judicious counsellor for all the Pandavas, is also the god Vishnu in disguise.[2] The Gita is therefore Krishna's response to Arjuna's moral quandary, in which Arjuna faces an excruciatingly painful choice: Should he or should he not fight? And is it all worth it?

What brought Arjuna and the others to this precipice? This whole saga is a small part of the magnificent epic known as the Mahabharata, which centers on the ongoing struggle between two clans, cousins to each other. The sons of the blind King Dhritarashtra, the Kauravas, had unjustly taken over the kingdom that rightfully belonged to the Pandavas. The Pandavas, as a result of a game of dice, are sent into exile. When they return from exile, they muster enough forces together to engage in one bitter battle against their cousins, and they finally take back their kingdom.

Not only is the epic a literary masterpiece, based partly upon historical events, but it also is a perennial source of inspiration and guidance on ethical conduct for Hindus. Its pages are filled with scenes in which the characters face moral predicaments and make ominous choices, some heroic and others more fainthearted. Krishna's response to Arjuna's inner struggle, which we discuss at the conclusion of this chapter, gives us a key to better understanding the meaning of *dharma,* translated as "right conduct," which is the centerpiece of Hindu ethics. However, before we go on to examine certain themes in Hindu ethics, let us briefly survey some moments in the development of Hindu philosophy.

BACKGROUND

Beginnings: The Veda and the Upanishads

A chronicle of Hindu philosophy is difficult to reconstruct for two reasons. First, its earliest teachings were passed down as sacred, authoritative truths, with little concern for who wrote what and when. Second, many of its diverse schools evolved around the same time, so that their interrelationship and influence are especially intricate. Nevertheless, after the northern tribe of Aryans overcame the indigenous Dravidian culture between 1700 and 1500 B.C.E., the seeds of Hindu (and all of Indian) philosophy were sown in the earliest collection of works, called the Veda (after 1500 B.C.E.).

The Veda was orally transmitted as four groups of works: Rig Veda, Sama Veda, Yajur Veda, and Atharva Veda. Of these, the oldest is the Rig Veda. The bulk of the Rig Veda contains prayers for rituals, sacrifices, and rites of passage, along with hymns to gods such as Indra, the god of thunder, rain, and war, who rules the sky and gives light as well as darkness; or Varuna, who guides the cosmos according to the principle of universal order, or *rita*. Nevertheless, it is the first work to raise deeply metaphysical questions concerning the meaning of reality and the source of all existence.

Later works known as the Upanishads (written from 800 to 300 B.C.E.) are more narrative in form. They number more than a hundred, yet eleven are considered as the most authoritative: the Katha, Isha, Kena, Prasna, Mundaka, Mandukya, Taittiriya, Aitareya, Chandogya, Brihadaranyaka, and Svetasvatara. Here, we touch the philosophical core of Hindu thought. These works attempt to describe the nature of the relationship between our own existence and all of being, not in strict systematic fashion, but in stories and splendid dialogues. The term *upanishad* literally means "sitting down near," so that we get a sense of the personal transmission of special teachings from teacher to student. Let us briefly review these most important teachings, the heart of Hinduism.

First of all, the driving question in all of Hindu thought is, What is our true nature? And its response is *atman. Atman* literally means "breath," so that it is what gives each one of us life; it is our essence. Therefore, *atman* constitutes my true self, my soul. It is eternal and divine. My bodily form is its temporary dwelling, and although my body will die, *atman* will never die.

Next, What is the nature of reality? What is the source of all Being, the principle of all that exists? This is *Brahman,* the absolute reality. The root of *Brahman* is the verb *bhr,* literally meaning "to grow." *Brahman* is, therefore, a fully dynamic principle, the principle of all that comes to be as well as all that goes away. *Brahman* is the unconditional principle of the universe, eternal, and without boundaries.

Given this, what is the relationship between *atman* and *Brahman?* We have so far asserted that whereas *atman* is the individual, personal soul, *Brahman* is the universal soul. But there is more. This leads us to the most penetrating insight in the Upanishads, revealed in the phrase *tat tvam asi* ("that art thou"). Consider the conversation between Uddalaka Aruni and his son Svetaketu in the Chandogya Upanishad in which the father compares our true self, *atman,* to the unseen, dissolved, but still savored salt in a cup of salt water. He instructs Svetaketu:

> "Please take a sip from this end." He [Uddalaka] said, "How is it?" "Salt" [Svetaketu replied] . . . [Uddalaka then says] "Verily indeed, my dear, you do not perceive Pure Being here? Verily, indeed, it is here.
> That which is the subtle essence this whole world has for its self. That is the true. That is the self. That art thou [*tat tvam asi*], Svetaketu."[3]

In this profound passage, "That which is the subtle essence this whole world has for its self" refers not only to *atman* but to the world essence, *Brahman.* In the phrase "that art thou," "that" (*tat*) refers to *Brahman,* while "thou" (*tvam*) refers to *atman.* Therefore, *atman* is in essence identical to *Brahman!* Here we have one of the most astounding teachings in intellectual history. I am, in essence, one with the universal essence, *Brahman.* This is why India is sometimes referred to as "the land of 300 million gods." At our deepest core, we are divine, as we read in the opening chapter of the Brihadaranyaka Upanishad:

> This [self] was indeed *Brahman* in the beginning. It knew itself only as "I am *Brahman.*" Therefore it became all. And whoever among the gods had this enlightenment, also became That [*Brahman*]. It is the same with the seers [rishis], the same with men. The seer Vamadeva, having realized this [self] as That, came to know: "I was Manu and the sun." And to this day, whoever in a like manner knows the self as "I am *Brahman,*" becomes all this [universe].[4]

Yet there is a catch to all of this. Despite our divine natures, we go through our lives oblivious of who we really are. We tend to think of our true self as ego. We thereby mistakenly associate who we are with things like our bodies, status, occupation, and material possessions, all of which have no real bearing on our real self. As to our real nature, we live in a state of ignorance, a condition referred to as *avidya.* Furthermore, we linger on in this condition because we are under the cloud of *illusion,* or *maya.*

And as long as we remain in ignorance, we endure the nearly infinite cycle of birth, death, and rebirth, called *samsara*. This means that because of my ignorance regarding my true self, when I die, I will be reborn—this constitutes my "second" death—in another psychophysical form. In this way, my soul travels through countless transmigrations, being reborn each time, as a human, a higher or lower animal, perhaps even as an insect, stuck in *samsara*, chained to the wheel.

Finally, What is the paramount aim in all Hindu teachings? Our ultimate goal is to realize our true nature, that is, to experience *atman*. This is my lifelong quest in every life I lead—to experience my true self. This experience is genuine enlightenment, called *moksha*, an awakening to my self. *Moksha* is the bliss that transports me beyond the bittersweet pale of birth, death, and rebirth. However, because the clouds of illusion, *maya*, are so powerful, I will most likely endure countless lifetimes before I realize my true self. And when I do, I will also recognize that my true self is one with the universal self, *Brahman*. And then, upon my death, I will be freed from the wheel. These are the core teachings in Hindu philosophy.

Epic Period

The two greatest Indian epic poems, the Mahabharata and the Ramayana, illustrated some of these early teachings in magnificent story form and in a beautifully composed literary style. Whereas the authorship of the Mahabharata is unknown, the Ramayana was composed by Valmiki around the fourth century B.C.E. The Mahabharata was most likely put together from 800 B.C.E. to 200 C.E. These epics contain heroic tales, whose characters encounter those timeless difficulties we all face in our complex human struggle to live moral and meaningful lives. Many of the questions posed in the epics therefore deal with the nature of ethical action, or *dharma*, and we examine some of these in this chapter.

During this same epic period, treatises (*shastras*) on social, moral, and legal issues and rules were also being written. One of the most important was the Manu Shastra (Code of Manu), which had a particularly far-reaching effect upon India's legal system. Also, during this time, certain prominent teachings disputed Hindu orthodoxy and its reliance upon the Vedic literature and the Upanishads. Three of these challenges consequently seized the popular imagination and became more widespread: the materialist school of Carvaka, the teachings of the Buddha, and the Jainist school.

The Carvakan school boldly claimed that the sole reality is matter, and thus it swept away the Hindu belief in a spiritual self as well as the belief in survival after physical death. Moreover, they urged the pursuit of material well-being and pleasure as the all-important goals in life, rather than the Hindu spiritual goal of *moksha*.

Buddhism originated with the teachings of Siddhartha Gautama (c. 6th century B.C.E.), who took issue with the Hindu concept of the individual self, *atman*. In fact, Buddhists went so far as to actually refute the idea of an individual, unique self. Buddhists also rejected the class, or caste, system, which appeared to be reinforced in Hindu teachings. We examine Buddhism more closely in Chapter Two.

Jainism was supposedly founded by Vardhamana (599–527 B.C.E.), who was also called Mahavira. By proposing a doctrine of hylozoism, which teaches of an infinite number of souls, or *jivas,* that need to be released from the burden of matter, Jainists supported a complete renunciation of all material concerns. Furthermore, they adhered to the principle of *ahimsa,* or noninjury, in the most literal sense, applying this to all life forms and through strict ascetic practices.

Sutras and Commentaries

These challenges to Hindu orthodoxy obliged Hindus to eventually furnish a more systematic exposition and defense of their teachings. In the form of discourses called *sutras,* Hindu writings became more philosophical in character. These sutras addressed Hindu teachings from unique perspectives and eventually led to the formation of six philosophical schools, each one based upon a specific set of writings.

The Nyaya school (c. 4th century B.C.E.) focused upon the principles of logical reasoning and argumentation. The school obviously assumed prominence in a time when more and more debates on doctrinal matters arose because of the proliferation of heterodox objections. The founder of the school was Gautama, author of the Nyaya Sutras.

The Vaisheshika school (c. 6th century B.C.E.) attempted to investigate the nature of the cosmos and reached the astonishingly modern conclusion that all of reality consists of unseen, indestructible atoms. This was its own cosmological support for the Upanishadic teaching of *tat tvam asi.* Kanada established the school, based upon his Vaisheshika Sutras.

The Samkhya school (7th century B.C.E.) addressed the process of the evolution of the self and the world and their relationship with each other. Founded by Kapila (c. 7th century B.C.E.), it is based upon the teachings in the Samkhyapravacana Sutra, along with the better known Samkhya Karika (c. 3rd century C.E.), written by the sage Ishvarakrishna.

The Yoga school (2nd century B.C.E.) studied disciplined methods to reach *moksha,* or liberation. *Yoga* refers to a "joining together" of body and mind, and the school was founded by Patanjali, centering on his famous *Yoga Sutra* (c. 2nd century B.C.E.).

The Mimamsa school elaborates further upon those parts of the Vedic literature that deal with ritual, sacrifice, and proper action. Jaimini founded the school, based upon the Purva-Mimamsa Sutra (c. 400 B.C.E.). This school also provides an interesting metaphysical view of *dharma,* moral action.

The most influential school is still the Vedanta system. *Vedanta* literally means "end of the Veda." Therefore the school is a commentary and interpretation of the essential teachings of the Upanishads as well as the Bhagavad Gita.

Vedanta thoroughly explores the meaning of *atman, Brahman,* and their dynamic interrelationship. Founded by Badarayana, its principal text is the revered Brahma Sutra (4th to 2nd centuries B.C.E., also called the Vedanta Sutra).

These sutras led to all sorts of commentaries, interpretations, and exegetical treatises by numerous scholars, of whom the most important were Sankara (788–820 C.E.) and Ramanuja (c. 1017–1137 C.E.). Even though they were both affiliated with the Vedanta school, they opposed one another regarding the nature of the relationship between the world, *atman,* and *Brahman.*

Sankara, often regarded as one of the most important of Hindu philosophers, produced his formulation known as Advaita Vedanta, or nondualism (*advaita* means "nondual"). He taught that since *Brahman* permeates all reality, there is no difference at all between the world and *Brahman.* In fact, the world is a manifestation of *Brahman,* not merely an illusion, as Sankara's predecessor, Gaudapada, contended. In turn, the key phrase in the Upanishads—*tat tvam asi*—asserts the literal identity of *atman* and *Brahman.*

Ramanuja, on the other hand, interpreted the Upanishadic idea as suggesting that although world, self, and *Brahman* are not completely different, they are, nevertheless, in some respects distinct from each other. Because he himself views *Brahman* as a more personal God, as Ishvara, Ramanuja is able to maintain their distinction. In any case, he offers us a more qualified nondualism and also allows for a more devotionalist approach to *Brahman.*

Modern Times

This more devotionalist approach eventually became widespread in India from the 1800s on, when the country felt the increasing presence of Islam and Christianity, accompanied by the diminishing influence of Buddhism. For instance, Gadadhar Chatterji (1834–86), later known as Ramakrishna, stressed the primacy of the Vedanta, while also incorporating elements of Tantra (or esoteric) Buddhism. By viewing meditation as a style of *bhakti,* or devotion, he sought to harmonize *bhakti* with Islamic and Christian teachings. And his disciple Narendranath Datta (1863–1902), better known as Swami Vivekananda, followed this up by accenting the essential oneness of all religions in their quest for the Absolute.

And as the powerful British presence led to its official rule over India in 1858, Hindu social reformers had been justifying their own efforts based upon Hindu teachings. For instance, Ram Mohan Roy (1772–1833) authenticated his Brahmo Samaj ("Divine Society") movement upon fundamental ideas in the Upanishads, whereas another reformer, Dayananda Sarasvati (1824–83), founded the Arya Samaj ("Noble Society"), spirited by the early Vedic hymns.

The name we tend to associate more closely with the end of British rule is Mohandas Karamchand Gandhi (1869–1948), surely a vital force in the drive to restore independence to India, which came about in 1947, the year before his assassination. Gandhi's teachings and lifestyle are integrally Hindu, grounded especially upon the Bhagavad Gita. Yet his global vision enabled him to incorporate ideas from the New Testament and Jainism as well. In fact, his view of *ahimsa,* nonviolence, stems from Jainist beliefs.

Sri Aurobindo Ghose (1872–1950) was another outspoken intellectual and defender of Indian independence from British rule. He was imprisoned for his teachings regarding social reform. After he was released, he set up an ashram in Pondicherry, where he composed his well-known *The Life Divine,* a discussion of the evolution and relationship between spirit and matter.

The philosopher Bhagavan Das (1869–1957) particularly influenced the moral and social climate of contemporary Hindu thought by promoting the traditional view that urges us to pursue four stages in our lives. To conclude our brief summation, let us now review these four stages, or spiritual turning points, in what appears to be a coherent Hindu philosophy of life.

Life's Four Stages

According to Hindu teachings, our journey through life should ideally occur in four distinct stages, called *ashramas* (literally meaning "rest-stops"): student, householder, forest-dweller, and hermit, or *sannyasin.*[5]

The student stage involves disciplined learning, which is not simply book learning, but a spiritual training whereby the student at an early age becomes aware of that intangible though ultimately real world that is deeper than the material and physical. The Hindu poet and 1913 Nobel Prize winner Rabindranath Tagore (1861–1941) says of this stage:

> Life being a pilgrimage, with liberation in Brahma as its object, the living of it was as a spiritual exercise to be carried through its different stages, reverently and with a vigilant determination. And the pupil, from his very initiation, had this final consummation always kept in his view.[6]

This *ashram* is totally dedicated to study, particularly the revered teachings of the Vedas and Upanishads.[7]

The householder stage reminds us that we cannot pursue our spiritual goal of enlightenment unless we are in touch with reality. Therefore, events such as marriage, the bearing and raising of children, and the caring for the security as well as enhancement of the entire family, elders as well as children, are viewed as noble in character and a necessary path to realization. House-holders are fully committed to the service of others, family and society. Their ultimate goal—"liberation in Brahma"—remains before their eyes as they throw themselves totally into their responsibilities. As Tagore tells us:

> Wisdom does not attain completeness except through the living of life; and discipline divorced from wisdom is not true discipline, but merely the meaningless following of custom, which is only a disguise for stupidity.[8]

Upon fulfilling his familial responsibilities, the householder is now ready for the next stage of forest-dweller. This does not mean that he literally enters a forest. The forest symbolizes a retreat, a weaning away from the world of practicalities, occupation, and family responsibilities in order to attend to interior matters, matters of self, so that he can nourish his spiritual side, his genuine self. Again, Tagore gives us an eloquent description:

> After the infant leaves the womb, it still has to remain close to its mother for a time, remaining attached in spite of its detachment, until it can adapt itself to its new freedom. Such is the case in the third stage of life, when man though aloof from the world still remains in touch with it while preparing himself for the final stage of complete freedom. He still gives to the world from his store of wisdom and accepts its support; but this interchange is not of the same intimate character as in the stage of the householder, *there being a new sense of distance.*[9] [italics mine]

Here, in contrast to American culture, the Hindu culture celebrates our maturing, our aging, for this is the time to replenish and reconnect with our true nature. At this point, we are blessed with our experiences and stored wisdom and continue to share these with others.

Finally, the hermit stage, or *sannyasin,* involves the radical disconnection from all material and earthly concerns in the effort to attain that supreme goal of spiritual awakening—*moksha.* This part of the journey is indeed solitary. As the Hindu philosopher Sarvepalli Radhakrishnan (1888–1975) reminds us, "The last part of life's road has to be walked in single file." The *sannyasin* is now detached, no longer connected to family and society, so that, it is hoped, as Tagore declares, "at last comes a day when even such free relations have their end, and the emancipated soul steps out of all bonds to face the Supreme Soul...."[10]

Thus, these are the four indispensable steps to our spiritual awakening. Bear in mind also that this awakening is within our grasp since our nature itself is divine. With this overview in mind, let us now examine some basic themes in Hindu ethics.

LIFE'S FOUR GOALS

Hindu teachings are deeply aware of our basic human needs. At the same time, they show an astute sensitivity to our more elevated need to grasp our true nature. With this in mind, they propose that we aspire to four basic goals, or *purusarthas,* in our human life. These are four worthy ambitions that should lead us to enlightenment. They are (1) material comfort and prosperity, (2) pleasure, (3) virtue or right conduct, and (4) spiritual awakening. The first two clearly address our material and bodily needs, while the latter two acknowledge our spiritual and moral natures. Of these four goals, spiritual awakening, or enlightenment, is definitely the most important, and the other three provide a blueprint to achieve this consummate end.

Material Comfort (*Artha*)

Artha has a variety of meanings, ranging from "advantage" to "property," "object," "wealth," and "money."[11] In his famous treatise on *artha*, the *Arthashastra*, Kautilya (3rd century B.C.E.) says that "The subsistence of mankind is termed *artha*, wealth; the earth which contains mankind is termed *artha*, wealth."[12] *Artha*, therefore, refers to material comfort, prosperity, and security. This is viewed as a fitting goal in life. After all, a safe level of material well-being is the condition for personal growth and development. And even though in themselves material goods do not cause personal happiness, they do appease our basic needs regarding comfort and security. Hindu teachings and ethics in particular therefore recognize this biological and social gratification as a prerequisite on our path to the supreme spiritual aim, the total realization of our true self.

However, we must add a critical caveat. Material comfort is a legitimate goal only if we attempt to obtain it through the proper means and in the right attitude. To illustrate, consider the relationship between means and end. Although the end of material well-being is posited as a respectable goal, that does not at all justify any means to achieve it. In principle, the end does not justify the means. Improper methods, such as those involving deceit, manipulation, greed, and all other acts driven by self-centeredness, can never bring about respectable *artha*. Kautilya also warns us against those means steered by unawareness or lack of restraint:

> Ignorance and absence of discipline are the causes of a man's troubles. An untrained man does not perceive the injuries arising from vices.[13]

Such vices naturally follow from a lack of *dharma*, or right conduct. Although we will examine the meaning of *dharma* more closely later, we can at least point out here that *dharma* is a vital ingredient in ascertaining whether or not material comfort is legitimate. Simply put, *dharma* means "right conduct" and "right duty," so that our pursuit of material comfort is morally sound only when it is conducted in the spirit of *dharma*. On the other hand, by acting contrary to *dharma* (this is called *adharma*), we corrupt our goal. Furthermore, this corruption has a polluting effect in that material gains improperly or unfairly acquired will consequently lead to further exploitation and misconduct. In short, the acquisition of material comfort through means that violate right conduct, or *dharma*, is not genuine *artha*.[14]

Pleasure (*Kama*)

Kama also embraces an assortment of meanings such as "desire," "pleasure," and "enjoyment." The definitive classic text that depicts *kama* is the Kamasutra by Vatsyayana (c. 5th century B.C.E.) and here we read:

Kāma is the enjoyment of the appropriate objects of the five senses of hearing, feeling, seeing, tasting, and smelling, assisted by the mind, together with the soul.[15]

The Kamasutra especially portrays *kama* in terms of physical and sensual pleasures. Actually, *kama* incorporates all sorts of enjoyments, not just sexual ones. For instance, those material goods represented by *artha* also produce pleasure, and Hindus claim that this pleasure is a worthwhile aim. Surely, we all seek pleasures and hope to avoid pain, and there is no doubting the powerful lure of sexual pleasure. Sensual pleasure satisfies a fundamental bodily need. Therefore enjoyment is a natural enough goal.

However, this goal of *kama* is appropriate only within certain boundaries. Again, we face the counterweight of *dharma*. As with material comfort, pleasure can be a fitting goal only if it is reasonably tempered with right action. That is, if we act improperly in our pursuit of *kama*—in other words primarily out of self-interest and attachment to *kama* as an end in itself—the *kama* that we achieve is not valid *kama,* and is, on that account, not a proper goal.

Dharma here acts as a principle of regulation. Consider the image of the chariot driver controlling wild horses. The driver, acting reasonably, represents the possibility of regulation. The horses epitomize the passions that if out of control, could lead to ruin. In fact, if things go wrong, there are three potential casualties: the individual driver, his horses, and the larger group to which he belongs. And in Hindu morality, under no circumstances does individual interest prevail over group interests. Therefore, *kama* regulated by *dharma* works to preserve the social order as well as personal well-being. Also bear in mind that without the horses the chariot is useless and goes nowhere. In other words, we need our desires and passions, for they breathe life into us. At the same time, acting according to *dharma* enables us to sensibly channel them.

It becomes clear that, in and of itself, pleasure is not a moral good. Instead, it is instrumental for developing other goods, the most important being the spiritual pleasure attained through self-realization. Thus we hear Krishna confess to Arjuna in the Bhagavad Gita, "I am pleasure (*kama*) that is not opposed to goodness (*dharma*)."[16] This is clearly expressed in the following passage from the Katha Upanishad, and is part of a discourse in which Death instructs Nachiketas about the secret of life. He points out the sometimes subtle but serious difference between what is pleasing, the "pleasanter," and what is good, the "better."

The better (*sreyas*) is one thing, and the pleasanter (*preyas*) quite another.
Both these, of different aim, bind a person.
Of these two, well it is for him who takes the better;
He fails of his aim who chooses the pleasanter.

Both the better and the pleasanter come to a man.
Going all around the two, the wise man discriminates.
The wise man chooses the better, indeed, rather than the pleasanter.
The stupid man, from getting-and-keeping, chooses the pleasanter.[17]

Plato, *Phaedrus*

As to soul's . . . nature there is this that must be said . . . Let it be likened
to the union of powers in a team of winged steeds and their winged charioteer. Now all the gods' steeds and all their charioteers are good, and
of good stock, but with other beings it is not wholly so. With us men, in
the first place, it is a pair of steeds that the charioteer controls; moreover
one of them is noble and good, and of good stock, while the other has
the opposite character, and his stock is opposite. Hence the task of our
charioteer is difficult and troublesome. . . . easy is that assent for the chariots of the gods, for they are well balanced and readily guided. But for
the others it is hard, by reason of the heaviness of the steed of wickedness, which pulls down his driver with his weight, except that driver have
schooled him well . . .

Of that place beyond the heavens none of our earthly poets has
yet sung, and none shall sing worthily. But this is the manner of it, for
assuredly we must be bold to speak what is true, above all when our
discourse is upon truth. It is there that true being dwells, without color
or shape, that cannot be touched; *reason alone, the soul's pilot, can behold
it,* and all true knowledge is knowledge thereof. [italics mine]

From Plato, *Phaedrus,* in Edith Hamilton and Huntington Cairns, eds., *The
Collected Dialogues of Plato* (Princeton, NJ: Princeton University Press, Bollingen Series LXXI, 1961), sec. 246–47, pp. 493–94.

Right Action (*Dharma*)

Dharma stems from the root *dhr,* meaning "to nourish" or "to support." It
therefore assumes a guiding role as a beacon to right conduct. *Dharma*
pertains to that which is morally commendable. We can trace its origin to the
meaning of *rita* (*rta*) in the Rig-veda. *Rita* literally means "the course of things"
and is the principle of universal order and harmony.[18] It ushers in the later
idea of *dharma.* This principle of *rita* also infused the moral realm. Belief in
the moral order of human existence inspired a rudimentary trust that all things
would eventually work out for the best.

How can we know what constitutes *dharma?* If we look to the Upanishads, we find no elaborate or systematic discussion of ethics. Nevertheless,
their teachings have a strong moral flavor. For example, they instruct us to
adhere to the Vedas for proper ritual and prayer. They also recommend that
we emulate the conduct of those who are virtuous because *dharma* is embodied in their actions. Note the advice that the teacher gives to his student in the

Taittiriya Upanishad. After he exhorts the student to follow the Vedic teachings, he then gives more specific instructions:

> Let your mother be a god to you; let your father be a god to you; let your teacher be a god to you; let your guest also be a god to you. Do only such actions as are blameless. Always show reverence to the great.
>
> If at any time there is any doubt with regard to right conduct, follow the practice of great souls, who are guileless, of good judgement, and devoted to truth.[19]

So also, the Brihadaranyaka Upanishad cites three traits or virtues of moral conduct:

> This same thing does the divine voice here, thunder, repeat . . . that is, restrain yourselves, give, be compassionate. One should practice this same triad: self-restraint, giving, compassion.[20]

If we look to some other writings, such as the Dharmasastras (Sciences of *Dharma*), we see that they are inspired by the Mimamsa school, and that they give us some concrete advice concerning the applications of *dharma*.[21] The Mimamsa school itself stipulates four criteria that can aid us in identifying *dharma:* Vedic prescriptions for rituals, prayers, sacrifices, and other social duties; commentaries; others' good example; individual conscience.[22] These codes are the bases for rules of social conduct, including strict rules of conduct among castes.[23]

Furthermore, the Mimamsa school seems to assign a more metaphysical status to ethical action.[24] *Dharma* is viewed as a foundational force, and ethical action is bestowed with a sense of ultimacy. The essence of reality lies in ethical action as potency, and to live is to act. Therefore, in view of the four fundamental aims of human existence—material comfort, pleasure, right action, and enlightenment, Mimamsa surely elevates our status as creatures of action.[25] And the starting point for ethical action lies in following the prescribed rules in the Vedas.

Ethical action goes beyond the mere observance of ritual, however. Considering the other three criteria—teachings from the commentaries, others' good example, and personal conscience—we see a movement from external to internal sources of moral authority. Perhaps all of this can be summed up by saying that morality in essence involves the ability to view others in the same way we view ourselves, similar to the Golden Rule. In fact, in the Mahabharata, this is pronounced as the heart of *dharma:*

> What is harmful to oneself, one should not do to others. This is the quintessence of *dharma*. Behavior which is contrary to this is born of selfish desire.[26]

Dharma therefore appears to have multiple meanings, and there is no absolute definition. Instead, it conveys a general principle with diverse shades of meaning depending upon the particular situation. We examine some of these shades and situations in the final section of this chapter. At this point, keep in mind *dharma*'s indispensable role as an absolutely necessary goal and a vital step toward spiritual insight.

Enlightenment (*Moksha*)

As we have said, in Hindu thought the supreme goal is *moksha*. The term *moksha* can mean "liberation," "release," and "freedom." It is a genuine spiritual awakening or enlightenment, whose corollary is freedom from the cycle of *samsara,* the wheel of birth, death, and rebirth.[27] As long as I am essentially ignorant of my true nature, I remain in bondage to this cycle, under the karmic influence that my soul, *atman,* has accumulated through all my previous lives. As we later explain, positive karma will lead to advantageous future lives, while negative karma will have a reverse effect. In any case, lacking self-realization, I will linger on in this seemingly endless sequence. *Moksha* occurs if and when I finally realize my true nature, that is, when I experience myself as *atman* and my integral oneness with *Brahman*. Hindu morality is viewed in terms of this final goal of emancipation.

This explains why the latter two stages in life, the forest-dweller and the hermit (*sannyasin*), demand detachment from the powerful desires for material comfort and sensual pleasure. For only this type of detachment can bring about genuine happiness, or inner peace. These last two stages therefore represent the final and most critical steps to our supreme goal of liberation, *moksha*. And even though we may ultimately experience *moksha* only after countless lifetimes, for each life that we live, the happiness and inner peace that accompanies our partial detachment is still thoroughly meaningful. The secret lies in being relatively free from the frustrations associated with attachment and desire, so that we can enjoy a gracious measure of peace of mind.

The Caste System

We cannot reach these four goals in a vacuum. Hindus recognized the need for a reasonable degree of social cohesion so that individuals could pursue these aims. This required a clear-cut, explicit class structure grounded upon specific roles and reciprocal obligations. And here is where the long-standing Indian class structure comes in.

The class system as it has evolved in India is rather complex. Nevertheless, it embraces four main categories, later referred to as *castes*.[28] First, *brahmanas* occupy the highest rung on the social ladder. They are responsible for being the spiritual guides of the community, and they are educators, teaching about the Vedas. Next, the *kshatriyas,* or warriors, are the community guardians, many working as soldiers and as enforcers of the laws. Quite a few also assume administrative positions. Third, the *vaishyas* consist of traders, merchants, farmers, and other trade and business occupations. As professionals in the economic sphere, they are responsible for sustaining the material status of the community through the distribution of resources. Finally, the *shudras* are the laborers and servants. It is important to bear in mind that the status of the laborer is not construed as being inferior to that of the other classes, for the laborer contributes a valuable share to the social order. These four composed the formal society. Those outside, or on the fringe, of this formal society were the *panchamas,* the "outcastes" or the "untouchables" (also called the "fifths"), who were involved with "polluting" tasks such as cleaning refuse and sewage.[29]

Each class possesses specific roles and duties unique to that class. It is important to bear in mind that, at least originally, the relationship among the various classes did not consist of a relationship of domination of those inferior by those superior. The relationship was organic, given the division of labor among the classes. With such a division of labor based upon particular talents and occupations, the Indian society was able to maintain harmony and complementarity among the different classes. The overriding goal was collective well-being and security.

Indeed, it was of the utmost importance that members of each caste would adhere to its prescribed rules. Yet, contrary to prevailing opinion, class rules were not necessarily absolute. For example, switching castes was generally discouraged as a social practice. However, the powerful Gupta dynasty, famous for its victory over the Huns, actually originated from the *vaishya* class.[30] Moreover, there are instances of individuals who violated social customs by following their own conscience. For instance, the respected elder in the Mahabharata, Bhisma, breached a social custom when he relinquished his title and assumed the vow of celibacy. Conscience plays a critical role in somehow indicating a level of discernment as to what is the right thing to do. Individual conscience is, therefore, bestowed a perhaps surprising degree of importance in Indian thought. As important as conscience is, however, it is imperative that we be able to critically differentiate between our genuine personal conscience and our personal inclinations, instincts, and desires. There is a distinction between what we deeply value, and thus cherish as a moral premium, and what we desire, being driven essentially by self-interest.

It is also interesting to note that the Sanskrit term for class, *varna,* literally means "color." However, even though *varna* may have originally referred to the pigmentation of the skin, the idea of color acquired a different meaning later when it was used to refer to one's character.[31] Therefore, at least originally, class membership, one's "color," was not ultimately determined by birth, as often understood, but by character.[32]

PATHS TO ENLIGHTENMENT

There are three specific paths, or *yogas,* through which we can attain *moksha,* the total experience of our true self: *karma* yoga (the way of action), *bhakti* yoga (the way of devotion), and *jnana* yoga (the way of knowledge). These address a triad of needs: to act, to pray (or to have faith in), and to know. Yoga is a fitting term for "path" since it literally means "yoke" in the sense of joining together, and, on one level, it means the joining together of body and mind. For instance, the four goals we just examined assume a unity of the physical, mental, and spiritual. The three types of yoga exemplify this same unity. On another, more penetrating level, yoga means the "joining together" of our true self, our *atman,* with the principle of Reality, or *Brahman.* For our purposes, our primary interest here lies with karma yoga. However, first let us briefly review the *bhakti* and *jnana* paths.

The three personal faces of Brahman. (Corbis)

Bhakti Yoga: The Path of Devotion

Bhakti yoga appeals to our more interior needs in terms of devotion and prayer. After all, the idea of *Brahman* as the "unconditional ground of existence" may be too abstract for us. We often need a more positive, concrete image with which we can identify. Thus the more devotional schools of Hinduism prefer the triad of *Brahman's* attributes—*sat-cit-ananda* ("being-consciousness-bliss")—as more satisfying. Another triad depicts *Brahman* as God with three faces: Brahma, Vishnu, and Shiva. Brahma manifests the creative aspect of God; Vishnu depicts the nourishing, life-giving quality; and Shiva represents God's destructive side.

In any case, *bhakti* yoga is the path of love of *Brahman*, as personal God. This may more suitably lead to union with the divine. *Bhakti* yoga is especially expressed in the Bhagavad Gita, and in the religious sects of Saivism (devoted to Shiva) and Vaisnavism (devoted to Vishnu).

Jnana Yoga: The Path of Knowledge

Jnana yoga meets another fundamental need—the need to know. It is the path to *moksha* through knowledge. Proper knowledge is necessary to root out the natural ignorance we have of our real nature. Our most fundamental error lies in mistaking our ego for our true self. Awakening to the truth revealed in the Upanishads, *tat tvam asi,* can occur through the cultivation of intellect and a proper state of mind. *Jnana* yoga, therefore, involves personal, moral cultivation, and intensive study and meditation. This is particularly important in Sankara's Advaita Vedanta.

Advaita Vedanta is the most influential philosophical system in Hindu thought. Lacking a rigorous, formal ethical structure, it still provides us with some moral guidelines. Since its raison d'etre underscores the oneness of *atman* and *Brahman,* the overriding moral standard in Advaita teachings lies in whether or not an act or thought contributes to this self-realization. In other words, to what degree are our actions and thoughts mired in ego-centeredness?

Thus, the purpose of Advaitin ethics is to liberate ourselves from the grip of self-interest. And this comes about through *jnana,* meaning "proper knowledge," which involves shattering the delusion of ego as self.

Arthur Schopenhauer, *The World as Will and Representation*

Nature flatly contradicts herself, according as she speaks from the particular or the universal, from inside or outside, from the centre or the periphery. Thus nature has her centre in every individual, for each one is the entire will-to-live. Therefore, even if this individual is only an insect or a worm, nature herself speaks out of it as follows: "I alone am all in all; in my maintenance is everything involved; the rest may perish, it is really nothing." Thus nature speaks from the *particular* standpoint, from that of self-consciousness, and to this is due the *egoism* of every living thing. On the other hand, from the *universal* standpoint, from that of the *consciousness of other things,* and thus from that of objective knowledge, from the moment looking away from the individual to whom knowledge adheres,— hence from outside, from the periphery, nature speaks thus: "The individual is nothing and less than nothing. . . . Every day I produce millions of new individuals without any diminution of my productive power; just as little as the power of a mirror is exhausted by the number of the sun's images that it casts one after another on the wall. The individual is nothing." Only he who really knows how to reconcile and eliminate this obvious contradiction of nature has a true answer to the question concerning the perishableness or imperishableness of his own self. . . .

. . . All genuine virtue proceeds from the immediate and *intuitive* knowledge of the metaphysical identity of all beings . . .

From Arthur Schopenhauer, *The World as Will and Representation*, Vol. II, trans. E. F. J. Payne (New York: Dover, 1958), pp. 599–601.

Karma Yoga: The Path of Action

On March 12, 1930, Mohandas Gandhi set out on foot with 78 men and women from their ashram in Ahmedabad on a 200-mile odyssey to the sea. By the time they reached Dandi, on the Gulf of Cambay, 24 days later, their numbers had swelled to several thousand. On the next day, Gandhi purified himself in the sea and then picked up some salt deposited there on the beach by waves. In doing so, he defied the infamous Salt Act, which banned Indians from making their own salt. The act also imposed a heavy sales tax on the salt, which was manufactured solely by the British government.

Authorities considered the march bizarre. Nevertheless, this symbolic act of defiance against an unjust law was not lost upon the people, and journalists throughout the world made the plight of the Indians under British rule headline news.

A few weeks later, the sixty-one-year-old Gandhi was arrested. The authorities could not have been more wrong in thinking this would silence the dissent he enkindled. As a protest against both his imprisonment and the Salt Act, twenty-five hundred Indians, led by Mrs. Sarojini Naidu, peacefully marched upon the Dharasana Salt Works, run by British officers. An American correspondent, Webb Miller, gives us a moving eyewitness account of the event:

In complete silence the Gandhi men drew up and halted a hundred yards from the stockade. A picked column advanced from the crowd, waded the ditches, and approached the barbed-wire stockade. . . . Suddenly, at a word of command, scores of native policemen rushed upon the advancing marchers and rained blows on their heads with their steel-shod lathis. Not one of the marchers even raised an arm to fend off the blows. They went down like ten-pins. From where I stood I heard the sickening whack of the clubs on unprotected skulls. The waiting crowd of marchers groaned and sucked in their breath in sympathetic pain at every blow. Those struck down fell sprawling, unconscious or writhing with fractured skulls or broken shoulders. . . . The survivors, without breaking ranks, silently and doggedly marched on until struck down. . . .

They marched steadily, with heads up, without the encouragement of music or cheering or any possibility that they might escape serious injury or death. The police rushed out and methodically and mechanically beat down the second column. There was no fight, no struggle; the marchers simply walked forward till struck down.[33]

Here, we have a remarkable example of the path of action, *karma* yoga. This is karma yoga in harmony with Gandhi's own conviction of the power of active nonviolence. And as a result of the steadfast spirit of all those who shared Gandhi's vision, it did more than any other act to raise global awareness of the plight of the Indians. Now let us define more clearly what this karma yoga means.

As a popular path to enlightenment, karma yoga is the path of work, whereby our efforts, labor, and occupation bring us closer to personal realization. It is therefore important to fulfill our duties in line with our position. Yet, there is an indispensable ingredient: *We ought to perform our duties without being attached to them.* In other words, it is all important that we work without being attached to the consequences of our work. For instance, we should not perform our responsibilities *in order* to be recognized or praised. This is a highly important teaching in the Bhagavad Gita: not to be attached to the fruits of one's efforts. As long as we are attached to what we do, we work from a self-interested reference point, still enmeshed by desires. The ultimate goal is *moksha,* and not recognition, praise, fame, or reward. Let us look again to the example of Gandhi.

Gandhi's life and teachings point to a common ground among religions—the ideal of nonviolence and compassion. Even with his eclectic interest, however, Gandhi considered himself first and foremost a Hindu. Influenced especially by karma yoga in the Bhagavad Gita, he taught that nonviolence and love are the keys to genuine self-determination and the governance of others. His Salt March particularly illustrates karma yoga because it embodies his teaching concerning *satyagraha,* literally meaning "passionate devotion to truth."[34] And for Gandhi, not only is God Truth, but the Truth of existence lies in Love. *Satyagraha* is therefore a manifestation of this Truth of Love. The Salt March was an extraordinary display of *satyagraha* within a political and social context. It represented nonviolent resistance to manifestations of nontruth, expressed in this case through unjust taxes and a monopoly. *Satyagraha* therefore embraces Gandhi's belief that truth will eventually prevail over injustice, and love will conquer the forces of malice.

KARMA AND REBIRTH

Toward the end of the bloody eighteen-day war between the Kauravas and the Pandavas, the great warriors Karna and Arjuna finally met each other in combat. They fiercely charged each other in their chariots. Just as Arjuna was ready to strike with an arrow, the wheel of Karna's chariot sunk into the mud, the chariot now paralyzed. This was his waterloo. He shot an arrow at Arjuna with such staggering force that Arjuna was momentarily stunned. Meanwhile, Karna dropped to the ground, struggling to lift the axle, which would not budge. He then decided to strike Arjuna with a Brahmasastra, a supernatural weapon he could invoke with a special mantra. He gasped and could not call his special saying to memory. And now Arjuna took aim:

> And he [Arjuna] drew his bow *Gandiva,* aimed his dart with stifled breath,
> Vengeance for his murdered hero winged the fatal dart of death,
>
> Like the fiery bolt of lightning Arjun's lurid arrow sped,
> Like a rock by thunder riven Karna fell among the dead![35]

Arjuna and Karna were equal in skill. But Karna's death resulted from two unexpected factors: His wheel was immovable, and he could not remember his secret saying, or mantra, to unleash his ultimate weapon.

But were these accidents? Karna, a warrior, or *kshatriya,* mastered the art of archery from his great teacher Parasurama only because he tricked his teacher into thinking that he was a Brahmana. One day, his aged teacher fell asleep on Karna's lap, and when an insect bit Karna, blood oozed from his leg. However, Karna did not flinch, not wanting to wake his teacher. When Parasurama awoke and saw the blood, he knew that Karna was a warrior, for only a warrior could stoically withstand such pain. He said to Karna:

> You have deceived your teacher. When your hour comes, your knowledge of the *astras* will fail you, and what you have learnt from me through deception will not be useful to you.[36]

One other time, Karna accidentally killed a Brahmana's cow with an arrow. The Brahmana swore at Karna:

> In battle your chariot wheel will get stuck in the mud, and you will be done to death even like this innocent cow which you have killed.[37]

So, again we ask: Did Karna's death result from bad luck, or was it destined to happen in this way?

Any discussion of ethics in Indian philosophy must take into account both karma and its role in survival after death. This is because our particular survival in another psychophysical form will depend upon the quality and accumulation of karma we have from our previous lives. Karma is, therefore, the interface between this life and the next.

Literally, *karma* means "act," or "deed." Generally, it refers to the law of cause and effect within the moral sphere. It is the principle of moral causality. This means that each deed and thought generates a specific effect that will inevitably occur, if not in this life, then in another. The effect is actually twofold: Not only does an act or thought produce its particular negative or positive effect, but it also contributes to the formation of an individual's moral character, in the same way that repeated acts produce a habit, and those habits bring about a condition. A habit of good deeds will result in good character, whereas the reverse is true with evil deeds. Therefore, each action or thought either enhances or detracts from our moral personality.

Throughout all this, what is especially notable is that we are the sole agents of what we become. Thus, Hindus believe that being born into a particular class is a result of past karma. Yet we are still free to affect our destinies. Although we are constrained in varying degrees by our circumstances, as humans we possess the free will to choose how we respond to those conditions. Karma emphasizes all the more the notion of individual responsibility for one's actions and for the consequences that result.

Rebirths usually occur in realms other than the human, such as the animal and insect realms. Just think of the phenomenal amount of karma we accrue in one day, let alone one lifetime. When we die, we will have karma that has not yet been actualized—we can call it our karmic residue. In other words, not all karma exhausts itself right away and, instead, becomes a latent force for later effects. Some of this residue is spent in our next rebirth. Yet, because our negative karma tends to outweigh our positive karma, only occasionally are we reborn in human form.

However, the human being holds a distinctive status. Only as humans can we generate karma. This is because only as humans do we possess the reason and will that brings about moral and immoral actions and thoughts. Only humans can act ethically or unethically. At the same time, only humans can experience *moksha,* the spiritual awakening that liberates us from the cycle of *samsara.*

G.W. Leibniz, *Monadology*

There is nothing wasted, nothing sterile, nothing dead in the universe; no chaos, no confusions, save in appearance. . . . We must not imagine. . . . that each soul has a mass or portion of matter appropriated or attached to itself for ever. . . . For all bodies are in a perpetual flux, like rivers, and parts are passing in and out of them continually. Thus the soul only changes its body bit by bit and by degrees, so that it is never despoiled of all its organs all together . . . neither are there any entirely separate souls, nor superhuman spirits without bodies.

From Mary Morris, trans., *Leibniz: Philosophical Writings* (London: J.M. Dent, 1934), p. 16.

SHADES OF DHARMA

As we said earlier, *dharma,* or "right conduct," can embrace a variety of meanings and actions ranging from performing class duties, fulfilling Vedic prescriptions, and obeying the law to following one's personal conscience. There is no
one absolute definition. Rather, *dharma* is a general principle of moral action
with various shades of application depending upon the circumstances. And
throughout Hindu literature, we find passages that convey the struggles involved
in ascertaining *dharma.* Morality is not that simple. For instance, the principal
characters in the epics often face moral predicaments that, in turn, force the
reader to wrestle with the question of *dharma.* Let us look at three instances of
moral conflict, and see whether we can discern the right action in each case.

A Friendly Game of Dice and Draupadi's Question

In one of the most curious episodes in the epic Mahabharata, Yudhisthira, the
oldest of the Pandava brothers, is invited to King Dhritarashtra's new Crystal
Palace to play a "friendly" game of dice with the king's sons. And he accepts the
challenge since it is against his code as a warrior to refuse. This leads to his undoing. Even though he is regarded as the most honorable of the Pandavas, he has
one fatal flaw—his passion for gambling. His Kaurava cousins know this, so they
eagerly look forward to the match. Having already seized the kingdom, which
by right belongs to the Pandavas, the Kauravas now see this dice match as a
golden opportunity to convincingly break the backs of their opponents.

   The hall fills up with visitors and members of the Kaurava clan, who are
led by Duryodhana and his uncle Sakuni, who will roll the dice on Duryodhana's behalf. Sakuni himself is a most clever and deceitful gambler. And as
the roll of the dice begins, the stakes are small. But as the game progresses,
with Sakuni winning every roll, the wagering increases as Yudhisthira becomes
more consumed by the game. The contemporary Indian novelist R.K. Narayan
gives us his rendition:

> Beginning modestly with a handful of pearls, the stakes grew in size. Yudhistira
> slipped into a gambler's frenzy, blind to consequences, his vision blurred to all
> but the ivory-white dice and the chequered board. He forgot who he was, where
> he was, who else was there, and what was right or wrong. All he knew was the
> clatter of the rolling dice, followed every few minutes by Sakuni's raucous chant,
> "I win," and the cheers that burst from Duryodhana's party. Yudhistira was
> provoked to raise his stakes higher each time Sakuni's voice was heard.[38]

   Soon, Yudhisthira loses all his wealth: his armies, elephants, territories,
houses, and attendants. Driven by ego and imprisoned in his obsession, he
continues to be taunted by Sakuni. The wise Vidura sees through Sakuni's
cunning and warns the king that "Those who collect honey after ascending
giddy heights never notice that they are about to step off the precipice at their
back."[39] Anticipating impending disaster, Vidura implores:

This has gone too far. Stop it, and if you are not obeyed, get that jackal in our midst, your son [Duryodhana], destroyed. Otherwise, I see the complete destruction of your entire family, sooner or later. To save a family or a clan it is proper to sacrifice an individual. Even at birth, Duryodhana never cried like a baby, but let out a howl like a jackal which everyone understood as an evil sign. They advised you to destroy that monster forthwith, but you have allowed him to flourish in your family. You are partial to him and accept all his demands, and you have sanctioned this monstrous game, which is undermining the Pandava family. But remember that this setback to them is illusory; whatever they lose now, they will recover later with a vengeance. Before it is too late, stop it and order Dhananjaya [Arjuna] to kill Duryodhana here and now, and you will save the entire race.[40]

The king pays little heed to Vidura. And to everyone's amazement, Yudhisthira, now nearly completely absorbed, puts up more serious stakes: each one of his four brothers—Nakula, Sahadeva, Arjuna, and Bhimsena.[41] Again, he loses. Spent and desperate, he then stakes himself. Again, he loses.

Sakuni is now relentless. He wants to press every drop of blood out of the helpless Yudhisthira. He baits him, "Only the Princess of Panchala [Draupadi] is left; will she not feel lonely with all her husbands gone suddenly in this manner?"[42] The assembly is stunned at the proposition that Yudhisthira bet his wife, Draupadi, who is also the wife of all five brothers. And despite loud protests, Yudhisthira, in his depleted state, shocks everyone by staking Draupadi. The final indignity. Again, he loses. It is now over—he has lost all his wealth, his brothers, himself, and his beloved wife to the Kauravas.

Greedily, Duryodhana orders an attendant to fetch Draupadi. However, the attendant returns empty-handed, except for a question she sent with him:

She has asked me to bring back an answer to this question, "Whom did Yudhistira lose first, me or himself? Whose lord were you at the time you lost me?"[43]

The question is posed to Yudhisthira, who just silently stares at the floor, still in shock. Finally, as we see in the following account, Draupadi is dragged into the hall where she insists that her question be answered by the august assembly:

FROM THE MAHABHARATA

With her tresses and sari in disarray through Dussasana's rude handling, Draupadi looked piteous as she stood in the centre of that vast assembly facing the elders and guests. "This is monstrous," she cried. "Is morality gone? Or else how can you be looking on this atrocity? There are my husbands—five, not one as for others—and they look paralysed! While I hoped Bhima alone could crush with his thumb the perpetrators of this horrible act, I do not understand why they stand there transfixed, speechless and like imbeciles. . . ."

Karna, Dussasana, and Sakuni laughed at her and uttered jokes and also called her "slave" several times. She looked at their family elder, Bhishma, pleadingly and he said, "O daughter of Drupada, the question of morality is difficult to answer. Yudhistira voluntarily entered the dice game and voluntarily offered the stakes. Sakuni is a subtle player, but Yudhistira went on recklessly. I am unable to decide on the question you have raised. While he played and staked out of his own free will, we can have nothing to say, as long as he was the master, but after he had lost himself, how far could he have the authority to stake his wife? On the other hand, a husband may have the absolute right to dispose of his wife in any manner he pleases, even if he has become a pauper and a slave. . . . I am unable to decide this issue. . . ."

Draupadi was undaunted. "How can you say that he voluntarily entered this evil game? Everyone knew that the King had no skill, but he was inveigled into facing a cunning gambler like Sakuni. How can you say that he played voluntarily, or that the staking was voluntary? He was involved and compelled and lost his sense. He acted like one drugged and dragged. Again, I ask the mighty minds assembled here, when he put up his stake, did anyone notice whether the other side put up a matching stake? Did Duryodhana offer his wife or his brothers? This has all been one-sided. The deceitful player knows he can twist the dice to his own advantage and so does not have to offer a matching stake. Yudhistira in his magnanimity never even noticed this lapse. All wise minds gathered here, saintly men, equal to Brihaspathi in wisdom, you elders and kinsmen of the Kauravas, reflect on my words and judge, answer the points I have raised here . . ." Saying this, she broke down and wept.

Bhima, who had stood silently till now, burst out, "Yudhistira, there have been other gamblers in this world, thousands of them. Even the worst among them never thought of staking a woman, but you have excelled others in this respect. You have staked all the women in our service, and also your wife, without a thought. I did not mind your losing all the precious wealth and gems we had, but what you have done to this innocent creature! Looking at her plight now, O brother, I want to burn those hands of yours. . . . Sahadeva, bring some fire. I shall scorch those hands diseased with gambling. Or give me leave to smash these monsters . . ."

Arjuna placated Bhima. "When you talk thus, you actually fulfill the aim of our enemies, who would have us discard our eldest brother. Yudhistira responded to the summons to play dice, much against his will."

Bhima answered rather grimly, "Yes, I know it. If I hadn't thought that the King had acted according to kshatriya usage, I would myself have seized his hands and thrust them into fire."

Seeing the distress of the Pandavas and of Draupadi, Vikarna, one of the younger sons of Dhritarashtra, said, "This unfortunate person has asked a question which has not been answered. Bhishma, Drona, Dhritarashtra, and even Vidura turn away and remain silent. Will no one give an answer?" He paused and looked around and repeated Draupadi's question, but no one spoke. Finally he said, "Whether you Kings of the earth answer or not, I will speak out my mind. It has been said that drinking, gambling, hunting, and the enjoyment of women in excess will bring down a king, however well protected and strong he might be. People should not attach any value or authority to acts done by anyone under the intoxication of wine, women, or dice. This rare being, Yudhistira, engaged himself in an unwholesome game, steeped himself in it, staked everything—including Draupadi—at the instigation of the wily Sakuni. She is the common wife of the other four also, and the King had first lost himself and then staked her. Reflecting on these things, I declare that Draupadi has not been won at all." A loud applause resounded through the hall and his supporters cursed Sakuni aloud.

At this point, Karna stood up and motioned everyone to remain quiet. "This Vikarna is an immature youth, not fit to address an august assembly of elders. It is not for him to tell us what is right or wrong, the presumptuous fellow! Yudhistira gambled and staked with his eyes wide open. Don't consider him an innocent simpleton, he knew what he was doing. He knew when he staked Draupadi, he was offering his wife. Whatever has been won has been won justly. Here take off the princely robes on those brothers. Moreover, what woman in any world would take five husbands? What does one call the like of her? I will unhesitatingly call her a whore. To bring her here, whatever her state, is no sin or act that should cause surprise. You, Yudhistira and the rest, take off your princely robes and come aside."

At this order, the Pandavas took off their coats and gowns and threw them down and stood in their loincloths. Duryodhana ordered, "Disrobe her too. . . ."

Dussasana seized Draupadi's sari and began to pull it off. She cried, "My husbands, warrior husbands, elders look on helplessly. Oh God, I can expect no help from any of you. . . ." As Dussasana went on tugging at her dress, she cried, "O God Krishna! Incarnation of Vishnu, Hari, help me." In a state of total surrender to God's will, she let go her sari with her hands raised to cover her face, eyes shut in deep meditation.

The god responded. As one piece of garment was unwound and pulled off, another appeared in its place, and another, and another, endlessly. Dussasana withdrew in fatigue, as a huge mass of cloth unwound from Draupadi's body lay in a heap on one side. But her original sari was still on her.

Everyone was moved by this miracle and cursed Duryodhana. Bhima loudly swore, "If I do not tear open this wretch's chest someday in battle and quaff his blood . . ."

When the novelty of the miracle wore off, the Kauravas engaged themselves again in bantering and baiting their victims. Duryodhana said, "Let the younger Pandava brothers swear here and now that they will not respect Yudhistira's commands any more. Then we will set Panchali free."

Bhimasena cried, "If Yudhistira commands me, I will slay you all with my bare hands. I don't need a sword to deal with rats."

Duryodhana bared his thigh and gestured to Draupadi to come to his lap. This maddened Bhimasena and he swore at that moment, "If I do not smash that thigh into a pulp some day . . ." The Kauravas all laughed.

Karna said, "O beautiful one, those ex-lords have no more right over you; slaves can have no rights. Now go into the inner chambers and begin your servitude as we direct. . . ."

Finally, Vidura said to Dhritarashtra, "Stop all this mean talk, O King. Although they stand here apparently in misery, they have the protection of God."

Dhritarashtra felt repentant, summoned Draupadi, and said, "Daughter, even in this trial you have stood undaunted, holding on to virtue. Please ask for any favour and I will grant it."

Promptly Panchali said, "Please free Yudhistira from slavery."

"Granted," said Dhritarashtra, and since he was in a boon-granting mood, he added, "Ask for another boon."

"Let all his brothers be freed."

"Granted," the king replied. "Now you may ask for a third boon."

"I do not want anything more."

Dhritarashtra turned to his nephew. "Yudhistira, you may take back all that you have lost—wealth, status, and kingdom. Now speed back to Indraprastha and rule in peace. Don't have any ill will for your cousins. Don't forget that you are all of one family. Go away in peace."

Presently the five brothers and Draupadi got into their chariots and started back for Indraprastha.

From *The Mahabharata*, copyright © 1978 by R. K. Narayan. Reprinted by permission of the Wallace Literary Agency, Inc.

In this case, what is the proper course of action? Aside from the related issues of gambling, the alleged authority of husband over wife, and the practice of polyandry, the most poignant issue pertains to Draupadi's question: Did Yudhisthira lose himself first to Duryodhana or did he first lose Draupadi? Her question suggests that if Yudhisthira lost himself first, then he, in effect, forfeits his authority to put her up for stakes. The resulting questions of *dharma* are, Is her alleged enslavement to Duryodhana legitimate? Is it legal? Is it moral? Where does moral integrity enter in?

The resulting silence to her question from the assembly is especially shocking, considering the presence of many wise and respected elders, who, in the past, often took articulate stances on certain moral tenets. Yet now they seem baffled, despite their erudite textbook knowledge of morality. Finally, only a few break the silence. For one, Vidura (in the original work) claims that since Yudhisthira lost himself first, he no longer has authority to stake Draupadi.[44]

Even the respected family elder, Bhisma, appears confused and does not offer a clear-cut response. Instead, he points out the inscrutable nature of morality—"the question of morality [*dharma*] is difficult to answer."[45] He admits that Yudhisthira may have lost his authority by losing first to Duryodhana. Yet at the same time, he also emphasizes (his culture's view of) the authority of the husband over the wife. Furthermore, although Yudhisthira's actions are reckless, he still voluntarily engages in the match. Finally, Yudhisthira's own silence betrays his acceptance of the outcome, or it indicates that he himself has no reasonable answer to the question raised by his wife. Bhisma thus seems to waver toward the side of Duryodhana.

Draupadi's response to Bhisma is riveting. She doubts whether Yudhisthira freely and willingly played dice by arguing that he was tricked into playing, and once involved in the game, "lost his sense . . . like one drugged and dragged."[46]

Another lone voice from the assembly is Vikarna, Duryodhana's younger brother. He speaks out in support of Draupadi by articulating four reasons. First, "acts done by anyone under the intoxication of wine, women, or dice" inherently lack validity because the excesses of these intoxications constitute vice. Second, Yudhisthira was beguiled into playing dice and into placing such high stakes "at the instigation of the wily Sakuni," and such trickery and deceit invalidate the transaction. Third, Draupadi "is the common wife of the other four also"; therefore, Yudhisthira did not have the sole right to bet her. Fourth, because Yudhisthira lost himself first, he forfeited his authority to bet her.

Clearly, Vikarna gives us a persuasive argument for *dharma* in making his case for the release of Draupadi. Yet it is noteworthy that these arguments do not persuade King Dhritarashtra. What sways him is not the voice of reason, but the miracle concerning Draupadi—her original sari cannot be removed. Deeply moved, the king grants her three wishes, and she, truly embodying moral integrity, requests the return of the brothers and all of their properties. She does not request her own emancipation since she does not believe that she was enslaved to begin with. In any case, due to her faith, efforts, and moral conduct, the kingdom of the Pandavas was spared from the Kauravas' greed.

But only temporarily. As the Pandavas start on their journey back home, the sly Duryodhana whispers into his father's ear that the Pandavas, now filled with anger and resentment, would seek all-out revenge upon the Kauravas:

We carefully trapped the cobra and its family, but before the fangs could be pulled out, you have removed the lid of the basket and let them loose. Don't imagine they will be gone; they will come back to finish us.[47]

The weak-willed king is easily coaxed. He sends a messenger to intercept
Yudhisthira. The king invites him for a rematch, which, of course, Yudhisthira
cannot refuse. The result of the rematch? Again, Yudhisthira's defeat. The
stakes? Twelve years of exile in the forest, "barefoot, and dressed in deerskin";
the thirteenth year to be spent in the city living in disguise and, if recognized,
to repeat the twelve-year exile. In this manner, the Pandavas, Draupadi, and
all of their attendants are banished for thirteen years.

Rama's Choice

The Ramayana is another landmark Indian epic, and, indeed, the most popular and beloved among Hindus. The story centers on Rama and Sita, husband
and wife. Rama is the noble son of the King Dasa-ratha. He wins the hand of
the beautiful Sita by being able to bend a miraculous bow owned by Sita's
father, King Janak.

As the aging King Dasa-ratha is about to bestow his rule to Rama, one
of the king's wives, Kaikeyi, convinces the king to hand the regency instead to
her son, Bharata, because of a former promise. At the same time, Rama is sent
into exile into a dark forest, where Sita and his devoted brother, Lakshman,
accompany him. While in exile, Sita is abducted by a demon-king, Ravan. Much
of the poem deals with efforts to rescue her. Rama is finally able to bring her
back only with the aid of the monkey-king, Hanuman, and his army. After
Sita's rescue, Rama is restored as king. Sita must then undergo all sorts of
ordeals in order to prove her virtue and loyalty. She is eventually sent into
the forest, and there gives birth to their two sons. Later on, they are all
reunited with Rama. In a final scene, the Earth Mother defends Sita's virtue
and transports her to the land of the gods.

The following selection is from the early part of the epic in which King
Dasa-ratha is about to hand over his rule to Rama, his favored son. However,
Queen Kaikeyi remembers that the king had once promised her two wishes,
and she reminds the king of this. The king agrees to grant her the wishes but
is thoroughly tormented when she tells him what they are. First, she insists,
"Let my son Bharata be consecrated with the very rite of consecration you
have prepared for Raghava [Rama]." Second, she says, "Let Rama withdraw
to Dandaka wilderness and for nine years and five live the life of an ascetic,
wearing hides and barkcloth garments and matted hair." Horrified, the king
pleads with her to change her mind, but she is ruthless: "She was misfortune
incarnate and had yet to secure her fortunes." Yet, despondent as he is, the
king, a man of honor, must nevertheless keep his word. And he is so over-
powered with grief that he faints:

> And as the king stared at the woman he loved but could not appease, whose
> demand was so perverse—for the exile of his own son—he once again was taken
> faint, overcome with grief, and dropped unconscious to the floor.[48]

This is where our reading begins. Rama enters this scene with the king and Kaikeyi and learns what has transpired.

FROM THE RAMAYANA

1. Rama saw his father, with a wretched look and his mouth all parched, slumped upon his lovely couch, Kaikeyi at his side.

2. First he made an obeisance with all deference at his father's feet and then did homage most scrupulously at the feet of Kaikeyi.

3. "Rama!" cried the wretched king, his eyes brimming with tears, but he was unable to say anything more or to look at him.

4. As if his foot had grazed a snake, Rama was seized with terror to see the expression on the king's face, one more terrifying than he had ever seen before.

5. For the great king lay heaving sighs, racked with grief and remorse, all his senses numb with anguish, his mind stunned and confused.

6. It was as if the imperturbable, wave-wreathed ocean had suddenly been shaken with perturbation, as if the sun had been eclipsed, or a seer had told a lie.

7. His father's grief was incomprehensible to him, and the more he pondered it, the more his agitation grew, like that of the ocean under a full moon.

8. With his father's welfare at heart, Rama struggled to comprehend, "Why does the king not greet me, today of all days?

9. "On other occasions, when Father might be angry, the sight of me would calm him. Why then, when he looked at me just now, did he instead become so troubled?

10. "He seems desolate and grief-stricken, and his face has lost its glow." Doing obeisance to Kaikeyi, Rama spoke these words:

11. "I have not unknowingly committed some offense, have I, to anger my father? Tell me, and make him forgive me.

12. "His face is drained of color, he is desolate and does not speak to me. It cannot be, can it, that some physical illness or mental distress afflicts him? But it is true, well-being is not something one can always keep.

13. "Some misfortune has not befallen the handsome prince Bharata, has it, or courageous Satrughna,* or one of my mothers?

14. "I should not wish to live an instant if his Majesty, the great king, my father, were angered by my failure to satisfy him or do his bidding.

15. "How could a man not treat him as a deity incarnate, in whom he must recognize the very source of his existence in this world?

16. "Can it be that in anger you presumed to use harsh words with my father, and so threw his mind into such turmoil?

17. "Answer my questions truthfully, my lady: What has happened to cause this unprecedented change in the lord of men?

18. "At the bidding of the king, if enjoined by him, my guru, father, king, and benefactor, I would hurl myself into fire, drink deadly poison, or drown myself in the sea.

19. "Tell me then, my lady, what the king would have me do. I will do it, I promise. Rama need not say so twice."

20. The ignoble Kaikeyi then addressed these ruthless words to Rama, the upright and truthful prince:

21. "Long ago, Raghava, in the war of the gods and *asuras,* your father bestowed two boons on me, for protecting him when he was wounded in a great battle.

22. "By means of these I have demanded of the king that Bharata be consecrated and that you, Raghava, be sent at once to Dandaka wilderness.

23. "If you wish to ensure that your father be true to his word, and you to your own, best of men, then listen to what I have to say.

24. "Abide by your father's guarantee, exactly as he promised it, and enter the forest for nine years and five.

*The fourth son of Dasharatha and close companion of Bharata.

25. "Forgo the consecration and withdraw to Dandaka wilderness, live there seven years and seven, wearing matted hair and barkcloth garments.

26. "Let Bharata rule this land from the city of the Kosalans, with all the treasures it contains, all its horses, chariots, elephants."

27. When Rama, slayer of enemies, heard Kaikeyi's hateful words, like death itself, he was not the least disconcerted, but only replied,

28. "So be it. I shall go away to live in the forest, wearing matted hair and barkcloth garments, to safeguard the promise of the king.

29. "But I want to know why the lord of earth, the invincible tamer of foes, does not greet me as he used to?

30. "You need not worry, my lady. I say it to your face: I shall go to the forest—rest assured—wearing barkcloth and matted hair.

31. "Enjoined by my father, my benefactor, guru, and king, a man who knows what is right to do, what would I hesitate to do in order to please him?

32. "But there is still one thing troubling my mind and eating away at my heart: that the king does not tell me himself that Bharata is to be consecrated.

33. "For my wealth, the kingship, Sita, and my own dear life I would gladly give up to my brother Bharata on my own, without any urging.

34. "How much more readily if urged by my father himself, the lord of men, in order to fulfill your fond desire and safeguard his promise?

35. "So you must reassure him. Why should the lord of earth keep his eyes fixed upon the ground and fitfully shed these tears?

36. "This very day let messengers depart on swift horses by order of the king to fetch Bharata from his uncle's house.

37. "As for me, I shall leave here in all haste for Dandaka wilderness, without questioning my father's word, to live there fourteen years."

38. Kaikeyi was delighted to hear these words of Rama's, and trusting them implicitly, she pressed Raghava to set out at once.

39. "So be it. Men shall go as messengers on swift horses to bring home Bharata from his uncle's house.

40. "But since you are now so eager, Rama, I do not think it wise to linger. You should therefore proceed directly from here to the forest.

41. "That the king is ashamed and does not address you himself, that is nothing, best of men, you needn't worry about that.

42. "But so long as you have not hastened from the city and gone to the forest, Rama, your father shall neither bathe nor eat."

43. "Oh curse you!" the king gasped, overwhelmed with grief, and upon the gilt couch he fell back in a faint.

44. Rama raised up the king, pressed though he was by Kaikeyi—like a horse whipped with a crop—to make haste and depart for the forest.

45. Listening to the ignoble Kaikeyi's hateful words, so dreadful in their consequences, Rama remained unperturbed and only said to her,

46. "My lady, it is not in the hopes of gain that I suffer living in this world. You should know that, like the seers, I have but one concern and that is righteousness.

47. "Whatever I can do to please this honored man I will do at any cost, even if it means giving up my life.

48. "For there is no greater act of righteousness than this: obedience to one's father and doing as he bids.

49. "Even unbidden by this honored man, at your bidding alone I shall live for fourteen years in the desolate forest.

50. "Indeed, Kaikeyi, you must ascribe no virtue to me at all if you had to appeal to the king, when you yourself are so venerable in my eyes.

51. "Let me only take leave of my mother, and settle matters with Sita. Then I shall go, this very day, to the vast forest of the Dandakas.

52. "You must see to it that Bharata obeys Father and guards the kingdom, for that is the eternal way of righteousness."

53. When his father heard Rama's words, he was stricken with such deep sorrow that he could not hold back his sobs in his grief and broke out in loud weeping.

54. Splendid Rama did homage at the feet of his unconscious father and at the feet of that ignoble woman, Kaikeyi, then he turned to leave.

55. Reverently, Rama circled his father and Kaikeyi, and withdrawing from the inner chamber, he saw his group of friends.

56. Laksmana, the delight of Sumitra, fell in behind him, his eyes brimming with tears, in a towering rage.

57. Reverently circling the equipment for the consecration, but careful not to gaze at it, Rama slowly went away.

58. The loss of the kingship diminished his great majesty as little as night diminishes the loveliness of the cool-rayed moon, beloved of the world.

59. Though he was on the point of leaving his native land and going to the forest, he was no more discomposed than one who has passed beyond all things of this world.

60. Holding back his sorrow within his mind, keeping his every sense in check, and fully self-possessed he made his way to his mother's residence to tell her the sad news.

61. As Rama entered her residence, where joy still reigned supreme, as he reflected on the sudden wreck of all his fortunes, even then he showed no sign of discomposure, for fear it might endanger the lives of those he loved.

The end of the sixteenth *sarga* of the *Ayodhyakanda* of the *Sri Ramayana*.

Here, we see the strong moral fiber of Rama. Throughout, he shows compassion ("his father's welfare at heart") and exceptional devotion. Furthermore, Rama, like his father, is a man of honor, and he realizes the importance of keeping one's word. Yet he does have a choice. He can either break his promise to the jealous and vindictive Kaikeyi and refuse to go along with his father's request, which was made out of a promise to Kaikeyi or else he can remain faithful to both his and his father's pledges. He chooses the latter. Why? Because he is a person of good character and integrity. His duty comes before his own interests, and honoring his promises and doing what his father requests constitute *dharma*.

So, Rama remains composed, and he dutifully consents. In the face of Kaikeyi's "hateful words," Rama remains "unperturbed." And even when he visits his mother one last time to bid her goodbye, he maintains his composure. He offers us the key to his composure when he says to her:

> My lady, *it is not in the hopes of gain that I suffer living in this world.* You should know that, like the seers, I have but one concern and that is righteousness. (italics mine)

Rama voices the meaning of *dharma* etched into the Bhagavad Gita (which we soon examine): to not be attached to the consequences of one's actions. This is why the thought of personal gain is foreign to him. And, for Rama, the highest expression of righteousness lies in his devotion and duty to his father, even if it means jeopardizing his own welfare.

Rama does not stand alone in the epic as a paradigm of *dharma,* or virtuous action. Sita and Lakshman also exemplify duty and devotion when, for example, they both accompany Rama in his long exile. And what is said of Rama can be applied to all three:

> The loss of the kingship diminished his great majesty as little as night diminishes the loveliness of the cool-rayed moon, beloved of the world.

Immanuel Kant, *Foundations of the Metaphysics of Morals*

[Thus the first proposition of morality is that to have moral worth an action must be done from duty.] The second proposition is: An action performed from duty does not have its moral worth in the purpose which is to be achieved through it but in the maxim by which it is determined. Its moral value, therefore, does not depend on the realization of the object of the action but merely on the principle of volition by which the action is done, without any regard to the objects of the faculty of desire. . . .

The third principle, as a consequence of the two preceding, I would express as follows: Duty is the necessity of an action executed from respect for law . . . that which is connected with my will merely as ground and not as consequence, that which does not serve my inclination but overpowers it or at least excludes it from being considered in making a choice—in a word, law itself—can be an object of respect and thus a command. . . .

> Thus the moral worth of an action does not lie in the effect which is expected from it or in any principle of action which has to borrow its motive from this expected effect.
>
> From Immanuel Kant, *Foundations of the Metaphysics of Morals,* trans. Lewis White Beck (New York: Macmillan, 1985), pp. 16–17.

Arjuna's Quandary and Krishna's Response

Now back to that most treasured book in the Mahabharata, the Bhagavad Gita.

After their thirteen-year exile, the Pandavas gathered together all of their forces, committed to restoring their rightful rule over the kingdom and to overthrowing the Kauravas. And so begins the outbreak of the great war, which was launched on the battlefield of Kuruksetra, the setting for the opening scene depicted at the beginning of this chapter—Arjuna's moral conflict.

Arjuna is despondent. Knowing that the outcome of the terrible battle will wreak countless deaths for his cousins, immediate family, and friends wrings his heart. So he casts aside his weapons, while his friend and charioteer, Krishna, attempts to console him and to persuade him to fight. Should Arjuna fight? What is his *dharma* in this case? Before we can resolve any of this, we first need to be clear about the problem Arjuna faces.

Duty versus emotions. One way to view Arjuna's conflict is to see it as a battle between his sense of duty and his overpowering emotions. In other words, it is not a genuine crisis in his conscience, since this presupposes some fundamental moral values clashing with each other within him.

On the day before battle, Arjuna reminded his elder brother that there is a just reason for war. They must regain the kingdom, which rightfully belonged to them. The Kauravas' forces certainly outnumbered the Pandavas and demonstrated far superior leadership, and this would mean formidable loss of life to the Pandavas. Nonetheless, Arjuna was convinced, as he had been all along, that the inevitable showdown was justified.

Now that he confronts the enemy, however, his feelings make an about-face. When he sees his cousins, friends, and respected elders—the enemy—his emotions prevail over his sense of duty. He does not suddenly transform into a pacifist, for this would be inconsistent with the lifestyle he so freely and willingly adopted as a warrior. There is no conflict between two predominant though incompatible values. The conflict lies between his duty to fight a just war versus his present emotions, between his long-held values versus his current desires.

Duty versus duty. Another way we could view Arjuna's predicament is that there is a real crisis in conscience. In other words, real moral duties within Arjuna oppose each other.

As we have said, Arjuna comes to the field of Kuruksetra intent upon conquering the Kauravas. What is at stake is more than human life—it is a matter of rectifying injustice after all other avenues have been exhausted. The Pandavas were wrongly disinherited from their kingdom. In the name of justice, they therefore feel vindicated in waging war.

Nevertheless, about to enter the fray, Arjuna is racked with pangs of distress for reasons that have to do with more than emotions. His prior convictions are now held in check by other considerations that rise to the surface at the critical moment. Arjuna realizes that the consequences of war will be nasty and brutish, not only destroying family and friends, but also, and even more serious, leading to the crumbling of the social order. Here, his reasoning is unmistakably utilitarian, for he is acutely aware of the long-term catastrophic results of war for all the parties involved. And these thoughts are in sharp conflict with what he intellectually knows to be his duty.

Arjuna finds this dilemma especially painful because it also involves the conflict between his duty toward his family versus his duty as a warrior, which represents his duty to society. In other words, Arjuna knows that he must wage war against his own kin. This is indeed plaguing for him because of his strong sense of commitment to his family. Taking up arms will wreak insurmountable suffering upon his kin, and he foresees a devastating aftermath: the loss of respect for ancestors and tradition and an eventual disruption of the social order.

At the same time, he belongs to the warrior class, and he must fulfill his duties as a member of this class in order to maintain the social order. Yet, what would be the consequences of vindicating the Pandavas? Destruction of his kinsmen, his revered elders, and his friends. And the death of the elders will most likely lead to the decline of authority, and the deterioration of social order and morality—the collapse of the entire social edifice.

We can therefore surmise that Arjuna presents both sentimental and reasonable grounds for his resistance to fighting. Caught on the horns of this dilemma, he both feels and reflects.

Krishna's response. Let us now read the Bhagavad Gita's "Second Teaching," Krishna's response to Arjuna's plight in a profound discourse about the nature of self, duty, and right conduct.

FROM THE BHAGAVAD GITA

Samjaya:
   1.   When sentiment had thus overcome him,
           while he despaired—his sight blurred,
       His eyes filled with tears—
           Krsna, the Slayer of Madhu, answered:

The Lord:

2. How is it possible that at a time of crisis
    you, Arjuna, should become so weak!
    Noblemen detest such weakness.
    It does not lead to heaven. It is degrading.

3. Be a man, Son of Pṛthā!
    This impotence does not suit you.
    Cast off this abject faintheartedness.
    Stand up, you Conqueror!

Arjuna:

4. O Slayer of Madhu, Slayer of Enemies,
    how can I fight Bhīṣma and Droṇa?
    How shall I send my arrows at those two,
    worthy of my worship?

5. It would be better
    To live on alms
    Without having slain
    Our spiritual guides,
    Men of authority—
    But after killing my elders,
    Even if they were greedy,
    My food here in this world
    Would taste of blood.

6. Still we do not know
    Which is best,
    Whether we should win
    Or they.
    There they are,
    Dhṛtarāṣtra's men,
    Drawn up before us.
    If we slay them,
    We'll no longer wish to live.

7. I am not myself:
    I am afflicted
    With feelings of pity.
    I am confused.
    What should be done?

I ask you:
Which is best?
Tell me that
With certainty.
I am your pupil.
Teach me.
I have thrown myself at your feet.

Saṃjaya:
9. Thus the thick-haired warrior
      spoke to Kṛṣṇa,
    And he concluded: "I shall not fight!"
      Then he was silent.

10. Hṛṣīkeśa seemed to smile
      when he answered
    The desperate man
      between the two armies:

The Lord:
11. You have spent your sorrow on beings who do not need it
      and pay lip-service to wisdom.
    Educated men do not sorrow
      for the dead nor the living.

12. There was no time at which I was not
      nor you nor these princes.
    Nor shall any of us
      ever cease to be.

13. Just as a person changes from
      childhood to youth to old age in the body,
    He changes bodies.
      This does not upset the composed man.

14. The world our senses touch, Son of Kuntī,
      is hot or cold, pleasant or unpleasant.
    Sensations come and go. They do not last.
      Learn to endure them, Son of Bharata!

17. But you must know that which is imperishable
      and which stretched forth the whole world.

No one is able to destroy that
   which is everlasting.

18.   Before you are the temporal bodies
         of the eternal, embodied one
      Who does not perish and cannot be measured.
         Therefore you must fight.

19.   Who thinks this one a slayer,
         or who thinks of him as slain,
      Both lack understanding.
         He neither slays nor is slain.

20.   He is never born.
      He never dies.
      You cannot say of him
      He came to be
      And will be no more.
      Primeval, he is
      Unborn,
      Changeless,
      Everlasting.
      The body will be slain,
      But he will not.

21.   How can the man who knows him as imperishable,
         eternal, unborn, and changeless,
      Kill anyone?
         Whom does he cause to be killed, Son of Pṛthā?

26.   Or, even if you think he is born and dies
         continually,
      Even then, O Warrior,
         you ought not to lament him.

27.   Whoever is born will certainly die,
         and whoever dies will certainly be born.
      Since this cannot be changed,
         your grief is inappropriate.

31.   Considering also the duty of your own class
         you should not waver.

To a warrior nothing is better than
   a just battle.

32. Happy the warriors, Son of Pṛthā,
    who find such a battle
Offered unsought—
    a gate to heaven wide open.

33. But if you will not engage
    in this just war,
You give up your duty and your fame
    and will incur demerit.

34. Also, the world will talk
    of your everlasting dishonor,
And dishonor is worse than death
    to a man of fame.

35. The great warriors will think
    you deserted out of fear.
Those who held you in high esteem
    will snap their fingers at you.

39. I have given you this understanding through the teachings
    of Reason. Now hear it in the tradition of Discipline.
Armed with its meditative knowledge you will be free
    from imprisonment by actions.

40. In Discipline no observance is lost,
    nor can any harm result from Discipline.
Even the least practice on this path
    can protect you from grave danger.

41. The knowledge meditation attains on this path consists
    in commitment and is whole.
Irresolute men have a fragmented
    and incomplete knowledge.

49. For ritual [performed for its effect] is far inferior
    to the Discipline of Meditation.
Seek refuge in meditative knowledge.
    Wretched are men when results are their incentive.

50. A man with meditative knowledge
     leaves behind him both good and evil deeds.
     Therefore, practice Discipline.
     Discipline is skill in works and rites.

Arjuna:
54. Please describe the man of firm judgment
     who is established in concentration.
     How would a man of firm mind speak,
     or sit, or move about?

The Lord:
55. A man is of firm judgment
     when he has abandoned all inner desires
     And the self is content,
     at peace with itself.

56. When unpleasant things do not perturb him
     nor pleasures beguile him,
     When longing, fear, and anger have left,
     he is a sage of firm mind.

57. That man has a firm judgment
     who feels no desire toward anything.
     Whatever good or bad he incurs,
     he never delights in it nor hates it.

62. A man gets attached to what the senses tell him
     if he does not turn his mind away.
     Attachment gives rise to desire,
     desire to anger.

63. Anger leads to a state of delusion;
     delusion distorts one's memory.
     Distortion of memory distorts consciousness,
     and then a man perishes.

64. But when a man wholly governing himself
     is roaming the sensual world
     With his senses under control, freed
     from likes and dislikes, he attains clarity.

68. Therefore, O Warrior,
        having your senses entirely withdrawn
     From the world of the senses
        means attaining a steadfast judgment.

69. The man of self-control is awake
        in what is night for all creatures;
     And when they are awake,
        it is night for the seer.

70. The sea gathers the waters;
     It fills and fills itself . . .
     Its equilibrium
     Is undisturbed.
     So also
     The man into whom
     All desires enter—
     Not he who goes after desires—
     Finds peace.

71. The man who has given up all desire
        and moves about without wanting anything,
     Who says neither *mine* nor *I,*
        wins peace.

72. This, Son of Pṛthā, is divine stability.
        Whoso reaches it is not again confused.
     Whoso abides in it even at death
        gains the freedom that is God's.

Let us condense Krishna's answer to Arjuna by considering two levels: the human level and the transcendent level.[49] First, let us see how this passage reflects on the human-to-human plane of morality. Bear in mind that Krishna is a god in disguise. Yet, he first must adapt Arjuna's human perspective. And in doing so, Krishna offers the following reasons why *dharma* in this case requires that Arjuna should fight.

First of all, he admonishes Arjuna for being overly sentimental. Arjuna is particularly, and emotionally, attached to the body, and he identifies with the body, whereas Krishna points out that as far as death is concerned, no one truly dies on the battlefield or elsewhere. Our true identities are invincible, for the self, *atman,* is immortal.

Arjuna, when a man knows the self
to be indestructible, enduring, unborn,
unchanging, how does he kill
or cause anyone to kill?

It makes little sense to grieve over bodily death. Therefore, we should not be attached to bodily existence, pain, or pleasure.

Krishna then assumes a utilitarian perspective, just as Arjuna does earlier, by describing some rather disagreeable consequences if Arjuna resists fighting: "People will tell of your undying shame"; "you will be despised by those who held you in esteem"; and "enemies will slander you."

If Arjuna does fight, the consequences will be favorable, regardless of whether or not he lives: "If you are killed, you win heaven; if you triumph you enjoy the earth." As far as Krishna is concerned, this is surely a just war (*dharmayuddha*). And for a *kshatriya,* there is no greater good than to fight for justice.

Arjuna must therefore do his duty as a warrior and fight. In this way, he champions the social order. Moreover, the true self never dies. However, a true understanding of this requires wisdom and insight, which Arjuna lacks as long as he remains fettered to his emotions.

Krishna is therefore compelled to supply an even more emphatic argument. As important as it is to consider the previous consequences, the reasoning is still morally weak as far as true *dharma* is concerned. In other words, fighting solely in order to win back the kingdom does not make Arjuna's action *dharma,* because he is still attached to the results of his actions, and this diminishes the moral merit of his fighting. The lesson? One must act without attachment to consequences, without regard to gain or loss. The sole motive must be duty and not personal gain. The following passage contains one of the most important statements in the Gita:

Be intent on action,
not on the fruits of action;
avoid attraction to the fruits
and attachment to inaction!

Perform actions, firm in discipline,
relinquishing attachment;
be impartial to failure and success—
this equanimity is called discipline.

Arjuna, action is far inferior
to the discipline of understanding;
so seek refuge in understanding—*pitiful*
are men drawn by fruits of action. [italics mine]

The key to this passage about *dharma* lies in the nature of detachment, and it elevates the level of reasoning about *dharma,* concerning which Arjuna lacks the proper understanding. *Dharma,* action without attachment to its results, is not purposeless action, for action is only meaningful because there is some purpose. Nor is *dharma* that which is without desire. Desireless action is also meaningless action. It is the essential attitude one assumes toward purpose and desire that matters. In other words, *dharma* requires the absence of self-interest. As long as I am motivated by self-interest, my action is not *dharma.*

Let us now consider the second level in Krishna's response to Arjuna, not found in the previous passage, but which composes a good part of the remainder of the Bhagavad Gita. This is the transcendent level. As convincing as the previous arguments may be, Krishna finally realizes that Arjuna can be stirred from his lethargy only through a radical transformation away from his limited human perspective. The peak of the drama occurs when Krishna reveals his true identity as the god Vishnu. And in this unfolding revelation, Arjuna experiences an immeasurable, indescribable vision, a vision so profound that it enables him to perceive the situation within the panorama of the entire drama of existence. His vision is thoroughly transformative. Arjuna thus experiences *moksha,* and from his now enlightened perspective, the ethical conflict disappears. As the scholar Agrawal states, "Virtue is necessary for moral choice, and enlightenment is necessary for virtue."[50] The truth sets him free. He realizes that he must do what he had known all along to be his duty.

Let us now summarize the Gita's key lessons concerning *dharma.* First, ethical action is grounded upon the relationship between our act and how attached we are to the results of that act. In other words, properly conducting our duty requires egoless action. Another lesson is that *dharma* must take into account specific circumstances. For example, noninjury is certainly a universal principle, but it is not a strict moral absolute, as in cases of a just war. Third, as Arjuna's vision illustrates, the ultimate source of morality comes from within, from the inner self, our divine center, *atman*—and not from external sources.

In conclusion, a précis of the three previous vignettes. The first episode gives no definite resolution to Draupadi's question about whether her enslavement, along with that of the Pandavas, constitutes *dharma.* However, it is reasonable enough to conclude that given her reasons and those of Vikara, their bondage violated *dharma* and was immoral.

In the Ramayana, faced with his apparent conflict—whether or not to honor his promise—Rama resolves the conflict on his own by choosing, without a second thought, integrity over personal gain. Rama embodies *dharma* in the most noble sense.

In Arjuna's case, he alone cannot resolve his quandary. He needs the guidance of Krishna, who actually can be said to represent many roles: friend, counsellor, god in disguise, but also Arjuna's "alter-ego," or inner self. Dire circumstances sometimes require dire measures. The stakes are high, and ordinary moral, philosophical reasoning is limited. Through the inspiration of Krishna, it is no longer earth-bound Arjuna who resolves his *dharma,* but his true self.

REVIEW QUESTIONS

1. Discuss the radical meaning behind *tat tvam asi.*
2. Examine the four stages of life. How do they represent moral progress along the lines of Hindu thought?
3. Explain why, according to Hindu teachings, both material comfort (*artha*) and pleasure (*kama*) are not necessarily construed as incompatible with moral development.
4. Since each path (yoga) to enlightenment is unique, how would each path address specific individual needs? Furthermore, how would each yoga interrelate with the others?
5. Discuss the meaning behind karma. How does karma relate to rebirth (or the transmigration of souls)?
6. What are the ethical implications of Draupadi's predicament and her specific question?
7. Discuss the nature of the choice that Rama faced. Why did duty win out for him?
8. Describe Arjuna's impasse in the Bhagavad Gita. How does Krishna attempt to settle this for him?
9. What lessons in ethical decision making can we learn from each of the crises faced by Draupadi, Rama, and Arjuna?
10. How can Hindu ethical teachings help us to live better lives?

NOTES

1. It is also the first Hindu document to be translated into a European language. The first translation was Charles Wilkins's translation in 1785. Its title literally means "Sung by the Lord" (Bhagavad-gitopanisad). This differs from the usual translation as "Song of the Lord."
2. Krishna is an example here of an *avatar,* a god who assumes human form. On another level, Krishna could also be viewed as Arjuna's alter-ego.
3. Chandogya Upanishad VI.13,2–3, in Sarvepalli Radhakrishnan, trans., *The Principal Upanishads* (London: George Allen & Unwin, 1953), p. 463.
4. Brihadaranyaka Upanishad I.iv.10, in Swami Nikhilananda, trans., *The Upanishads,* abridged edition (New York: Harper Torchbook, Harper & Row, 1964), pp. 191–92.
5. *Ashram* also means "training points."
6. From Rabindranath Tagore, "The Four Stages of Life," in William Gerber, ed., *The Mind of India* (New York: Macmillan, 1967), p. 185.
7. During this training, the pupil also realizes the special relationship that exists between the teacher and student, in which the teacher lives as a model of instruction and is viewed as a spiritual mentor.

8. Tagore, in Gerber, *The Mind of India,* p. 185.

9. Ibid., p. 186.

10. Ibid.

11. Y. Krishan, "The Meaning of the Purusarthas in the Mahabharata," in Bimal Krishna Matilal, ed., *Moral Dilemmas in the Mahabharata* (Delhi: Motilal Banarsidass, 1989), pp. 55–56.

12. Kautilya Arthashastra, 15.1, in Sarvepalli Radhakrishnan and Charles A. Moore, eds., *A Sourcebook in Indian Philosophy* (Princeton, NJ: Princeton University Press, 1957), p. 223.

13. Kautilya Artha-Sastra, 8.3, in ibid., p. 221.

14. See discussion in Krishan, in Matilal, *Moral Dilemmas,* pp. 57f.

15. From The Kama Sutra of Yatsyayana, note 7, in John M. Koller, *Oriental Philosophies,* 2nd ed. (New York: Charles Scribner's Sons, 1985), p. 45.

16. From the Bhagavad Gita, VII, 11, cited in Charles A. Moore, ed., *The Indian Mind: Essentials of Indian Philosophy and Culture,* p. 155.

17. Katha Upanishad II.1–2, in Radhakrishnan and Moore, *Sourcebook,* p. 45.

18. The opposite of *rita* is *anrita,* the absence of order.

19. From Taittiriya Upanishad (I.XI.2,4), in Swami Prabhavananda and Frederick Manchester, trans., *The Upanishads: Breath of the Eternal* (New York: Penguin Books, Mentor, 1948), p. 54.

20. Brihadaranyaka Upanishad, 5.2.3, in Radhakrishnan and Moore, *Sourcebook,* p. 89.

21. S. Radhakrishnan, *Indian Philosophy,* Vol. II (London: George Allen & Unwin, 1923), p. 376.

22. According to the Manu-samhita, there are basically four grounds for morality, or *dharma.* These are (1) Vedas, (2) smrti writings elaborating Vedas, (3) examples of virtuous persons, and (4) individual conscience. See Moore, *Indian Mind,* p. 344.

23. In fact, the rules for higher castes appear more difficult than those for the lower castes. This may explain why sudras did not necessarily seek to become brahmins, since the latter caste was the most stringent.

24. See P.T. Raju, *Structural Depths of Indian Thought* (Albany: SUNY Press, 1985), pp. 54ff.

25. See ibid., pp. 61ff.

26. Mahabharata, in Moore, *Indian Mind,* p. 156.

27. The Samkhya and the Nyaya-Vaisheshika schools define *moksha* in a somewhat more negative tone as the liberation from anguish and misery. The more influential Vedanta school describes *moksha* in more positive terms as the highest, ineffable bliss-filled experience. This bliss transcends our ordinary notions of happiness since "happiness" in this mundane sense confines itself within the conventional duality of happiness-sorrow.

28. Four specific estates are proposed within the poem called Purusasukta (Hymn of the Primeval Man) in the Rig Veda 10.90. Scholars such as

Basham consider this to be a precursor of the later system of castes in India. Here, the centrality of sacrifice is evident within the cosmic plan. Out of a primordial sacrifice, humanity originates and evolves. Not only is humanity the product of this original sacrifice, but a human hierarchy also results. This is the unique thesis of Basham. See A.L. Basham, *The Origins and Development of Classical Hinduism* (Boston: Beacon Press, 1989), p. 25.

29. There is a growing movement today to assign more equal rights to these "untouchables," who, for more than three thousand years, have not at all enjoyed the same status as other classes in India. See Barbara Crossette, "Caste May Be India's Moral Achilles Heel," in *New York Times,* Sunday, Oct. 20, 1996, p. 3.

30. See Raju, *Structural Depths,* pp. 205f. He notes that castes first determined profession; later professions determined castes. He also points out instances of brahmins who became warriors in the *kshatriya* class.

31. In Hindu thought, the three primary temperaments, or *gunas,* were purity, virility, and dullness. The Samkhya school especially emphasizes this. And these three, respectively, were represented by the colors white, red, and black. It was held that each individual possesses these three gunas in varying degrees. This pertained to certain groups as well. For example, the *brahmanas* possessed more of *sattva* (purity); the warriors possessed more *rajas* (activity, virility); and the *vaisyas* possessed more of *tamas* (dullness), while the *sudras* had little development of any of these *gunas.* See Moore, *Indian Mind,* pp. 162–63.

32. See Moore, ibid., p. 163. The history of India attests to the many races that have occupied its territories. India managed to assimilate the various racial groupings: the indigenous Dravidians, the conquering Aryans, then the Persians, Greeks, and Huns, etc. There was most likely a growing class consciousness which reflected an awareness of differences in skin color, the Aryans generally being lighter in skin color than the indigenous peoples.

33. From William L. Shirer, *Gandhi: A Memoir* (New York: Simon & Schuster, 1979), pp. 97–98.

34. Raju, *Structural Depths,* p. 547.

35. From the Mahabharata, Book X, in Romesh C. Dutt, trans., *The Ramayana and The Mahabharata* (London: Everyman's Library, 1910), p. 297.

36. T.S. Rukmani, "Moral Dilemmas in the Mahabharata," in Matilal, *Moral Dilemmas,* p. 25.

37. Ibid., p. 24.

38. R.K. Narayan, trans. and abridged, *The Mahabharata* (New Delhi: Vision Books, 1987), p. 73. All excerpts from *The Mahabharata* copyright © 1978 by R.K. Narayan. Reprinted by permission of the Wallace Literary Agency, Inc.

39. Ibid., p. 75.
40. Ibid.
41. Note that the conventional rules for gambling here were already being violated. It was not at all allowed to stake living beings.
42. Narayan, *The Mahabharata,* p. 77; indeed an odd example of polyandry in Indian culture.
43. Ibid., p. 78.
44. This is mentioned in the original account though not in Narayan's rendition.
45. Narayan, *The Mahabharata,* p. 79.
46. Ibid.
47. Ibid., p. 83.
48. Ramayana, Book 2, Sarga 11; this and previous passage are cited from Mary Ann Caws and Christopher Prendergast, eds., *The HarperCollins World Reader: Antiquity to the Early Modern World* (New York: Harper Collins, 1994), pp. 528–29.
49. See discussion in M.M. Agrawal, "Arjuna's Moral Predicament," in Matilal, *Moral Dilemma,* pp. 132f.
50. Ibid., p. 142.

TWO

☺ You have a potential urge and the ability for accomplishment. ☺

2/14/2004

Buddhist Ethics

THE LOST SON

A man parted from his father and went to another city; and he dwelt there many years. . . . The father grew rich and the son poor. While the son wandered in all directions [begging] in order to get food and clothes, the father moved to another land, where he lived in great luxury, . . . wealthy from business, money-lending, and trade. In course of time the son, wandering in search of his living through town and country, came to the city in which his father dwelled. Now the poor man's father . . . forever thought of the son whom he had lost . . . years ago, but he told no one of this, though he grieved inwardly, and thought: "I am old, and well advanced in years, and though I have great possessions I have no son. Alas that time should do its work upon me, and that all this wealth should perish unused! . . . It would be bliss indeed if my son might enjoy all my wealth!"

Then the poor man, in search of food and clothing, came to the rich man's home. And the rich man was sitting in great pomp at the gate of his house, surrounded by a large throng of attendants, . . . on a splendid throne, with a footstool inlaid with gold and silver, under a wide awning decked with pearls and flowers and adorned with hanging garlands of jewels; and he transacted business to the value of millions of gold pieces, all the while fanned by a fly-whisk. . . . When he saw him the poor man was terrified . . . and the hair of his body stood on end, for he thought that he had happened on a king or on some high officer of state, and had no business there. "I must go," he thought, "to the poor quarter of the town, where I'll get food and clothing without trouble. If I stop

51

here they'll seize me and set me to do forced labor, or some other disaster will befall me!" So he quickly ran away. . . .

But the rich man . . . recognized his son as soon as he saw him; and he was full of joy . . . and thought: "This is wonderful! I have found him who shall enjoy my riches. He of whom I thought constantly has come back, now that I am old and full of years!" Then, longing for his son, he sent swift messengers, telling them to go and fetch him quickly. They ran at full speed and overtook him; the poor man trembled with fear, the hair of his body stood on end . . . and he uttered a cry of distress and exclaimed, "I've done you no wrong!" But they dragged him along by force . . . until . . . fearful that he would be killed or beaten, he fainted and fell on the ground. His father in dismay said to the men, "Don't drag him along in that way!" and, without saying more, he sprinkled his face with cold water—for though he knew that the poor man was his son, he realized that his estate was very humble, while his own was very high.

So the householder told no one that the poor man was his son. He ordered one of his servants to tell the poor man that he was free to go where he chose. . . . And the poor man was amazed [that he was allowed to go free], and he went off to the poor quarter of the town in search of food and clothing. Now in order to attract him back the rich man made use of the virtue of "skill in means." He called two men of low caste and of no great dignity and told them: "Go to that poor man . . . and hire him in your own names to do work in my house at double the normal daily wage; and if he asks what work he has to do tell him that he has to help clear away the refuse-dump." So these two men and the poor man cleared the refuse every day . . . in the house of the rich man, and lived in a straw hut nearby. . . . And the rich man saw through a window his son clearing refuse, and was again filled with compassion. So he came down, took off his wreath and jewels and rich clothes, put on dirty garments, covered his body with dust, and, taking a basket in his hand, went up to his son. And he greeted him at a distance and said, "Take this basket and clear away the dust at once!" By this means he managed to speak to his son. [And as time went on he spoke more often to him, and thus he gradually encouraged him. First he urged him to] remain in his service and not take another job, offering him double wages, together with any small extras that he might require, such as the price of a cooking-pot . . . or food and clothes. Then he offered him his own cloak, if he should want it. . . . And at last he said: "You must be cheerful, my good fellow, and think of me as a father . . . for I'm older than you and you've done me good service in clearing away my refuse. As long as you've worked for me you've shown no roguery or guile. . . . I've not noticed one of the vices in you that I've noticed in my other servants! From now on you are like my own son to me!"

Thenceforward the householder called the poor man "son," and the latter felt towards the householder as a son feels towards his father. So the householder, full of longing and love for his son, employed him in clearing away refuse for twenty years. By the end of that time the poor man felt quite at home in the house, and came and went as he chose, though he still lived in the straw hut.

Then the householder fell ill, and felt that the hour of his death was near. So he said to the poor man: "Come, my dear man! I have great riches, . . . and am very sick. I need someone upon whom I can bestow my wealth as a deposit, and you must accept it. From now on you are just as much its owner as I am, but you must not squander it." And the poor man accepted the rich man's wealth, . . . but personally he cared nothing for it, and asked for no share of it, not even the price of a measure of flour. He still lived in the straw hut, and thought of himself as just as poor as before.

Thus the householder proved that his son was frugal, mature, and mentally developed, and that though he knew that he was now wealthy he still remembered his past poverty, and was still . . . humble and meek. . . . So he sent for the poor man again, presented him before a gathering of his relatives, and, in the presence of the king, his officers, and the people of town and country, he said: "Listen, gentlemen! This is my son, whom I begot. . . . To him I leave all my family revenues, and my private wealth he shall have as his own."

From *The Saddharma-Pundarika,* in H. Kern, trans., *The Sacred Books of the East,* Vol. XXXI, ed. F. Max Müller (London: Clarendon Press, 1912).

"The Lost Son" belongs to one of the most treasured masterpieces in Mahayana Buddhist literature, the Lotus Sutra, or Saddharmapundarika (Lotus of the Good Law). And while "The Lost Son" may remind us of the Prodigal Son in the Gospel of Luke 15:11–32, the Buddhist account reveals some noticeable differences. For instance, in the Buddhist rendition, the father is the only one who recognizes the true relationship between "rich man" and "poor man." Furthermore, he keeps the secret of his son's identity to himself, even though he obviously desires that his son realizes the same truth; indeed, he urges his son to "think of me as a father. . . . From now on you are like a son to me!" And even though the son's initial feelings of estrangement and apprehension gradually dissolve, he still remains ignorant of his true identity until his father's disclosure.

According to Buddhist teachings, we are very much like the estranged son. We also do not recognize our true identity, that is, our Buddha-nature. No matter how many clues we uncover, we generally remain ignorant. We go through life bound to a false view of ourselves as separate and individual entities, and thereby we remain "poor" in a spiritual sense. Buddhism insists that we awaken to our true nature, our Buddha-nature, which all beings share.

Furthermore, in the Buddhist narrative, not only does the father conceal his identity from his son, but he intentionally allows his son to go through a rather long stretch of service, cleaning his household and "clearing away the refuse"— for twenty years! Only after the son proves himself to be "humble and meek" does his father, nearing death, publicly confess the truth of their relationship.

In the same way, we can awaken to our true identity only after we have *earned* enlightenment. The son's Buddha-nature was revealed to him by his father because he deserved it through his actions and attitude. Like the son, we need to be diligent and disciplined in our work while maintaining an attitude of humility. Just as the son who, living now in wealth, still "cared nothing for it, and asked for no share of it, not even the price of a measure of flour," we need to cultivate the same spirit of detachment. Can we likewise choose to live in our own "straw hut" in any type of situation? This is Buddhism's challenge to us, one that has been undertaken by billions of its adherents for well over two thousand years, a challenge that has profoundly influenced the flow of world history.

BACKGROUND

The Buddhacarita, or Deeds of the Buddha, tells us that as a young boy Siddhartha Gautama, who later became the Buddha, coaxed his charioteer into taking him beyond his father's palace walls, against his father's wishes. His father, ruler of the Sakya clan, evidently sought to shield his son from the outside world's unkind realities. Still, the youth beheld four scenes beyond the walls that left an indelible imprint in his heart. He saw an elderly person, a person afflicted by some illness, a corpse, and laborers sweating in misery. These encounters planted the seeds for what he later called the First Noble Truth of existence: All reality is filled with suffering. And it provided the groundwork for a philosophy that centered on the key idea of LIBERATION FROM SUFFERING.

The historical unfolding of the Buddha's teachings is exceedingly complex. Our main concern, however, lies in how it relates to Buddhist ethics. Therefore, let us modestly start by reviewing Buddhism's early formation within the context of its "Three Jewels": the Buddha's own life and enlightenment experience, the Buddha's teachings (*Dharma*), and the Buddha's community of followers (*sangha*).

First Jewel: The Buddha's Life

Siddhartha Gautama (c. 536–476 B.C.E., born at Lumbini) left the safety of his wife, son, and familiar surroundings in order to attain insight into his true nature. After undergoing various meditative and ascetic practices with others, he eventually struck out on his own. He consequently acquired his "awaken-

The world's largest image of the Buddha, 100 meters
tall, inlaid with more than a mile of gold, in Thailand.
(AP Photo/Charles Dharapak)

ing" or enlightenment experience just outside of the town of Bodh Gaya,
under what was later called the *bodhi* ("enlightenment") tree. Thereupon, he
was known as the Buddha ("the awakened one"), and until his death at Kusi-
nagara, he shared his profound insights with countless followers.

Second Jewel: The Buddha's Teachings (*Dharma*)

Three signs. In his first official sermon, at Sarnath, the Buddha delivered his
celebrated teachings concerning the Four Noble Truths and the Middle Path.
These constitute his prescription for emancipation from suffering, and they

form the bedrock of his teachings, or *Dharma*. They can also be understood through what are known as the Three Signs, or characteristics, of existence: All life is filled with suffering (*dukkha*); everything is impermanent (*anicca*); and there is no self (*anatta*). We will later address the first of these, the universality of suffering, within the context of the Four Noble Truths. As to impermanence, all Buddhists believe that every facet of existence undergoes constant change. Each moment carries within itself being and nonbeing, and each moment experiences a rising and a falling.

In this same light, Buddhists contend that there is no self, no substantive, permanent entity. In contrast to the Hindus, who insist upon an individual and separate self called *atman*, Buddhists claim there are no empirical grounds for assuming that this separate self exists. And so long as we sustain the illusion that we are separate selves, we remain ignorant as to our true nature, which, for lack of a better term, Buddhists prefer to call *anatman*, or no-self. Although *anatman* is a negative depiction of our true nature, Buddhists more positively assert that our genuine nature is a Buddha-nature, a nature that all creatures share.

Nirvana. Thus, the ultimate aim in Buddhism is to awaken to our genuine Buddha-nature. The attainment of this enlightenment is called *nirvana*. Nirvana is nearly impossible to describe since it is an experience that transcends our normal categories of time and space. Yet we can glean a clue from the word itself: *Nirvana* literally means "extinguishing," as in putting out a flame. What is extinguished? The false notion of a separate, individual self.

Nirvana is the extinction of the illusion of a distinct self. Furthermore, the experience of nirvana liberates us from the wheel of birth, death, and rebirth (*samsara*). Yet as long as we continue to crave permanence and be ignorant of the illusion of self, we remain fettered to *samsara*, sentenced to rebirth.

However, if there is no individual self, then just what is it that is reborn? Indeed, this is perhaps the most enigmatic question in Buddhism. And suffice it to say here that what is reborn is, in contrast to Hindu teachings, not some enduring, permanent entity called self or soul. Instead, what is reborn can be likened to a "stream of consciousness" characterized by the karma that this stream had accumulated over its many lives.

Dependent origination. This brings us to another item in the Buddhist *Dharma*—dependent origination (*pratityasamutpada*), also referred to as "co-dependent origination" or "dependent arising." It essentially means that all physical and mental phenomena interact so that ultimately nothing occurs solely by itself or without affecting everything else. This intrinsic interdependency of all phenomena further reinforces the ideas of impermanence and nonsubstantiality in that there can be no underlying permanent substance since all things are in a state of constant flux.

We all participate in an intricate web of cause and effect: "no person is an island" in the most literal sense. We are all somehow linked with one another so that our individual actions have far-reaching consequences. For instance, my eating a steak dinner in some way affects all other living creatures. Normally, under the false spell that only the local is real, we do not think of ourselves and our actions in this way. And the impetus behind Buddhist thought lies precisely in emancipating us from this mistaken view.

Third Jewel: The Sangha

The Third Jewel of Buddhism is the *sangha,* the community of monks and nuns who devoted themselves to following the Buddha's teachings. These devotees were originally itinerants (*bhikkus,* or "beggars") who eventually settled down to form pockets of communities that adopted strict regulations and ethical standards, all centering on the necessity of both conscientious discipline and detachment.

The *sangha* was especially instrumental in establishing Buddhist ethical ideals. For instance, both *sangha* monks and laypersons were prohibited from killing (taking life, one's own as well as others'), theft, indulgence in sensuality and adultery, lying and deceit, and drinking intoxicants.[1] And if a layperson joined the *sangha,* strict rules were required, such as abstaining from sexual activity, owning private property, and the handling of money. The monk's only possessions consisted of his robe and begging bowl. Such strict rules aimed to encourage detachment and discipline, with the attainment of nirvana as the ultimate goal.

There was a vital link between the *sangha* and the lay community. When monks went begging in neighboring towns, their presence would be for laypersons a living reminder of Buddhist teachings. Indeed, their act of begging enabled others to demonstrate compassion and charity.

Growth and Decline in India

After the Buddha's death, general councils of monks eventually set Buddhism on a more definite course and produced official teachings known as the Tripitaka or "Three Baskets," clusters of texts containing rules (*Vinaya-pitaka*), sayings (*Sutra-pitaka*), and doctrine (*Abhidharma-pitaka*). Consequently, conflicting interpretations of these teachings led to numerous Buddhist schools, the most traditional and conservative of these schools being the Theravada school.

Yet even within the ranks of the orthodox Theravada school, there was a major rift having to do with the status of those individuals, known as *arhats,* who attained the state of nirvana. Once we become *arhats,* we are then free from the cycle of birth, death, and rebirth, and we do not return to ordinary existence. Theravadins upheld the *arhat* as the ideal. And since the most important prerequisite for becoming an *arhat* is wisdom, or *prajna,* Theravadins clearly underscored the role of wisdom.

However, many Theravadins challenged the status of the *arhat* as an ideal, arguing that it exaggerated a private, individualized liberation while downplaying the real Buddhist message of compassion for others. These dissidents eventually broke away from the Theravadin school to form their own school, calling themselves *Mahayana,* meaning "Great Vehicle." ("Vehicle" refers to the teachings of the Buddha, the means by which one can be transported across the river from the shore of ignorance to that of awakening.) Mahayanists in turn designated the Theravada school by the derogatory term *Hinayana,* meaning "Lesser Vehicle."

Instead of the *arhat*, Mahayanists professed the *bodhisattva* as the Buddhist ideal, viewing the *arhat* as inferior to the *bodhisattva*. The *bodhisattva* is one who achieves his awakening experience and is therefore fully qualified to experience nirvana. Yet, out of genuine compassion, or *karuna,* he renounces nirvana and freely chooses to be reborn and remain in our samsaric cycle in order to help free all living creatures from suffering. He pledges to assist in the enlightenment of all creatures by taking four vows: to help save all other beings, to abolish unhealthy passions, to share the truth with others, and to guide all others toward Buddhahood. The bodhisattva therefore embodies a critical balance between genuine compassion and wisdom.[2] In this way, Mahayanists maintain that we are all potential bodhisattvas, and thus we are all capable of attaining Buddhahood.

To this day, the two foremost schools in Buddhism continue to be Mahayana and Theravada, and they have profoundly influenced Asia. Much of Southeast Asia (e.g., Burma, Thailand, Cambodia) has inculcated the teachings of Theravada Buddhism, whereas Vietnam, China, Korea, and Japan have adopted Mahayanist teachings. Nevertheless, despite their differences, these two schools essentially share a common ground in the *Dharma,* that core of Buddhist teachings we mentioned previously.

The most pivotal figure in the spread of Buddhism was the emperor Ashoka (ruled 269–232 B.C.E.). He first expanded his domain in the most brutal fashion. Then, influenced by Buddhist teachings, he made an about-face and embarked upon a reign of peace. He is famous for having carved his edicts on great rocks and sandstone pillars throughout his vast empire, and he is acknowledged as India's most enlightened emperor. Ashoka also constructed more than eighty thousand *stupas,* Buddhist burial mounds. These stupas later became sites for pilgrimages by Buddhists.

Ashoka is regarded as the living example of *Dharma* and was called the true *chakravartin* ("he for whom the wheel of the law [*Dharma*] turns").[3] His rock edicts contain moral admonitions such as urging compassion, pursuing truth, being generous to all others, and respecting parents. One edict states the following:

Both this world and the other are hard to reach, except by great love of the law [*Dharma*], great self-examination, great obedience, great respect, great energy

... this is my rule: government by the law, administration according to the law, gratification of my subjects under the law, and protection through the law.[4]

Throughout the remainder of his rule he stressed benevolence, placing special emphasis upon spiritual cultivation, nonviolence to humans as well as animals, and religious toleration. His example inspired millions, enabling Buddhism to spread beyond the borders of India into Burma and Ceylon.

One of the most prolific proponents of Mahayana teachings was also its most celebrated philosopher, Nagarjuna (c. 150 C.E.). A fabled account describes how he discovered key scriptural texts, or *sutras,* which later formed the core of Mahayana teaching. These include the revered Prajnaparamita ("Perfection of Wisdom") and Saddharmapundarika ("Lotus") sutras.

Nagarjuna's own landmark text, Madhyamika Karika ("Fundamentals of the Middle Way"), elaborates on the Buddha's teachings of the Middle Path within the context of *sunyata,* or "emptiness," the idea that all things lack substantiality, permanence, and "self-nature." Ethically, this Middle Path means avoiding the extreme positions of materialism (the sole aim being material and physical well-being) and nihilism (when material well-being counts for nothing at all).

Buddhism continued to be a powerful influence in India until the revival of Hinduism eclipsed Buddhist prestige by the thirteenth century. In addition, Muslim invasions in the twelfth century helped to further erode Buddhist authority, particularly when Muslim troops completely decimated the Buddhist Vikramasila Monastery. By the end of that same century, Buddhism had all but disappeared from the land of its origin, an astounding fact given its ongoing stamina and influence elsewhere in Asia.

Buddhism in China and Japan

Buddhism's passage into China was as equally remarkable as its virtual departure from India. Indigenous Chinese worldviews were nearly totally absorbed in Confucianism and Taoism, perspectives that, at least on the surface, seemed to be worlds apart from Buddhism. Moreover, Buddhist ideas about emptiness and no-self must have surely been alien to the Confucian, whose primary interest was in a social ethic that stressed communal interaction and social responsibilities. Nevertheless, the Chinese detected in Buddhism, particularly the Mahayana branch, a feasible complement to Confucian and Taoist beliefs.

How did Buddhism enter China? We can give credit to the untiring efforts of two missionaries, Kumarajiva (c. 343–413 C.E.) and Bodhidharma (460–534 C.E.). Kumarajiva not only transported Madhyamika teachings to China, but also translated major works from Sanskrit into Chinese. Bodhidharma introduced the *dhyana,* or meditational components, of Buddhism into China, and he planted the seeds of what later blossomed as the Ch'an Buddhist school.

Buddhist teachings first arrived in Japan by way of Korea in the sixth century. Despite the prevailing native, animistic beliefs of Shinto, before long

Buddhist beliefs were held in high esteem by the royalty, thanks to the efforts of Prince Shotoku (574–622 C.E.), who also labored significantly to spread Buddhist teachings among the populace.

Among the many Buddhist schools that evolved in Japan (*Tendai,* Pure Land or *Jodo,* and Lotus or *Hokke*), we find the most radical expression of Buddhist teachings in Zen Buddhism, the Japanese counterpart of the Chinese Ch'an school. Zen stresses meditation as a necessary means to awakening. And of all the schools, Zen has had the most penetrating effect upon Japanese culture and habit. More will be said of Zen in the next chapter.

In summary, Buddhism's sweeping power throughout the course of Asian history is irrefutable, a vital testament to the human quest for deliverance from suffering. Insisting upon the intimate link between wisdom and virtue, insight and ethics, Buddhism has inspired countless followers for more than two millennia, and it will continue to articulate humane values for an inhospitable planet.

THE MIDDLE PATH

There was once a monk named Sona who was exceptionally zealous in practicing bodily mortification. He would practice walking meditation so rigorously that his feet bled. Yet, despite his efforts, he did not achieve enlightenment and was disheartened. The Buddha, knowing that as a layman, Sona had been a lute player, addressed him:

> "Now what do you think, when the strings of your lute become too tight, could you get the right tune, or was it then fit to play?"
> "No indeed, Sir."
> "Likewise, when the strings became too slack, could you get the right tune, or was it then fit to play?"
> "No indeed, Sir."
> "But when the strings were neither too tight nor too slack but were keyed to an even pitch then did it give the right tune?"
> "Yes indeed, Sir."
> "Even so, Sona, too much zeal conduces to restlessness and too much slackness conduces to mental sloth." So saying, the Master admonished the young monk to strike a balance between these two extremes and develop an even tempo of spiritual equilibrium.[5]

It is said that Siddhartha Gautama, the Buddha-to-be, practiced such austere bodily renunciation that his own clothes hung as tattered rags on his emaciated body. He was so desperate for a garment that he even stole a shroud that draped the corpse of a young girl waiting to be cremated.[6] His fasting was so exacting that after abandoning his five fellow ascetics, he passed out from exhaustion under a tree.

According to one legend, a maiden regularly came to this same tree to leave offerings of food to the gods. Upon seeing the wasted Siddhartha, she believed him to be a god incarnate and set the food before him. When he awoke, he ate the portions and eventually felt revived and regained his strength. More important, he realized a most profound truth: The way to enlightenment does not demand bodily deprivation. Nor does it require that we indulge in physical and sensual pleasures. We can awaken to our true Buddha-nature only by steering a balanced path that avoids the extremes of deprivation and excess, asceticism and extravagance. This path requires stability and is known as the Middle Path. Herein lies our redemption. This Middle Path is the unequivocal cornerstone of Buddhist ethics.

This realization clearly made personal sense for Siddhartha, for it enabled him to persist in his long period of concentration, meditation, discipline, and patience, which led to his awakening experience. From that time on, his disciples referred to him as "the Buddha," meaning "the one who is awakened."

Buddhist teachings continually advise us to pursue this passage between excess and deficit—those two perennial traps we tend to lapse into throughout our lives. For instance, we fall into excess by overindulging in material comforts or superfluous "needs." Out of habit, we deceive ourselves into believing that these "essentials" are necessary. Yet excess too easily enslaves us in a prison of self-concern and self-centeredness.

On the other hand, sinking into deficit is equally perilous. Consider Siddhartha's utter depletion of energy after experimenting with all sorts of harsh austerities. Not only would such behavior literally consume us, but by acting in this way, we are still held captive to our preoccupation with liberation. That is, I am still enslaved to my chronic desire to free my self, my *atman*, from its bodily prison, even if it means sacrificing my personal health. In contrast, the Buddha sends us a clear message: Live a life of balance.

Herbert Marcuse, *One-Dimensional Man*

We may distinguish both true and false needs. "False" are those which are superimposed upon the individual by particular social interests in his repression: the needs which perpetuate toil, aggressiveness, misery, and injustice. Their satisfaction might be most gratifying to the individual. . . . The result then is euphoria in unhappiness. Most of the prevailing needs to relax, to have fun, to behave and consume in accordance with the advertisements, to love and hate what others love and hate, belong to this category of false needs. . . .

The prevalence of repressive needs is an accomplished fact, accepted in ignorance and defeat, but a fact that must be undone in the interest of the happy individual as well as all those whose misery is the price of his satisfaction. The only needs that have an unqualified claim for satisfaction are the vital ones—nourishment, clothing, lodging at the attainable level of culture. The satisfaction of these needs is the prerequisite for the realization of *all* needs, of the nonsublimated as well as the sublimated ones.

From Herbert Marcuse, *One-Dimensional Man* (Boston: Beacon Press, 1964), pp. 4–5.

According to traditional accounts, when the Buddha delivered his first sermon, his former fellow ascetics were among the crowd of listeners. Upon seeing the Buddha, they were convinced that he had forsaken the path of holiness by succumbing to indulgence. They therefore resolved among themselves not to address him with any titles of esteem. Still, they felt mysteriously drawn to his presence. And the Buddha spoke to them:

> "Neither abstinence from fish or flesh, nor going naked, nor shaving the head . . . will cleanse a man who is not free from delusions. . . .
>
> "Let me teach you, O bhikshus [referring to the ascetics], the middle path, which keeps aloof from both extremes. By suffering, the emaciated devotee produces confusion and sickly thoughts in his mind. Mortification is not conducive even to worldly knowledge; how much less to a triumph over the senses! . . .
>
> "On the other hand, sensuality of all kind is enervating. The sensual man is a slave of his passions, and pleasure-seeking is degrading and vulgar."[7]

The ascetics' lifestyle is one in which they are so preoccupied with their own salvation that they still remain chained to self, to ego. And it is precisely this attachment to self that is the root of the problem. So the Buddha continues, "All mortification is vain *so long as self remains, so long as self continues to lust after either worldly or heavenly pleasures*" [italics mine].[8]

This allegiance to an illusory self constitutes the real quandary and is the reason why we are so often ensnared by extremes. The Buddha proposes that we can be free to follow the Middle Path by freeing ourselves from the illusion of self:

> But he in whom self has become extinct is free from lust; he will desire neither worldly nor heavenly pleasures, and the satisfaction of his natural wants will not defile him. Let him eat and drink according to the needs of the body. . . .
>
> But to satisfy the necessities of life is not evil. To keep the body in good health is a duty, for otherwise we shall not be able to trim the lamp of wisdom, and keep our mind strong and clear.
>
> This is the middle path, O bhikshus, that keeps aloof from both extremes.[9]

The Buddha's message certainly speaks to all of us. The tendency to fall into excess or defect is universal, as is our ungrounded faith in a separate self. Let us now proceed further into the heart of the Buddha's first sermon and the core of his teachings—the Four Noble Truths.

THE FOUR NOBLE TRUTHS

All Buddhists, regardless of their school or sect, accept the Four Noble Truths. These four axioms render the most profound existential framework for Buddhist ethics. And since the Buddha offers his teachings, the *Dharma,* as an elixir for our human condition, we can more fittingly portray his Four Truths in terms of a medical diagnosis and prognosis.

The Diagnosis

First Truth: Our condition constitutes suffering (dukkha).

> [T]his is the Noble Truth of Sorrow. Birth is Sorrow, age is sorrow, disease is sorrow, death is sorrow; contact with the unpleasant is sorrow, separation from the pleasant is sorrow, every wish unfulfilled is sorrow—in short all the *five components of individuality* are sorrow.[10] [italics mine]

In sweeping fashion, our physician, the Buddha, tells us that suffering is our universal condition, a malady from which no one of us is exempt. Heartache, in all manner and form, permeates our existence. The Buddhist term for "suffering," *dukkha* [Sanskrit: *duhkha*], literally means "dislocation" and excruciatingly conveys sorrow's ubiquitous face, for the sense of painful dislocation seems nearly boundless and without end.

This suffering that the Buddha speaks of comes in various guises. Its most obvious form is the physical pain we all commonly experience. Yet it also incorporates the mental anguish that often accompanies such pain. Suppose I have a terrible accident that results in the loss of the use of my limbs. The thought of living my life without embracing another, swimming, playing tennis, or playing the piano may be unbearable. And I could become thoroughly depressed, for we often take our health for granted. Yet unforeseen events have a way of reminding us of our fragility.

Sorrow also speaks to us in more fundamental ways. Perhaps the most rudimentary aspect of our existence is that it is everchanging. Nothing stays the same. Existence, by its nature, is saturated with impermanence. Therefore, whatever pleasures we do experience are essentially short-lived, leading to all sorts of frustration. I am shocked into this awareness through my accident, now knowing that I can no longer do the things I loved doing. All things pass. Our vacations come to an end. Our bodies grow older, our reflexes less sharp, our vision weaker. The intensity of our feelings for another changes over time. In many respects, we are not the same persons we were yesterday, or even an hour ago. Change is the canvas of our being, while frustration fills the landscape.

Since all things are impermanent, so too are our identities. Buddhists teach us that there is no individual, unchanging, permanent self, soul, or entity we call "I". In fact, what we think of as a separate self or "I" is essentially an everchanging pattern of physical and mental energies. As the previously quoted passage tell us, "in short all the five components of individuality are sorrow."

We now address an even more profoundly philosophical meaning behind the notion of suffering. What are these "five components of individuality"? Buddhists tell us that these components refer to the five aggregates, or *skandhas,* that constitute the physical and mental facets of our individuality: physical forms or matter, feelings and sensations, perceptions, mental activities (especially will), and consciousness.

Suppose I have been studying all evening for my final exam tomorrow in ethics. I now have a raging headache. What is going on? According to Buddhist beliefs, my experience of a headache can be broken down into these five forces. First of all, there is matter: the area of my head and the more localized regions behind my eyes or around my temples. Second, sensation: I certainly have the sensation of a dull, lingering pain. Third, perception: I have the perception of the pain localized in the region of my head. Fourth, mental activities: I conceptualize the feeling of pain as a headache, and I therefore will that the feelings of pain stop. Volition is an important aspect of mental activities. Fifth, consciousness: There is an overall awareness of what is going on. It consists in an awareness of the region, the pain, and the desire to be rid of the pain. In other words, there is the awareness of what is called "headache." It is important to note that this consciousness of "my headache" is entirely dependent upon the other four components. It cannot exist on its own.

It is now apparent that this experience of "my headache" can be broken down only into these five physical and mental components. In no way do we find any enduring, substantial, permanent entity called "I" that undergoes the experience. There is only the experience itself and an awareness of the experience. Furthermore, each of these five components undergoes constant change. It is like a flowing river. The water at point C is not the same as the water at point O. Just as there is nothing about the river that is permanent (other than its stream of impermanence), in no way can I find an irreducible, enduring, autonomous entity called "self." Nevertheless, I still persist in presuming that I am a "self." The illusion is tenacious. And as long as I cling to this fallacy, I continue to generate sorrow, seeking permanence where there is none, for this separate self (*atman* as Hindus would call it) is a false idea. In the most profound way, these five components constitute sorrow since they induce this false idea.

Second Truth: The source of our condition is **trishna.**

> [T]his is the Noble Truth of the Arising of Sorrow. It arises from craving [*trishna*], which leads to rebirth, which brings delight and passion, and seeks pleasure now here, now there—the craving for sensual pleasure, the craving for continued life, the craving for power.[11]

Now that we have identified our disease, what can we know about its etiology? What is the real source of suffering? This is crucial. If we can ascertain the cause of our disorder, we can establish a course of treatment and propose a remedy.

Moreover, our physician, the Buddha, is not interested in merely relieving the symptoms. He radically approaches our illness by getting to the heart of the matter, the root cause of our condition. He informs us that the root cause of suffering lies in craving, that is, our tendency to cling to what we desire. The term for craving is *trishna* (Pali: *tanha*). Also translated as "desire," "thirst," and "clinging," *trishna* translated as "craving" is more fitting since it conveys the extreme measure of both our desire and our tendency to cling to some form of permanence.

Now the previous quote cites three objects of our craving: "sensual pleasure," "continued life," and "power." Our craving for pleasure inescapably incurs sorrow since pleasures are by their nature fleeting. The satisfaction of our physical desires remains temporary, and our craving can become insatiable. And clinging to "continued life" means denying life's impermanence as well as our own bodily mortality. This sort of craving can breed an extreme vitalism whereby life is to be preserved at any and all costs. Clinging to power spawns corruption, since the possession of power can lead to unscrupulous behavior. For Buddhists, craving these three—physical pleasures, immortality, and power—spells disaster, creating iniquities as well as begetting sorrow.

Clinging or craving occurs on an even deeper, perhaps more insidious level. Not only do we cling to material things like prestige, power, and pleasures, but we also cling to ideas, points of view, beliefs, and concepts. In fact, attachment to our ideas can produce the worst order of harms. For instance, the strife in Northern Ireland continues to flare up despite recent peace agreements partly because there are unhealthy attachments to ideas such as "freedom from the British" and a "united Ireland." Attachment to these ideas can permit extremists on both sides to view themselves as "freedom fighters" rather than as "terrorists."

Using the earlier example of my accident, since I can no longer use my arms and legs, I naturally experience an extended period of depression, sadness, and loss. Yet if I remain fixed to a former image of myself capably using arms and legs, my depression can enslave me. I will fail to readapt to my changed world, all because I choose to remain attached to an idea.

This attachment to an idea or image represents craving in its most subtle guise, a craving that seems to inhabit our human condition. For example, is it not natural for us to resist not only death but the *idea* of death, and instead to crave life? Consider the well-known and poignant tale of Kisagotami.

THE STORY OF KISAGOTAMI

Kisagotami became in the family way, and when the ten months were completed, gave birth to a son. When the boy was able to walk by himself, he died. The young girl, in her love for it, carried the dead child clasped to her bosom, and went about from house to house asking if any one would give her some medicine for it. When the neighbours saw this, they said, "Is the young girl mad that she carries about on her breast the dead body of her son!" But a wise man thinking to himself, "Alas! this Kisagotami does not understand the law of death, I must comfort her," said to her, "My good girl, I cannot myself give medicine for it, but I know of a doctor who can attend to it." The young girl said, "If so, tell me who it is." The wise man continued, "Gautama can give medicine, you must go to him."

Kisagotami went to Gautama, and doing homage to him, said, "Lord and master, do you know any medicine that will be good for my body?" Gautama replied, "I know of some." She asked, "What medicine do you require?" He said, "I want a handful of mustard seed." The girl promised to procure it for him, but Gautama continued, "I require some mustard seed taken from a house where no son, husband, parent, or slave has died." The girl said, "Very good," and went to ask for some at the different houses, carrying the dead body of her son astride on her hip. The people said, "Here is some mustard seed, take it." Then she asked, "In my friend's house has there died a son, a husband, a parent, or a slave?" They replied, "Lady, what is this that you say! The living are few, but the dead are many." Then she went to other houses, but one said, "I have lost a son"; another, "I have lost my parents"; another, "I have lost my slave." At last, not being able to find a single house where no one had died, from which to procure the mustard seed, she began to think, "This is a heavy task that I am engaged in. I am not the only one whose son is dead. In the whole of the Savatthi country, everywhere children are dying, parents are dying." Thinking thus, she acquired the law of fear, and putting away her affection for her child, she summoned up resolution, and left the dead body in a forest; then she went to Gautama and paid him homage. He said to her, "Have you procured the handful of mustard seed?" "I have not," she replied; "the people of the village told me, 'The living are few, but the dead are many.' " Gautama said to her, "You thought that you alone had lost a son; the law of death is that among all living creatures there is no permanence." When Gautama had finished preaching the law, Kisagotami was established in the reward of Sotapatti; and all the assembly who heard the law were also established in the reward of Sotapatti.

Some time afterwards, when Kisagotami was one day engaged in the performance of her religious duties, she observed the lights in the houses now shining, now extinguished, and began to reflect, "My state is like these lamps." Gautama, who was then in the Gandhakuti building, sent his sacred appearance to her, which said to her, just as if he himself were preaching, "All living beings resemble the flame of these lamps, one moment lighted, the next extinguished; those only who have arrived at Nirvana are at rest." Kisagotami, on hearing this, reached the stage of a Rahanda possessed of intuitive knowledge.

From Buddhaghosa, *Vissudhi Magga.*

In this story, we see an affirmation of the first two truths. Suffering is universal: "The living are few but the dead are many." And Kisagotami's open-hearted grief for her dead child brings about further sorrow if she remains attached to the idea of continued life. We cannot blame her for feeling the way she does, for the sting of craving infects all of us. Yet if this is native to our condition, then are we not chained to sorrow? Can we ever be freed from our agitation? Is peace of mind possible?

The Prognosis

Third Truth: We can be cured.

[T]his is the Noble Truth of the Stopping of Sorrow. It is the complete stopping of that craving, so that no passion remains, leaving it, being emancipated from it, being released from it, giving no place to it.[12]

The diagnosis looks bleak. Given what we now know about the disease as well as the patient, can we be cured? Since we seem tied to our congenital condition of craving, is the likelihood of recovery impossible? The answer is No. This third truth is the turning point in our analysis. The Buddha's message is hopeful: Not only can we alleviate our suffering; we can even be cured!

His optimism is logically compelling. After all, since the source of our disease lies within us, then so is the cure. If our suffering ultimately emanates from our innate tendency to crave, then any cure must rest upon whether or not our tendency can be altered. To this, the Buddha says "Yes!"

The root cause of suffering is craving, a clinging that accompanies ego and self-interest. Yet our sense of ego and self is actually a false sense since, as we described previously, there is no separate self, and our experiences can be reduced to the five components. Of these five, craving derives from the mental faculty of volition or will and is the extreme form of desire. Now since volition is an intrinsic component of our individuality, volition can also act to counter the force of craving. In other words, we can control volition and thereby will to cease craving.

To again illustrate, losing the use of my limbs from my accident was quite beyond my control and is a tragedy. It is even more tragic if I remain attached to images of myself as a completely functioning and athletic body. However, *I choose* whether or not to remain attached to these images. I can will to free myself from such images. My volition can liberate me from further suffering.

Here's the point. I can will to cease further craving, and this is absolutely necessary to be free from suffering. This is why the final state for Buddhists is called nirvana, for *nirvana* is that state of being in which complete cessation of craving comes about through realizing that the independent self is a fiction. What all this means is that genuine freedom is within our reach, and it comes about when we shatter the illusion of a separate self, which, in turn, means our willing to cease craving. Now we ask—*How can we cease craving? Through the diligent practice of the Eightfold Path.*

Fourth Truth: The prescription lies in the Eightfold Path.

> [T]his is the Noble Truth of the Way which Leads to the Stopping of Sorrow. It is the Noble Eightfold Path—Right Views, Right Resolve, Right Speech, Right Conduct, Right Livelihood, Right Effort, Right Mindfulness, and Right Concentration.

Herein lies the centerpiece of Buddhist ethics. The Eightfold Path requires both *mental discipline* and *moral behavior.* In Buddhist ethics, these two cannot be separated. Only by faithfully following the Eightfold prescription can we heal ourselves from our diseased condition of craving. This requires hard work and sincere effort, as we see in the story of the estranged son who worked dutifully for twenty years. Furthermore, our redemption is not contingent upon extraneous forces: no saints, no gods, no others to save us but ourselves. What does this prescription entail? It requires that we live morally by observing the following:

- right views
- right resolve

- right speech
- right conduct
- right livelihood
- right effort
- right mindfulness
- right concentration

Rather than observing each of these in isolation, it makes better sense to view them as interdependent, so that practicing each one entails cultivating the others as well. Moreover, these stages remind us of the critical importance of following the Middle Way, so as to avoid excess and deficit, and to help steer a course between living a life consumed by material pleasures and one that completely rejects material comfort. To see this more closely, let us examine each path.

Right view consists of embracing the Four Truths in more than simply an intellectual fashion. It means understanding them so that we accept the Three Signs mentioned earlier: All things are impermanent; there is no self; all of life is suffering. Otherwise, we can acquiesce to the Four Perverse Views that stain our ordinary, unenlightened state: seeking permanence in the impermanent, finding happiness in someone else's suffering, inventing a self where there is no-self, and seeing beauty in what is ugly.[14] These perverse views derive from our fixation upon a permanent, individual self, in turn, exposing our attachment to the idea of permanence itself. Actually, our desire for permanence illustrates the extreme of excess. In contrast, we could descend into the other extreme of deficit and adopt the nihilistic view that nothing whatsoever exists.

In this regard, right view signals a Middle Path in that we understand that all things both rise and fall, exist and nonexist simultaneously. This includes what we mistakenly think of as a permanent self or "I". Yet as long as we cling to this wrong view of self, we deviate from the right view and remain enslaved to sorrow.

Right resolve means having the determination and tenacity, or purity of heart, to follow these eight steps. Right resolve underscores our intention behind our actions and signifies our motive to pursue the morally appropriate path as a principal factor in assessing ethical behavior.

Another meaning for right resolve is "right thought"—the right mental content, which consists of thoughts of selflessness and love. These in turn require thoughts of the need for detachment as well as the notion of the absence of any permanent entity called self.

Right speech compels us to refrain from lying, maligning, gossiping, and cursing. Any form of abusive, malicious, and useless speech is prohibited. Buddhists deal with the role of language for two principal reasons. First, our speech may be untrue and/or useless. It may be either entirely or partially ungrounded, as, for instance, rumors generally tend to be. Yet, even though many of our conversations produce no real benefit, we still expend a great deal of our energies in this "idle talk."[15]

Second, our speech can precipitate injury or blessing. This pertains not only to falsehoods, but to rumor, gossip, cursing, and slander. Buddhists believe that our speech indicates our character. We ought, therefore, to restrict our speech to that which benefits others and alleviates sorrow. Although the following counsel from the Vinaya-pitaka describes the exemplary monk, it sets forth a model for laypersons as well:

> He abandons falsehood and speaks the truth.
> He abandons slanderous speech, and does not tell what he has heard in one place to cause dissension elsewhere. He heals divisions and encourages friendships, delighting in concord and speaking what produces it.
> He abandons harsh speech, his speech is blameless, pleasant to the ear, reaching the heart, urbane and attractive to the multitude.
> He abandons frivolous language, speaks duly and truly and in accordance with the Dhamma and Vinaya. His speech is such as to be remembered, elegant, clear, and to the point.[16]

Martin Heidegger, *Being and Time*

What is said-in-the-talk as such, spreads in wider circles and takes on an authoritative character. Things are so because one says so. Idle talk is constituted by just such gossiping and passing the word along—a process by which its initial lack of grounds to stand on becomes aggravated to complete groundlessness . . .

The groundlessness of idle talk is no obstacle to its becoming public; instead it encourages this. Idle talk is the possibility of understanding everything without previously making the thing one's own.

From Martin Heidegger, *Being and Time,* trans. J. Macquarrie and E. Robinson (Oxford: Basil Blackwell, 1967), pp. 212–13.

Right conduct prohibits murder, theft, living unchastely, harming others, destroying property, and all other actions that bring about unnecessary harm to oneself or to any other creature. For instance, the Buddha advises his son Rāhula that his bodily actions should be performed only after careful reflection on the merit and consequences of the intended act.

> If you, Rāhula, are desirous of doing a deed with the body, you should reflect on that deed of your body, thus: "That deed which I am desirous of doing with the body is a deed of my body which might conduce to the harm of myself and that might conduce to the harm of others and that might conduce to the harm of both; this deed of body is unskilled, its yield is anguish, its result is anguish." If you, Rāhula, reflecting thus, should find [this to be the case] . . . a deed of body like this, Rāhula, is certainly not to be done by you.[17]

Thus the standard for determining the rightness or wrongness of an action centers on whether or not the action itself would bring about harm to self and/or others.

Up to this point, note how these first four paths begin with our most interior mental behavior (right view, right resolve) and then unfold outwardly to right speech (our verbal behavior) and right conduct (our bodily behavior). This outward manifestation now reaches its peak in the following emphasis upon right occupation or livelihood.

Right livelihood requires us to engage in an occupation or profession that does not bring about unnecessary suffering to others, human and animal. Does our lifestyle induce harm or benefit? This path therefore warns us against engaging in professions such as butchering, hunting, and making and/or selling liquor, as well as those that involve the manufacturing or operating of weapons.

We must also avoid occupations that deliberately arouse attachments and desires on the part of others. For instance, a profession that intentionally lures us into commercialism is naturally risky because it inspires attachments. In view of the inordinate degree of consumerism in our society, Buddhist teachings would frown upon, for example, careers in advertising, since such work seeks to foster desires for commodities.

Of course, it would be inappropriate to presume that any one occupation is intrinsically superior to all others. Nevertheless, we need to make an earnest effort to pursue a lifestyle that alleviates suffering. This path squarely challenges us to recognize our moral duties within a community that comprises all sentient creatures, as well as to assess our participation in contributing to the suffering of others.

Right effort involves guarding the mind against unhealthy thoughts and desires. It reminds us to stay focused on what truly counts in life, and to not allow ourselves to be sidetracked. Like the song of the Sirens, which led all sailors before Odysseus to shipwreck, distractions can be our undoing.

In this way, right effort requires us to realize the significance of volition and free will. Despite the effects of both positive and negative karma, our volition still plays a definitive role. Our free will and capacity to make choices channel the direction our lives take.

Right mindfulness means being fully attentive to our state of mind and body, especially when they become agitated. Being aware in the fullest sense requires that we strike a balance between body and mind. And Buddhists recommend a meditative technique known as *vipassana,* which means "insight." It involves being totally aware of the four domains of bodiliness, feelings and sensations, mind, and ideas.[18]

One way bodily awareness occurs is through concentrating on our breathing. This is at first difficult since we take our breathing for granted. Yet, with practice we can cultivate an awareness of breathing that becomes second nature and provides both mental equilibrium and positive physiological effects. Another manner of mindfulness through *vipassana* is the total awareness of what we do as we do it. This enables us to enhance our powers of attention and to be fully engaged in our actions. For example, reading the newspaper while eating our breakfast does not permit us to be fully engaged in either reading or eating. Or, if we read while riding an exercise bicycle, we cannot reap the full benefits of exercising. This lack of focus can take more dangerous routes, such as speaking on a cellular phone while driving.

Staying focused is thereby all the more difficult in a culture such as ours that is so obsessed with distraction. And the whole point behind right mindfulness is to disengage ourselves from thinking in terms of "I". For instance, if I am reading, right mindfulness entails that I be completely focused upon reading so that "I" am lost in the activity. It does *not* mean being aware that "I am reading."

As for feelings, right mindfulness means being aware of sensations and feelings as they arise and observing them as if from a distance. It means seeing my feelings for what they are. It means observing our states of mind in such a way that we are able to view them as objectively as we can. For instance, what about my attitudes toward certain events or ideas? Am I being swept away by my emotions, passions, and ideas?

In these final paths (right effort, right mindfulness, and right concentration), note our return inward from right livelihood. We resort once more to the primacy of mental activity, and right mindfulness is especially important because it allows us to live fully in the moment.

Right concentration is also known as *samadhi*. It comes from practicing the proper meditative techniques so that we are free from the contents of our mind. That is, thoughts and feelings can no longer distract us—we are in a state of pure consciousness, a condition of "neither-perception-nor-nonperception." And this can only occur after I have perfected a series of techniques to help eliminate any differentiation between "I" as subject and my experience as object.

Right concentration involves four stages of meditation, or *dhyana*. The purpose in the first stage is to purge ourselves from all negative desires and thoughts while maintaining positive feelings such as happiness. In the second stage, we eliminate all intellectual efforts. Because Buddhists maintain that the feeling of joy itself is still an "active sensation," in the third stage, we remove that as well. In the final stage, we are rid of all sensations so that we are purely aware, undistracted, and in a state of pure balance and equanimity.[19]

It is important to note that Buddhists actually profess right mindfulness as being more significant than right concentration because right mindfulness more closely approaches nirvana, the ultimate experience of extinguishing the false idea of a permanent "I", the complete state of detachment. In any case, throughout all eight steps, it is entirely up to the patient to comply with the treatment plan, a prescription requiring neither bodily mortification nor material indulgence. There are no strict ritual sacrifices or offerings here. Instead, we have a composite of correct knowledge and proper behavior, a synthesis of insight and morality.

IN THE WAKE OF KARMA

There was once a monk named Cakkhupala. In one of his past lives, he was a successful eye surgeon. However, his state of mind got the worst of him when he performed surgery on a patient toward whom he bore all sorts of ill feelings and evil intentions. Not only did the surgery turn out to be disastrous for his patient, who ended up becoming blind, but the monk Cakkhupala himself has now irreparably lost his sight.[20]

As a prelude to our discussion of the Buddhist virtues, let us first review the highly relevant doctrine of karma. Even though the Buddhists inherited this from their Hindu predecessors, they gave it a different twist.

The general view of most Hindus was that karma pertained to the strict law of moral cause and effect in that each of our moral and immoral thoughts and deeds brings about consequences that are proportional to the act. These effects can occur either in this life or in some future life after reincarnation. Hindus also asserted that it is the same "I", as individual self or *atman* (unique and eternal), who actually creates karma as well as undergoes karmic effects.

Buddhists challenge these claims. First, they emphasize more strongly the volitional aspect of our actions. In other words, it is not simply the case that every action produces its results, but that "volitional actions" do.[21] Volition here refers to our will, intention, and motive and thereby signifies the degree of attachment that compels the action. Karma therefore refers to this volitional action itself and not to the consequences of the action.

At the same time, Buddhists, along with Hindus, recognize that certain other factors can play a hand in the actual outcome of a deed. In other words, the consequence of an action does not depend merely upon the action itself. Other aspects of the situation may also apply, such as the specific context within which the action occurs, for example, the differences in the sound created by a pianist who plays in a small room with low ceilings and the same pianist who plays the same piano in a large concert hall with high ceilings. And the most important contextual feature germane to karma is an individual's character. The Buddha instructs his listeners:

> Here, O Bhikkhus, a certain person is not disciplined in body, is not disciplined in morality, is not disciplined in mind, is not disciplined in wisdom, is with little good and less virtue, and lives painfully in consequence of trifles. Even a trivial act committed by such a person will lead him to a state of misery.
>
> Here, O Bhikkhus, a certain person is disciplined in body . . . in morality . . . in mind . . . in wisdom, is with much good, is high souled. . . . A similar act committed by such a person is expiated in this life and not even a small effect manifests itself (after death), not to say a great one.[22]

By stressing the distinctive role that character plays in the karmic process, Buddhists broaden the scope of karmic factors to include bodily action, conscious motives, and unconscious motives.[23] A bodily action, for example, rescuing a drowning person, may on the surface bring about a significant measure of karma. Yet as to whether this same action is a morally good one depends upon the conscious motivation. Buddhists point out the critical distinction between the action itself and the intent behind the act. Taken together, both aspects constitute a moral or immoral act. The important point is this. The key factor lies in motivation, and here is where our volition is critical.

Buddhists also admit that our unconscious motives may influence our actions. For instance, unbeknownst to myself, I may harbor an unconscious desire to gain from the inheritance of the relative I saved from drowning. Now although this unconscious motive is nondeliberate, I am *still somewhat responsible for it*. David Kalupahana, in his insightful analysis states,

> These motives, though unconscious, result from mistaken understanding of the nature of human existence. Hence an individual may be held responsible for behavior determined by them.[24]

This surely widens the scope of personal responsibility. For instance, occasionally having greedy desires may carve out the negative condition of greed. And this may produce greedy acts. To be sure, by taking into account conscious and unconscious motives, Buddhists reject a strictly deterministic idea of karma whereby the act alone automatically registers a future effect, thus widening the scope of individual accountability.

Aristotle, *Nicomachean Ethics*

Virtue, then, is of two sorts, virtue of thought and virtue of character. Virtue of thought arises and grows mostly from teaching, and hence needs experience and time. Virtue of character results from habit: hence its name 'ethical', slightly varied from '*ethos*'. . . .

Hence it is also clear that none of the virtues of character arises in us naturally . . .

Thus the virtues arise in us neither by nature nor against nature, but we are by nature able to acquire them, and reach our complete perfection through habit . . .

A state [of character] arises from [the repetition of] similar activities. Hence we must display the right activities, since differences in these imply corresponding differences in the states. It is not unimportant, then, to acquire one sort of habit or another, right from our youth; rather, it is very important, indeed all-important.

From Aristotle, *Nicomachean Ethics,* trans. T. Irwin (Indianapolis, IN: Hackett, 1985), pp. 33–35.

Second, in contrast to Hindus, Buddhists insist that there is no "self" (*atman*) as an individual, enduring entity. They refer to our true nature as *anatman,* or no-self. Yet they still maintain the efficacy of karma and believe in rebirth. This being so, what about the relationship between karma and *anatman,* or no-self? How can we untangle the meaning of karma without appealing to an individual self? The question plagues us, since we are so conditioned to think of individual personality in terms of a separate self.

As discussed earlier, Buddhists pare down individuality to five components (together they are called *nāma-rūpa,* meaning "name-form"): physical body, sensations and feelings, perceptions, mental activities such as volition, and consciousness. As far as "I" am concerned, "I" am a composite of these five aggregates. And these five undergo constant change so that there are no grounds for postulating a permanent self. Yet, through all this change, my stream of consciousness assumes a particular pattern or continuity. It is precisely this continuity that survives bodily death and immediately reenters another psychophysical form. What is reborn is not a fixed, immutable entity, a "self," but a continuity or stream of awareness, "no-self," or *anatman* for lack of a better term.

Suppose I lit a candle at the beginning of this chapter. By now, is the flame of the candle the same exact flame? Is it in essence different? *It is neither the same, nor is it different.* The flame has endured as a steady continuity, yet has been everchanging. There is no permanent flame-entity. The flame's "essence" consists in movement, in process.[25] Consider a point in the ocean two miles off the coast, and the movement at this point as the water gains momentum and becomes a sizable wave by the time it reaches the shore. Has this point in the sea changed, or has it stayed essentially the same? It is neither the same sea nor is it different. The sea's "essence" is movement, an unbroken continuity. Are you the exact same person today that you were yesterday? An hour ago? In like manner, Buddhists claim that we are everchanging yet continue on in an unbroken series. Now how does this relate to our discussion of karma?

In view of the features that produce karma—bodily actions, conscious motives, unconscious motives—all five components mentioned previously help to generate karma. In turn, this karmic activity eventually assumes a pattern or continuity that we can call personality, or better still, character. Thus, it is my character that is reborn, molded by my moral and immoral behavior in this life and in previous lives.[26]

My character is ultimately the offspring of my thoughts, conscious as well as innermost. A classic illustration of this power of mind lies in the opening chapter of the matchless Buddhist text *Dhammapada.* It reveals the supreme role of karma in our lives and repeatedly reminds us that we are the controllers of our own destiny. We become what we make of ourselves. And contrary to ordinary opinion, our thoughts are ultimately in our control, and redemption is literally a matter of mind.

THE TWIN VERSES

1. All that we are is the result of what we have thought: it is founded on our thoughts, it is made up of our thoughts. If a man speaks or acts with an evil thought, pain follows him, as the wheel follows the foot of the ox that draws the wagon.

2. All that we are is the result of what we have thought: it is founded on our thoughts, it is made up of our thoughts. If a man speaks or acts with a pure thought, happiness follows him, like a shadow that never leaves him.

3. 'He abused me, he beat me, he defeated me, he robbed me,'—in those who harbour such thoughts hatred will never cease.

4. 'He abused me, he beat me, he defeated me, he robbed me,'—in those who do not harbour such thoughts hatred will cease.

5. For never does hatred cease by hatred here below: hatred ceases by love; this is an eternal law.

6. The world does not know that we must all come to an end here; but those who know, their quarrels cease at once.

7. He who lives looking for pleasures only, his senses uncontrolled, immoderate in his food, idle and weak, him Māra (the tempter) will surely overthrow, as the wind throws down a weak tree.

8. He who lives without looking for pleasures, his senses well controlled, moderate in his food, faithful and strong, him Māra will certainly not overthrow, any more than the wind throws down a rock mountain.

9. He who wishes to put on the yellow robe though still impure and disregardful of temperance and truth is unworthy of the yellow robe.

10. But whoever has cleansed himself from impurity, is well-grounded in all virtues, and regards also temperance and truth, is indeed worthy of the yellow robe.

11. They who imagine truth in untruth, and see untruth in truth, never arrive at truth, but follow vain desires.

12. They who know truth in truth and untruth in untruth, arrive at truth and follow true desires.

13. As rain breaks through an ill-thatched house, lust breaks through an ill-trained mind.

14. As rain does not break through a well-thatched house, lust will not break through a well-trained mind.

15. The evil-doer mourns in this world and he mourns in the next; he mourns in both. He mourns and suffers when he sees the evil of his own work.

16. The virtuous man delights in this world, and he delights in the next; he delights in both. He delights and rejoices when he sees the purity of his own work.

17. The evil-doer suffers in this world and he suffers in the next; he suffers in both. He suffers when he thinks of the evil he has done: he suffers even more when he has gone in the evil path (to hell).

18. The virtuous man is happy in this world and he is happy in the next; he is happy in both. He is happy when he thinks of the good he has done. He is even happier when he has gone on the good path (to heaven).

19. The slothful man even if he can recite many sacred verses, but does not act accordingly, has no share in the priesthood, but is like a cowherd counting another's kine.

20. If a man can recite but few sacred verses but is a follower of the Law, and, having forsaken lust and ill-will and delusion, possesses true knowledge and serenity of mind, he, clinging to nothing in this world or that to come, has indeed a share in the priesthood.

From *The Dhammapada,* trans. Irving Babbitt (New York: Oxford University Press, 1969), pp. 3–5.

THE FOUR SUPREME VIRTUES

Of the numerous virtues cataloged in the immense corpus of Buddhist literature, the four supreme or "sublime" virtues are

- compassion (*karuna*)
- lovingkindness (*metta*)

- sympathetic joy (*mudita*)
- impartiality (*upekkha*)[27]

The regular practice of these virtues along with faithful observance of the Eightfold Path leads to wisdom, further reminding us of the inseparable link in Buddhism between wisdom and morality. As the Buddha tells his beloved disciple Ananda, "So you see, Ananda, good conduct gradually leads to the summit."[28] And this summit is the most profound insight, nirvana—the obliteration of the false idea of an independent, permanent self, and the awakening to one's true Buddha-nature as well as the Buddha-nature inherent in all things. Let us now examine these supreme virtues, particularly noting how each represents the Middle Path.

Compassion

Without a doubt, compassion, or *karuna,* is the consummate Buddhist virtue. It requires that we empathize with the suffering of others. Moreover, it possesses an active quality in that it "has the characteristic of *devotion to removing* [others'] suffering"[29] [italics mine]. Whether or not the suffering is actually removed, what matters is that the compassionate person is *fully committed* to alleviating that suffering.

Compassion avoids two extremes. I can have a cold heart and be hardened to another's pain. This clearly shows my inability to transcend self-concern. Or else I can completely drown in the other's sorrow. Yet total identification with another's suffering impairs my capacity to improve the situation.

Compassion is a predominant trait in Buddhist ethics—after all, the Mahayana school set forth the *bodhisattva* as its prototype of both wisdom and compassion. In contrast to the *arhat*'s solitary journey of awakening, Mahayanists contend that a genuine awakening necessitates an ardent commitment to facilitate awakening for all other beings. Thus the seventh-century Buddhist Shāntideva describes in his *Compendium of Doctrine* the bodhisattva's resolve:

> He will not lay down his arms of enlightenment because of the corrupt generations of men, nor does he waver in his resolution to save the world because of their wretched quarrels.[30]

As the incarnate fusion of wisdom and compassion, the bodhisattva announces that

> I must not wait for the help of another, nor must I lose my resolution and leave my tasks to another. I must not turn back in my efforts to save all beings nor cease to use my merit for the destruction of all pain. And I must not be satisfied with small successes.[31]

The *Jataka Tales* are immensely popular stories of the former lives of the Buddha, in which he is depicted as various bodhisattvas. They often portray the bodhisattva, or the Great Being, as an animal who not only saves other animals but who ends up cooperating with willing humans as their spiritual guide. (For Buddhists, animals are not inferior to humans since we all share the Buddha-nature.)

Jeremy Bentham, *An Introduction to the Principles of Morals and Legislation*

The day *may* come when the rest of the animal creation may acquire those rights which never could have been witholden from them by the hand of tyranny . . . a full grown horse or dog is beyond comparison a more rational, as well as a more conversable animal, than an infant of a day or a week, or even a month, old. But suppose they were otherwise, what would it avail? The question is not, Can they *reason?* nor Can they *talk?* but, *Can they suffer?*

From Jeremy Bentham, "An Introduction to the Principles of Morals and Legislation," in James Rachels, ed., *The Elements of Moral Philosophy*, 2nd ed. (New York: McGraw-Hill, 1986), pp. 97–98.

Here is a well-known tale in which the Buddha is a monkey who sacrifices his safety to enable his fellow monkeys to cross the river. The crossing also represents going from the shore of ignorance to the shore of awakening. The king, who nurtures the monkey back to health, covers him with a yellow robe (symbolizing immortality) and seeks to learn from him the secret of crossing over.

CROSSING OVER BY BRIDGE

Once upon a time the Bodhisatta was born a monkey. When he grew up he lived in the Himalayan region with 80,000 monkeys. There was a splendid mango tree near the Ganges, and the monkeys, led by the Bodhisatta, used to eat its fruit, although he feared danger would come from eating the fruit of a great branch that overhung the Ganges. In spite of all precautions, a ripe mango that had been concealed by an ants' nest fell from this branch into the river and was hauled in by some fishermen.

They showed it to the King who then tasted mango for the first time, and so enraptured was he by its sweet flavour that he decided to visit the mango tree. Travelling upstream by boat with his retinue, he pitched camp at the root of the tree but was wakened in the night by the herd of monkeys as they moved from branch to branch and ate the mangoes. So he roused his archers and ordered them to shoot the monkeys: "Tomorrow we shall eat both mangoes and monkey-flesh." The monkeys, seeing the archers surrounding the tree, were stricken with the fear of death and, unable to run away, asked the Great Being what they should do.

The Bodhisatta said: "Do not fear, I will give you life." And while comforting the monkeys he climbed onto the branch that stretched towards the river, and leaping from its end and covering as much as a hundred bow-lengths, he alighted on top of a thicket on the river bank. On coming down, he measured the space, thinking: "This much will be the distance I have come," and cutting off a rattan-rope at the root and stripping it, he thought: "So much will go round the tree, so much will be in the air," but in determining these two lengths he did not think of the part to be tied round his own waist. He took the rattan-rope, bound one end round the tree and the other round his waist, and cleared the space of the hundred bow-lengths with the speed of a cloud rent by the winds. But because he had not thought of the part bound round his waist, he could not reach the tree. So taking the mango branch firmly in both hands, he beckoned to the herd of monkeys and said: "Trampling on my back, go quickly to safety along the rattan-rope."

The 80,000 monkeys, having saluted the Great Being, apologizing to him, went as he had told them.

At that time Devadatta was a monkey among that herd. He thought: "This is the time for me to see the back of my enemy," and climbing on to a high branch he put forth speed and fell on the Great Being's back. The Bodhisatta's heart was broken and anguished feelings beset him. But he who had caused that pain went away. The Great Being was as though alone. The King, being awake, saw all that was done by the monkeys and the Great Being, and he thought: "This animal, not recking of his own life, gave safety to his company." And as the night waned, he further thought: "It is not right to destroy this monkey king. By some means I will get him down and look after him." So, turning a raft downstream and building a platform there, he made the Great Being come down gently, spread yellow garments over his back, had him bathed with Ganges water, offered him sugared water to drink, had his body cleansed and anointed with highly refined oil, and having an oiled skin spread over a bed he made him lie down there, and himself sitting on a low seat, he spoke the first stanza:

"Having made of yourself a causeway
You helped them across to safety.
What are you then to them,
And what they to you, great monkey?"

Jātaka III, 370–73, no. 407 (condensed).

How can we cultivate compassion? Compassion centers on one key idea—namely, detachment from both self-interest and material goods. This involves acquiring the habit of being other-directed. Other-directedness and self-detachment go hand-in-hand.

Yet achieving a state of detachment is exceedingly difficult. It requires keeping our minds constantly on guard, for our minds can be like stampeding elephants, and our thoughts, desires, and fears can steer us to disaster. As the Second Noble Truth tells us, all suffering originates ultimately in our tendency to crave things and to cling to permanency. And craving comes from our volition, generated by the mind, thus the need to keep careful vigilance over our minds.

We can also cultivate compassion through practicing the six moral "perfections" (*pāramitās*). The great translator Kumārajiva interpreted *paramita* as a "crossing over to the other shore." These six practices involve giving (*dāna*), moral precepts (*sila*), patience (*ksanti*), strength of purpose (*virya*), meditation (*dhyāna*), and wisdom (*prajna*). They all demand detachment from self-reference. We can cultivate compassion only if we are able to let go of the "I" as a separate self. For instance, we can practice genuine giving, or charity, only if we give without any thought of personal gain. It also means giving without making any distinctions among creatures. Being charitable to friends but not to strangers is not true charity.

Lovingkindness

The virtue of lovingkindness does not refer to physical or sensual love, but to a genuine concern for the well-being of others. Cultivating this lovingkindness demands that we foster an attitude of beneficence in all our behavior—be it physical, verbal, and mental.

Other terms for lovingkindness, such as friendliness and benevolence, avoid the two extremes of total attachment and absolute indifference. Utter attachment to another hinders my ability to demonstrate genuine concern, whereas indifference derives from my inability to transcend the circle of self-interest. Each extreme exhibits an outright lack of balance.

To whom are we obliged to show this kind of love? Ideally, Buddhists urge us to show regard for all others without discrimination, to "break down the barriers" among four generic categories: ourselves, those with whom we are close, those toward whom we are neutral, and those toward whom we are hostile (as in the story of the four monks that follows).[32] It is easy enough to care for those with whom we are close. The challenge lies in showing concern both for those toward whom we are indifferent and, particularly, for our enemies. Obviously, breaking down the barriers grows exceedingly demanding as we extend further outward from our own circle of self-concern.

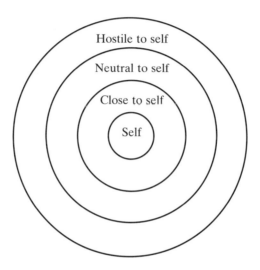

The key here is patience. We read in the Dhammapada that "Patience, long-suffering, is the highest form of penance."[33] The Dhammapada then compares patience to the endurance of an elephant:

> Patiently shall I endure abuse as the elephant in battle endures the arrow sent from the bow: for the world is ill-natured.
> They lead a tamed elephant to battle, the king mounts a tamed elephant; the tamed is the best among men, he who patiently endures abuse.[34]

This is why lovingkindness is a sublime virtue. Moreover, the force of this love reaches beyond the individual who expresses it and the person who directly receives it. Those who love emit an energy that sustains those whom they love. But Buddhists also believe that continual acts of kindness have a positive ripple effect upon the rest of the world. The following tale of the cow gives this idea a slightly different spin:

> A cow was standing giving milk to her calf. A hunter, playing with a spear in his hand, thought, "I will hit that [cow]." He threw the spear, which struck her body but bounced off like a palm leaf. . . . It was due to the fact that she had a strong state of mind [wishing] for the welfare of the calf. Love has great power in this way.[35]

Sympathetic Joy

Whereas compassion entails the desire to soothe another's suffering, sympathetic joy obliges us to share in another's happiness. This is harder than it first seems, particularly when the sphere of concern again extends outward beyond our circle of friends. Why should we share in the happiness of a stranger, let alone our enemy?

Again, we seek to avoid two extremes. One is resentment, envy, or jealousy toward another because of his or her good fortune. The other is to overly indulge in another's happiness. In either case, we lose that necessary balance, because of our inability to transcend self-interest. How can we follow this Middle Path and avoid these extremes? This is where the virtue of impartiality comes in, for it sustains the previous three.

Impartiality

Impartiality is also called equanimity, neutrality, or steady-mindedness. It guards us against falling into the extremes and is the virtue of level-headedness so that we can maintain the Middle Path. Consider the following encounter between bandits and four monks (*bhikkus,* literally meaning "beggars") in the Visuddhimagga:

> Suppose a person is sitting in a place with a dear, a neutral, and a hostile person, himself being the fourth; then bandits come to him and say, "Venerable sir, give us a *bhikku,*" and on being asked why, they answer "So that we may kill him and use the blood of his throat as an offering." Then if that *bhikku* thinks "Let them take this one, or this one," he has not broken down the barriers. And also if he thinks "Let them take me but not these three," he has not broken down the barriers either. Why? Because he seeks the harm of him whom he wishes to be taken and seeks the welfare of the others only. But it is when he does not *see* [italics mine] a single one among the four people to be given to the bandits and he directs his mind impartially towards himself and towards those three people that he has broken down the barriers.[36]

Moral Significance of Dependent Origination

To conclude our discussion of the supreme Buddhist virtues, recall the Buddhist teaching of *pratityasamutpada,* or dependent origination. It relates that most penetrating truth: We are intrinsically connected with all other things. Dependent origination thus joins hands with the idea of *anatman,* or no-self. We are not isolated, independent entities. Dependent origination therefore enhances our sense of responsibility to and for all other beings. This point is crucial, for it downplays the domain of purely private interests and rights. And Buddhism repudiates the primacy of the individual, since there is no individual as such.

This in fact subordinates the notion of individual autonomy, which reserves a primary spot in much of modern Western ethical theory. Dependent origination permits us to view the previous supreme virtues as inescapably natural.

To clarify, dependent origination has at least two major implications. First, by realizing that there is no essential difference between myself and others, I can more easily *view all others in terms of myself* and thus treat others as I myself would want to be treated. Second, I *view myself in terms of others* in that I recognize the dependency I have on others. This means that I weigh the communal contours of my existence. In light of this communal context, let us now examine the social quality of Buddhist ethics along with some contemporary examples.

WHAT IS A BUDDHIST SOCIAL ETHIC?

Buddhist teachings have always been a formidable voice in social and political commentary. For example, the later Mahayanists sternly objected to what they perceived as the static social order reinforced by orthodox Hindu teachings that appeared to give a sacred stamp of approval to the caste system. Buddhists thoroughly rejected the doctrine that membership in a caste occurs through birth:

> No brāhman is such by birth.
> No outcaste is such by birth.
> An outcaste is such by his deeds.
> A brāhman is such by his deeds.[37]

Buddhists were especially critical of those Brahmins of the highest caste who flagrantly exploited their privileges. This kind of spiritual elitism attended the unfair subjugation of the lowest caste of laborers, or *sudras*. The orthodox Hindu legal handbook, the *Laws of Manu,* states the following:

> A Sudra, whether bought or unbought, may be compelled to do servile work; for he was created by the Self-Existent to be the slave of a Brahamin.[38]

Undoubtedly the Buddha's teaching—that we are all fundamentally equal—was a bombshell for his contemporaries. By opposing the prevailing class structure and advocating the startling notion that all four classes were in truth no different from one another, he certainly swam against the stream, particularly when he pointed out that persons from any class were eligible for membership in his *sangha*. According to his teachings, all persons have the potential to achieve enlightenment.

Buddhists are not advocating a classless society. A need for structure as well as order of rank exists even within the *sangha*. Instead, they claim that affiliation in the different classes should simply have a pragmatic rationale to accommodate the different professions. Buddhists urge an evenhanded inter-action among the classes with equitable rights and responsibilities. This is the advice that the Buddha gives to Sigala, a Hindu householder. Reciprocal rights and duties are described for parents and children, teachers and students, husbands and wives, masters and dependents, laypersons and priests, and among friends. Moreover, Sigala is warned against slipping into the four vices (taking life, theft, licentiousness, and malicious speech), the four evil motives (partial-ity, enmity, stupidity, and fear), and the six ways of wasting one's resources:

> Being addicted to intoxicating liquors, frequenting the streets at unseemly hours, haunting fairs, being infatuated by gambling, associating with evil companions, the habit of idleness.[39]

This reciprocity of rights and responsibilities among various relations under-scores an imperative social cohesion, a class structure in which the real outcaste is not the untouchable as asserted in orthodox Indian teaching. For the Buddhist, being an outcaste has nothing to do with birthright, but every-thing to do with the degree to which we fail to live a morally sound lifestyle. The true outcaste is the immoral person. Regardless of the caste one is in, the karma that an individual effects is still karma. Our deeds define us, not the class into which we are born.

Aung San Suu Kyi

Aung San Suu Kyi, the charismatic leader in Burma's struggle for human rights, vividly illustrates the Buddhist social ethic. Against an oppressive military regime, she has bravely spoken out against the government's numerous viola-tions of human rights and has helped to establish the National League for Democracy (NLD), which won an overwhelming popular vote in the May 1990 elections. Yet the military junta refused to acknowledge the party's victory and still continues to rule Burma ("Land of the Pagodas"), now officially called the Union of Myanmar, through a brutal policy of repression, torture, and impris-onment.

Nevertheless, in the spirit of both Gandhi and the Buddha, Suu Kyi's protest has been strictly nonviolent, including her successful twelve-day hunger strike in 1989, demanding that her imprisoned supporters be treated humanely. Through her testimony, she has brought international attention to the Burmese plight, and the London *Times* has called her "Burma's Gandhi."[40] In 1991, while still under house arrest, she was awarded the Nobel Peace Prize. She was finally released in July 1995 after a six-year-long detention.[41]

Suu Kyi regularly reminds the Burmese people that their struggle for human rights rests upon their own Theravada Buddhist heritage, which has left its lasting imprint upon societal affairs. For instance, in 1917 the highly influential Young Men's Buddhist Association flatly condemned the practice of having "Europeans only" train carriages.[42] And it comes as no surprise that throngs of Buddhist monks marched in silent protest against the government at the start of Suu Kyi's hunger strike.

Moreover, Suu Kyi frequently reminds her people that the principles for proper government have a Buddhist basis. According to Theravada teachings, the ruler must ensure peace, order, and justice among his people.[43] He must see to it that the basic material and physical needs of his people are fulfilled, for this would enable them to cultivate spiritual growth. Furthermore, he is under a singular moral imperative to be a paragon of virtue and to live according to *Dharma,* the Buddhist teachings.

Just before she was placed under arrest in 1991, Suu Kyi was writing "In Quest of Democracy," in which she outlined the Buddhist view of good government. Good government demands good leadership, and the Buddhist teaching of the "Ten Duties of Kings" provides a fitting basis for the safeguarding of human rights and impress upon the ruler a special obligation grounded on Buddhist teachings. These ten duties are generosity, observance of moral precepts, "selfless public service," integrity, kindness, austerity, composure, nonviolence, patience, and "non-opposition to the will of the people."[44]

Generosity (*dana*), the first duty, is the pivotal Buddhist virtue and underlies all the others. The second, acting morally (*sila*), entails practicing the five Buddhist precepts, which require abstaining from destroying life, from stealing, from lies, from adultery, and from alcohol. The third requires subordinating self-interest to the needs of the people. The fourth duty is to maintain absolute integrity. As Suu Kyi remarks, "Truth is the very essence of the teachings of the Buddha, who referred to himself as the *Tathagata,* or the 'one who has come to the truth.' "[45] The duties of kindness, austerity, composure, nonviolence, and patience signal the implicit, sacred, moral covenant that exists between the ruler and his people. As Suu Kyi tells us,

> The ruler must bear a high moral character to win the respect and trust of the people, to ensure their happiness and prosperity and to provide a proper example. When the king does not observe the *dhamma* [Buddhist teachings, also *Dharma*], state functionaries are corrupt, and when state functionaries are corrupt the people are caused much suffering. . . . The root of a nation's misfortunes has to be sought in the moral failings of the government.[46]

As for democracy, Suu Kyi insists that it is unquestionably endorsed in the tenth duty—"non-opposition to the will of the people." There are Jataka tales of kings who have been expelled from the community because of their unwillingness to honor the people's mandate. For instance, Pawridasa was exiled from his kingdom because of his refusal to stop his unacceptable habit of cannibalism.[47] The implicit contract between ruler and ruled thus works both ways. The people themselves may legitimately force a ruler out of office if the ruler refuses to act in their best interests.

Nonviolence is another of the king's Ten Duties, imposing upon the king a genuine commitment to peace and to the avoidance of war by all means: "Violence is totally contrary to the teachings of Buddhism. The good ruler vanquishes ill-will with loving kindness, wickedness with virtue, parsimony with liberality, and falseness with truth."[48]

Aung San Suu Kyi represents for the Burmese a dynamic voice of hope, dignity, and universal values, which find their expression in Buddhist teachings. On the occasion of awarding her the Nobel Peace Prize, Francis Sejersted, the chairman of the Nobel Committee, honored her by echoing her words:

> Where there is no justice there can be no secure peace. . . . That just laws which uphold human rights are the necessary foundation of peace and security would be denied only by closed minds which interpret peace as the silence of all opposition and security as the assurance of their own power. The Burmese associate peace and security with coolness and shade:
>
> The shade of a tree is cool indeed
> The shade of parents is cooler
> The shade of teachers is cooler still
> The shade of a ruler is yet more cool
> But the coolest of all is the shade of the Buddha's teaching.[49]

Aung San Suu Kyi, 1991 Nobel Peace Prize winner. (AP Photo/Richard Vogel)

Sarvodaya Shramadana: "We Build the Road and the Road Builds Us"[50]

The Sarvodaya Shramadana movement in Sri Lanka is one of the most inspiring examples of a Buddhist social ethic. With its grass-roots approach, it offers a new alternative to the idea of "development," rejecting the idea that progress is measured solely in terms of material gain and profit. Instead, genuine development must balance economic concerns with an equal emphasis upon personal, spiritual, and cultural formation. The movement therefore sweeps away capitalism, Marxism, and nationalist socialism since they all underscore acquisition as the measure of success. For instance, capitalism creates counterfeit needs as well as fostering material acquisition, and it is therefore driven by what Buddhists call the poisons of delusion and greed.

Sarvodaya literally means the "awakening of all"—real development must enrich all peoples and classes. And even though the predominant religion in Sri Lanka is Buddhist, the movement involves Hindus, Muslims, and Christians, evidence of the capacity of Buddhism to reach out to different religious viewpoints on the basis of shared common ground.[51]

The movement started in 1958 when a high school science teacher, A.T. Ariyaratna, urged his students to live with poor villagers in order to heighten their awareness of the plight of the poor and of the need to improve living conditions. Though initially inspired by the Gandhian experiences in India, work camps (*shramadana*) were organized and the movement gained momentum, eventually grounding itself more upon Buddhist teachings. The term *shramadana*, for instance, consists of *shrama* ("human energy") and *dana* ("giving"), the thread that runs through the four central Buddhist virtues of lovingkindness, compassion, sympathetic joy, and impartiality. Sarvodaya clearly embraces the social nature of these virtues. For example, sympathetic joy means sharing in the happiness that results from community service, such as "a completed road to the village or in the altered lives of its inhabitants."[52] And impartiality ultimately demands nonattachment to any achievements, along with nonattachment through political nonpartisanship. In fact, this nonpartisanship is one of the most striking features of Sarvodaya, and it stands out in a country that has become intensely fragmented because of political and religious allegiances.

Sarvodaya also imparts the prominent Buddhist teaching of self-reliance. When villagers construct their own windmills, power generators, and preschool programs, they gain a sense of self-esteem, which is crucial since the lure of Westernization can generate feelings of inferiority. Sarvodaya stresses the need to cast off the destructive need to imitate the ways of the West.

Buddhist teachings undergird Sarvodaya's emphasis upon the Ten Basic Needs—food, water, clothing, shelter, health care, education, communication, fuel, a livable and sustainable environment, and spiritual and cultural growth— as key components of development. Furthermore, these needs are addressed within the context of the Four Awakenings: individual, village, national, and world. These demonstrate Sarvodaya's global sensitivity as well as local focus. These Four Awakenings also illustrate the Buddhist notion of interdependence since individual awakenings bring about community awareness and, in turn, influence how the community views the nation as well as the world.

Along these same lines, Sarvodaya centers on what is called the "economics of sufficiency."[53] This is a critical Buddhist idea in that it stresses an economy that strives for a modest attainment of material needs and comforts. It therefore embodies the Buddhist Middle Way by avoiding deficiency (poverty) and excess (affluence) and offers "an alternative to classical Western economics"[54]:

> From the perspective of the Dharma, economic interest includes not only production and profit, but also the "externalities" of human and environmental costs. The conservation of material resources, their humane use, and their equitable distribution are taken as legitimate and indeed preeminent concerns.[55]

And modest consumption is "not only conservative of resources, but essential to spiritual health and self-reliance."[56] The goal of living is not to accumulate wealth or acquire prestige and fame, but to achieve genuine happiness through spiritual cultivation and the enhancement of personal character. Sarvodaya, therefore, recognizes the necessity of addressing material needs without becoming attached to them as intrinsic goods. Thus Sarvodaya boldly challenges the dominant view of development in the West.

Sulak Sivaraksa

Sulak Sivaraksa, the Thai activist and co-founder of the International Network of Engaged Buddhists, energetically applies Buddhist teachings in criticizing various forms of corruption. After Thailand's bloody coup, in which hundreds of students were killed and Sivaraksa's life threatened and his books burnt, Sivaraksa was forced into exile and fled to the United States. He still spoke out boldly against government corruption in Thailand when he returned to Bangkok, and, after further arrests, he now remains in exile.

Sivaraksa delivers a scathing critique of Western-style capitalism. For him, both capitalism and socialism betray the fundamental teachings of Buddhism because they place too much emphasis upon material acquisition at the cost of real personal and spiritual growth. For him, the dominant ethic in the world is the "religion of consumerism," the obsession with acquiring profit and striving for excesses of comfort and convenience as ends in themselves.

A case in point is his own country. Thailand (or Siam, as Sivaraksa prefers to call it) has emerged as one of the fastest growing economies in the world— at the price of abdicating its traditional spiritual Buddhist values. For example, Sivaraksa sternly chastises Bangkok for allowing its natural resources to be plundered and exploited. He criticizes policies that have allowed shopping centers to replace Buddhist temples as centers of social activity.

This consumerist "religion," inspired by Western nations, particularly the United States, is an ideology that measures "progress" and "development" solely in quantitative terms, as measured by economic standards such as the Gross National Product (GNP). He calls this the "think-big strategy" of development. And it has seduced us into thinking that real growth is measured in monetary and material terms:

> It [this "think-big strategy"] has convinced us to think in terms of money and has cornered us into believing that if we can just get the economics right, the rest of life's pieces will fall comfortably into place.[57]

This strategy, thinking solely in terms of profit, has enabled rich companies to secure further wealth at the expense of the labor and sweat of the poor.

Moreover, this strategy produces a way of thinking that turns a blind eye to the world scandal of poverty. It all too easily leads to the vicious circle of "progress": Once we become enamored with our own material comfort, we desire more, and at the same time our own personal vision narrows as we turn a blind eye to the all-encompassing reality of suffering throughout the world. Sivaraksa reminds us that at least forty thousand people die daily from hunger and malnutrition, and 75 percent of them are children![58]

The "religion" of consumerism also begets various forms of exploitation, dominance, and corruption. Sivaraksa boldly attacks the corruption he finds in the Thai government, currently ruled by the National Peacekeeping Council (NPKC). He claims that the government's concern for democracy is cosmetic, and that its real interests center on profit making, for instance, in arms dealings with China and other countries.

Where do Buddhist teachings fit into all this? Sivaraksa points out that the roots of consumerism lie in what Buddhists call the three poisons: greed, hatred, and delusion: "All three are manifestations of unhappiness, and the presence of any one poison breeds more of the same."[59] Given the seductive force of these poisons, is there any antidote to stem the tide of consumerism?

As a start, Sivaraksa urges us to be fully mindful of the first Buddhist Noble Truth of *dukkha* and of the suffering that billions of people undergo daily. This requires extra effort since consumerism easily lulls us into a state of complacency if we live comfortable lifestyles.

Next, Sivaraksa cautions us to pursue a Middle Way between an excess of material goods and a deficiency of them, between hedonism and strict austerity. We need to address the basic material and physical needs of food, clothing, shelter, and health care since these set the conditions for us to fulfill our human potential. Yet, consumerism can entice us into believing that things we genuinely do not need are "necessities" without which we could not live, and "it is imperative that items of necessity are distinguished from those of luxury."[60]

Sivaraksa believes that "Western material values have not merged with

Asian culture; they have overwhelmed and diluted it."[61] That is, although he does not advocate a simplistic return to traditional lifestyles, he encourages a Middle Way that both assimilates aspects of modernization and still manages to sustain the long-standing teachings of Buddhism and other faiths.

Finally, Sivaraksa reminds us of Buddhism's necessarily social dimensions, particularly in the teaching of interdependence, whereby all things interact and mutually affect everything else. We are not private, isolated, selves. Instead, we are in essence intertwined with all other creatures, past, present, and future. Those OTHERS who suffer and die from malnutrition are not in essence different from who we are. The Rwandan refugee is not a stranger. Those persons starving in the streets of Bangkok are not outsiders. Sivaraksa gives us the metaphor of a seed—each of us is like a seed planted in our society, and our own individual tendencies, whether toward greed or compassion, naturally affect the society we live in.

The XIVth Dalai Lama

> Between the two countries no smoke nor dust shall be seen. There shall be no sudden alarms and the very word "enemy" shall not be spoken. . . . All shall live in peace and share the blessing of happiness for ten thousand years.[62]

Etched on the stone monument at the entrance to Tibet's famous Jokhang Temple, these words record the 821–22 treaty between Tibet, the Kingdom on the Roof of the World, and its powerful neighbor China.

All this changed in 1950 when eighty thousand Chinese Communist troops stormed into Tibet. Tibet's fourteenth Dalai Lama, Tenzin Gyatso, or *Kundun* ("the Presence"), was then fifteen years old. By March 1959, tensions became so taut that the Chinese occupiers threatened to open fire upon the sacred palace of the Dalai Lama at Norbulingka. As tens of thousands of Tibetans risked their lives by assembling outside the palace to protect their *Kundun,* he and his entourage, including his mother, sister, and brother, managed to escape to Dharamsala, India. There, he boldly established his own independent Tibetan Government in Exile. He has not yet returned to Tibet, but he has remained steadfast in gathering international support for Tibetan independence.

The Dalai Lama has indeed embodied key Buddhist teachings. For instance, he viewed the presence of the Chinese as an opportunity to cultivate nonviolence and patience:

> Still, I took note of the Buddha's teaching that in one sense a supposed enemy is more valuable than a friend, for an enemy teaches you things, such as forbearance, that a friend generally does not. To this I added my firm belief that no matter how bad things become, they will eventually get better. In the end, the innate desire of all people for truth, justice, and human understanding must triumph over ignorance and despair. So if the Chinese oppressed us, it could only strengthen us.[63]

Having to mediate between Chinese military officials and the growing tide of Tibetan resistance against the Chinese occupation, he spoke out strongly against any use of force. He reminded Tibetans that the use of violence was contrary to Buddhist teachings as well as counterproductive to the Tibetan cause. Tibetan resistance regularly met with violent suppression. For instance, in 1956 when Khampa/Amdowa rebels (or "freedom-fighters") destroyed key roads and bridges used by the Chinese military, the Buddhist monastery at Lithang was decimated by aerial bombings and forty thousand more Chinese troops were sent in. In addition, women and children, along with nuns and monks, were ruthlessly tortured and slaughtered.[64]

The Dalai Lama also continues to exemplify Buddhist compassion. Tibetans believe the Dalai Lama to be the reincarnation of previous Dalai Lamas, who are in turn the manifestations of Avalokiteshvara, the Bodhisattva of Compassion.[65] And for the Dalai Lama, "The essence of Buddhism is kindness, compassion."[66] For instance, feeling sad for the yaks who were sold for slaughter during festivals, he would often instruct his emissary to buy the yaks and save them from their fate.[67] And Buddhism especially requires the extension of this compassion to enemies: "By living in a society we should share the sufferings of our fellow beings and practice compassion and tolerance, not only toward our loved ones but also toward our enemies."[68]

The Dalai Lama also stresses the Buddhist teaching of interdependence. After Deng Xiaoping became China's new leader in 1978, the Dalai Lama sent a fact-finding mission (which included his brother Lobsang) to Tibet to investigate conditions there.[69] The mission discovered gross violations of human rights. Under Chinese rule, there were years of famine and numerous accounts of executions and torture. Yet the Dalai Lama discovered that many Westerners seemed less concerned about matters far away and "foreign" and thus had little awareness of the Buddhist idea of the interconnectedness of all things. He tirelessly reminds us of the need to cultivate a sense of "Universal Responsibility," the "responsibility that we all have for each other and for all sentient beings and also for all of Nature."[70]

This emphasis upon nonviolence, compassion, and interdependence surfaced when the Dalai Lama put forth his Five-Point Peace Plan before the Human Rights Caucus of the U.S. Congress in 1987. First, he urged that all of Tibet become a "zone of *Ahimsa*"—a zone of peace whereby all weapons production and all exploitation of natural resources be prohibited. This would in turn require the entire demilitarization of Tibet and the withdrawal of all Chinese troops. Second, all attempts at the Sinicization of Tibet must stop. Since the occupation, China has imposed its own population control policies of two children per couple. And the massive relocation of Chinese into Tibet has virtually left the native Tibetans disempowered. Third, Tibetans' fundamental human rights must be recognized: "Human rights violations in Tibet are among the most serious in the world."[71] And the Tibetans face almost full-scale discrimination on all counts. Fourth, Tibet's natural environment must be restored. Tibet has been the dumping ground for China's nuclear waste, and China intends to dump the waste from other countries into Tibet as well. This threatens all forms of life and poses a solemn threat to future generations. Finally, the Dalai Lama advocates sincere negotiations between the Chinese and the Tibetans on all of the previous points. This will require genuine dialogue and the willingness to critically examine each position.[72]

As expected, Beijing denounced the Five-Point Plan as advocating separatism. And in March 1989, the same year that the Dalai Lama was awarded the Nobel Peace Prize, the Chinese imposed martial law in Lhasa after nearly twenty demonstrators were shot and killed by armed police during protests. Despite *Kundun*'s pleas to Deng Xiaoping, martial law remained throughout that year.

Since the Chinese occupation of Tibet in 1950, nearly 1.25 million Tibetans have died from starvation, torture, executions, and forced labor. And even though the Chinese government still refuses to officially acknowledge the Government in Exile, the Dalai Lama offers his message of conciliation:

> Learning to forgive is much more useful than merely picking up a stone and throwing it at the object of one's anger, the more so when the provocation is extreme. For it is under the greatest adversity that there exists the greatest potential for doing good, both for oneself and others.[73]

Now living in a small, humble cottage in Dharamsala, India, the Dalai Lama views himself as "a simple Buddhist monk, no more, no less." And he assures us that once Tibet achieves independence, he will live plainly as a private citizen without any claim to authority.

REVIEW QUESTIONS

1. How does the story of the "Lost Son" reflect Buddhist moral teachings?
2. Describe the interrelationship among the three signs, nirvana, and dependent origination.
3. How does the Middle Path strike a balance? And how is this morally relevant?
4. The Four Noble Truths have profound moral consequence. How do the first three underscore the absolute necessity of realizing individual responsibility for one's actions and attitudes?
5. Discuss the ethical impact of the Eightfold Path.
6. How can we associate karma with the Buddhist teaching of no-self? That is, how can we address issues of "personal" responsibility if there is no personal self?

7. Compassion is a supreme Buddhist virtue. What is the scope of Buddhist compassion, and how does this tie into the idea of no-self? How does this affect our view of what constitutes a "moral community"?

8. Explain how each of the supreme Buddhist virtues involves the realization of dependent origination, that is, our fundamental interconnectedness.

9. In what ways do the contemporary figures and movements (e.g., Aung San Suu Kyi) embody Buddhist virtues? What balance do they advocate through their teachings and actions?

10. In what ways do Buddhist moral teachings guide us along the path to living a better life?

NOTES

1. See Gunapala Dharmasiri, *Fundamentals of Buddhist Ethics* (San Francisco, CA: Golden Leaves, 1989), p. 79.

2. One of the more popular bodhisattvas is Avalokitesvara. He bestows comfort and safety, and his name combines the words *ishvara* ("lord") and *avalokita* ("he who watches with compassion"). Manjusri embodies "wisdom" (*prajna*), and is also popular. Another favorite is Maitreya, whom Mahayanists believe to be the future Buddha.

3. On top of many of his pillars are four sculptured lions. The lions carry a large stone "wheel of *dharma*" (Buddha's teachings), and three of these lions are today part of the national symbol of India. See Stanley Wolpert, *A New History of India,* 3rd ed. (New York: Oxford University Press, 1989), p. 67.

4. Ibid., pp. 66–67.

5. From the Vinaya-pitaka, in Lucien Stryk, ed., *World of the Buddha: A Reader* (New York: Doubleday, Anchor Books, 1968), pp. 211–12.

6. A. Foucher, *La Vie du Bouddha* (Paris: Editions Payot, 1949).

7. From the Sermon at Benares in Stryk, *World of the Buddha,* pp. 50–51.

8. Ibid., p. 50.

9. Ibid., pp. 50–51.

10. From Samyutta Nikaya, 5.421ff; in William Theodore de Bary, ed., *The Buddhist Tradition in India, China and Japan* (New York: Random House, Vintage Books, 1969), p. 16.

11. Ibid.

12. Ibid., pp. 16–17.

13. Ibid., p. 17.

14. See Anguttaranikaya, Pali Text Society of London, 4, 49, 1 II P. 52, in Hans Wolfgang Schumann, *Buddhism: An Outline of Its Teachings and Schools* (Wheaton, IL: Theosophical Publishing House, 1973), p. 69.

15. In his Discourse to Prince Abhaya, the Buddha lays down rules for proper speech in terms of whether it is true, useful, and pleasant. See Abha-

yarājakumāra-sutta and discussion in David J. Kalupahana, *A History of Buddhist Philosophy: Continuities and Discontinuities* (Honolulu: University of Hawaii Press, 1992), pp. 50–52.

16. From the Vinaya-pitaka in Stryk, *World of the Buddha,* pp. 233–34.
17. From Majjhima-nikaya 1.415, in Kalupahana, *A History of Buddhist Philosophy,* p. 106.
18. See the discussion in Walpola Rahula, *What the Buddha Taught,* 2nd ed. (New York: Grove Press, 1974, 1959), pp. 68–74.
19. Ibid., pp. 48–49.
20. Alluded to in Dharmasiri, *Fundamentals of Buddhist Ethics,* p. 38.
21. See the discussion in Rahula, *What the Buddha Taught,* p. 32.
22. From Anguttara-nikāya, in Stryk, *World of the Buddha,* p. 211.
23. See the excellent analysis in David J. Kalupahana, *Buddhist Philosophy: A Historical Analysis* (Honolulu: University of Hawaii Press, 1976), pp. 44–55.
24. Ibid., p. 47.
25. This refers to a famous discussion in the Buddhist text, The Questions of King Milinda.
26. Keep in mind that Buddhists believe that humans produce karma because of volition and intellect. At the same time, rebirth into other nonhuman realms such as animals or insects is rather likely since we need to burn away our enormous karmic residue. Nevertheless, as the Jataka tales indicate, nonhumans such as animals and demons, even though they are more restricted in the exercise of their volition, can still produce karma to some degree by virtue of their volition.
27. See the insightful discussion of these in Dharmasiri, *Fundamentals of Buddhist Ethics,* pp. 42ff.
28. Anguttara-nikaya, V.2, in ibid., p. 22.
29. Visuddhimagga, ix. 94, in ibid., p. 48.
30. From Siksasamuccaya, in de Bary *The Buddhist Tradition in India,* p. 84.
31. Ibid., p. 85.
32. "Break down the barriers" is an expression from H. Aronson, *Love and Sympathy in Theravada Buddhism,* alluded to in ibid., p. 47.
33. Irving Babbitt, trans., *The Dhammapada,* 184 (New York: New Directions, 1936), p. 30.
34. Ibid., 320, 321, p. 49.
35. From Anguttara Nikaya Atthakatha, in Dharmasiri, *Fundamentals of Buddhist Ethics,* p. 47.
36. From Visuddhimagga, 305–07, in ibid., p. 47.
37. Sutta Nipāta, v. 136, in Stryk, *World of the Buddha,* p. 49.
38. Laws of Manu, *Sacred Books of the East,* XXV, Chap. 10.
39. From Sigalovada Sutta in Dharmasiri, *Fundamentals of Buddhist Ethics,* p. 64.
40. *The Times* (London, August 8, 1989). In a way, she has embraced the distinguished legacy of her father and mother. Her father, Aung San, was

a national hero who had helped to bring about Burmese independence through peaceful arbitration with the British. He was assassinated when she was only two, and her mother, Daw Khin Kyi, held the post of ambassador to India until 1967.

41. While she was under house arrest, her own NLD party members felt threatened by the military and eventually proclaimed their own rival government, the National Coalition Government of the Union of Burma (NCGUB), under the leadership of Dr. Sein Lewin, Aung San Suu Kyi's cousin.
42. Aung San Suu Kyi, *Freedom From Fear* (London: Penguin Books, 1991), p. 142.
43. This is found particularly in the text Anguttara Nikaya.
44. Suu Kyi, *Freedom From Fear,* pp. 171–72.
45. Ibid., p. 171.
46. Ibid.
47. Ibid., p. 173.
48. Ibid., p. 172.
49. Ibid., p. 233.
50. This is a popular slogan for the Sarvodaya Movement.
51. This acts to help counter the long-standing political, religious, and linguistic tensions between the Sinhalese majority, who are Buddhists, and the Tamil minority, who are Hindus. Remember that Tamil Hindus were involved in the assassination of Prime Minister Rajiv Gandhi in 1991.
52. Joanna Macy, *Dharma and Development: Religion as Resource in the Sarvodaya Self-Help Movement,* rev. ed. (West Hartford, CT: Kumarian Press, 1983, 1985), p. 39.
53. The term "sufficiency" is borrowed from E.F. Schumacher in his popular *Small is Beautiful* (New York: Harper & Row, 1973). See ibid., pp. 45ff.
54. Ibid., p. 45.
55. Ibid.
56. Ibid., p. 46.
57. Sulak Sivaraksa, *Seeds of Peace: A Buddhist Vision for Renewing Society,* ed. Tom Ginsberg (Berkeley, CA: Parallax Press, 1992), p. 24.
58. Ibid., p. 28.
59. Ibid., p. 8.
60. Ibid., p. 30.
61. Ibid., p. 9.
62. Cited in Tenzin Gyatso, *Freedom in Exile: The Autobiography of the Dalai Lama* (New York: Harper Collins, 1990), p. 43.
63. Ibid., p. 81.
64. Ibid., p. 110.
65. This bodhisattva is called *Chenrezig* in Tibetan.

66. Gyatso, *Freedom in Exile,* p. 28.
67. Ibid., p. 50.
68. Ibid., p. 29.
69. The Dalai Lama believes that Lobsang's death in 1985 is attributed to the profound depression he experienced when he revisited his homeland and encountered the terrible suffering and living conditions faced by the Tibetans.
70. Gyatso, *Freedom in Exile,* p. 200.
71. Ibid., p. 251.
72. Ibid., p. 247.
73. Ibid., p. 261.

THREE

Zen Buddhist Ethics

Mrs. Ota's tear fell onto the shoulder of the tea kettle that had once belonged to Kikuji's deceased father. It was almost as if her tear was a kiss to her former lover. If tea kettles could speak, what stories we would hear!

The kettle was first owned by Mrs. Ota's husband. But after he died, it made perfect sense to sell it to Kikuji's father who had an abiding interest in matters of tea. Now, even he was gone. This time the kettle was being used to prepare tea for Mrs. Ota and Kikuji.

As soon as her tear fell, it sizzled dry on the kettle's surface, signaling her own brief sojourn in this fragile life. Was it perhaps a premonition of her suicide on the following day? One fact remained clear: this kettle would outlive her just as it had outlived its previous owners. Even so, the memory of her tear lingered on in Kikuji long after she had died.

This incident is from the story *Thousand Cranes,* written by Yasunari Kawabata (1899–1972), winner of the 1968 Nobel Prize for Literature. His haunting tale of love and destiny is both austere and complex, and it unfolds against the backdrop of the tea ceremony, or *chanoyu.* The story centers on Kikuji's relationship with his father's former mistresses, Chikako and Mrs. Ota, as well as his growing affection for Fumiko, Mrs. Ota's daughter. On a more enigmatic level, however, the principal characters in the story are actually various tea utensils, which in an odd way take on a life of their own.

For instance, the story opens with a tea ceremony whose participants are Kikuji, Mrs. Ota, Fumiko, and Chikako. Chikako was the mistress of Kikuji's father before he turned to Mrs. Ota. She thus harbors a deep-seated hostility toward Mrs. Ota. Chikako also instructs in the art of tea, and her student, Yukiko, assists in the ceremony, carrying some of the tea utensils in her kerchief, a white and pink print of a thousand cranes. Chikako, choosing to remain unwed, intends the ceremony to be an occasion for a *miai,* or arrangement between the unknowing Yukiko and Kikuji, hopefully leading to their marriage.

If tea bowls could speak! During the tea, there is another presence, strangely enough embodied in the Oribe tea bowl—the spirit of Kikuji's father. Like the kettle, the tea bowl evokes memories of its owners. The bowl had again passed from Mr. Ota to his wife, who then gave the bowl to Kikuji's father. He in turn relinquished the bowl to his former mistress Chikako. During the ceremony, Chikako speaks admiringly of the Oribe bowl and its resemblance to Kikuji's father. Kikuji, however, would rather overlook the recent past and cite only the bowl's wider history:

> "But what difference does it make that my father owned it for a little while? It's four hundred years old, after all—its history goes back to Momoyama and Rikyū himself [famous tea masters]. Tea masters have looked after it and passed it down through the centuries. My father is of very little importance." So Kikuji tried to forget the associations the bowl called up.
> It had passed from Ota to his wife, from the wife to Kikuji's father, from Kikuji's father to Chikako; and the two men, Ota and Kikuji's father, were dead, and here were the two women. There was something almost weird about the bowl's career.[1]

If tea jars could talk! Let us illustrate further. Long after his father's death, Kikuji becomes involved with Mrs. Ota. She initiates him with "an extraordinary awakening" into manhood. She, however, grows increasingly burdened with guilt and sadness. Soon after her last tea with Kikuji, when her "tear wet the shoulder of the kettle," she takes her life. Thoroughly distraught, Kikuji visits her home. And he learns that Mrs. Ota uncustomarily had been using her Shino water jar, meant for the tea ceremony, as a flower vase. Furthermore, Fumiko has emulated her mother's habit. The Shino jar, filled with flowers, now occupies a space next to the urn containing her mother's ashes. As a memorial, Fumiko gives the jar to Kikuji, and its "voluptuous and warmly cool surface" reminds him of Mrs. Ota, "soft, like a dream." Out of reverence for her, he intends to continue to use it as a vase.

Chikako, however, has other plans. She regularly cleans Kikuji's tea cottage. And when she recognizes the Shino jar that once belonged to Mrs. Ota, she shows her vindictiveness to both Mrs. Ota and Fumiko by planning to restore it to its original use for tea.

> Before Mrs. Ota's ashes it had been a flower vase, and now it was back at its old work, a water jar in a tea ceremony.
> A jar that had been Mrs. Ota's was now being used by Chikako. After Mrs. Ota's death, it had passed to her daughter, and from Fumiko it had come to Kikuji.
> It had a strange career. But perhaps the strangeness was natural to tea vessels.
> In the three or four hundred years before it became the property of Mrs. Ota, it had passed through the hands of people with what strange careers?[2]

Kikuji becomes more and more drawn to the Shino jar. It elicits warm memories of Mrs. Ota. But these begin to mingle with thoughts of Fumiko as well, and "His heart would rise even at the touch of the jar, and he had put no more flowers in it."[3]

If tea bowls could speak! So far we have seen how these tea vessels take on a life of their own by somehow embodying the presence of their owners. This is particularly evident near the end of the story when Fumiko offers another Shino piece to Kikuji—her mother's everyday tea bowl. What is striking about the tea bowl is that it appears as if her mother's lipstick graces the edge of the cup. And with this indelible token of her presence, it now becomes Kikuji's.

The story beautifully depicts certain Zen Buddhist qualities, more of which we will examine in this chapter. For now, one example of Zen is the total attentiveness shown by some of the characters during tea. This is what we will later refer to as the virtue of presence: the ability to be completely focused upon the present moment in all its meaningfulness. It entails an awareness of the harmony of permanence and impermanence, in that the durability of tea contrasts with the fleeting presence of the humans. And the participants themselves are suspended in timelessness, caught in the intersection between past and present.

Another Zen feature is the discovery of the extraordinary in the ordinary, beauty in the mundane. The tea vessels themselves are not ornate, but ordinary and common. Therein lies their special quality. And they evoke memories that are, in a sense, eternal. Thus there is no difference between the commonplace and the spiritual. The following scene depicts this transcendent quality of the mundane. Here, long after her mother's suicide, Fumiko shares tea with Kikuji, and they both behold two Raku tea bowls.

Yasunari Kawabata

THOUSAND CRANES

Fumiko brought in two bowls on a tray.

They were cylindrical, a red Raku and a black Raku.

She set the black before Kikuji. In it was ordinary coarse tea.

Kikuji lifted the bowl and looked at the potter's mark. "Who is it?" he asked bluntly.

"Ryōnyū,* I believe."

"And the red?"

---

*Raku, a Kyoto ware, was first produced in the sixteenth century. Ryōnyū (1756–1834) was the ninth master of the Raku kiln.

"Ryōnyū too."

"They seem to be a pair." Kikuji looked at the red bowl, which lay untouched at her knee.

Though they were ceremonial bowls, they did not seem out of place as ordinary teacups; but a displeasing picture flashed into Kikuji's mind.

Fumiko's father had died and Kikuji's father had lived on; and might not this pair of Raku bowls have served as teacups when Kikuji's father came to see Fumiko's mother? Had they not been used as "man-wife" teacups, the black for Kikuji's father, the red for Fumiko's mother?

If they were by Ryōnyū, one could be a little careless with them. Might they not also have been taken along on trips?

Fumiko, who knew, was perhaps playing a cruel joke on him.

But he saw no malice, indeed no calculation, in her bringing out the two bowls.

He saw only a girlish sentimentality, which also came to him.

He and Fumiko, haunted by the death of her mother, were unable to hold back this grotesque sentimentality. The pair of Raku bowls deepened the sorrow they had in common.

BACKGROUND

Indian Roots

In the first centuries after the Buddha's death, various groups engaged in some rather fervent disputes over interpretations of the Buddha's original message. Consequently, a major assembly of Buddhists broke away from the early, more conservative Theravada school and referred to themselves as *Mahayana,* meaning "Greater Vehicle." These Mahayanist reformers gave the Theravada school the derogatory name *Hinayana,* or "Lesser Vehicle." Both schools do share some common streams of thought, such as the belief in the Four Noble Truths and the disbelief in a separate self, as was discussed in Chapter 2. Yet, their differences run deep. For instance, Mahayanists hold that all beings are capable of attaining enlightenment, awakening to their true Buddha-nature. Hinayanists are reluctant to make such a claim. Furthermore, the Mahayana ideal is the *bodhisattva,* an enlightened being who works for the salvation and enlightenment of all humans, and whose primary virtues are wisdom (*prajna*) and especially compassion (*karuna*). This ideal is one step up from the Theravadin ideal of the *arhat,* which embodies the sole virtue of wisdom. Moreover, the *bodhisattva*'s compassion extends itself to *all sentient beings,* not just humans. This means that for Mahayanists, all psychophysical organisms participate in the Buddha-nature. This belief in the Buddhahood of all sentient beings is perhaps the chief contribution of the Mahayana school.

Reaffirming our original point, Zen Buddhism's bloodline goes back to the Mahayana teachings, which are revealed in their sacred groups of texts called *sutras*. The principal sutras are Lankavatara, Vimalikirti, Prajnaparamita, and Avatamsaka. The Lankavatara Sutra stresses the conditions necessary for enlightenment. The Vimalikirti Sutra addresses the nonduality of all things. The Prajnaparamita Sutra discusses the meaning of true wisdom, therefore its title is translated as Sutra of Transcendental Wisdom. The Avatamsaka Sutra examines the interconnectedness of all beings and their Buddha-nature.

In addition, all four sutras had profound impacts upon key figures in the history of Zen. The Prajnaparamita influenced the Middle Way theory of the great Indian Buddhist philosopher Nagarjuna (c. 150 C.E.) in the second century C.E. The Lankavatara was taught by the venerable Bodhidharma, the great teacher who brought Buddhism from India to China. And the Vimalikirti influenced Prince Regent Shotoku (fifth–sixth centuries C.E.), who first officially promoted Buddhism in Japan. Zen students continue to study these sutras.

The leading ideas from these sutras thus became major axioms in Zen Buddhism. Therefore, Zen went on to reaffirm the need for enlightenment, that is, awakening to our true Buddha-nature. And it continued to underscore the nonduality of all things, manifested in their interconnectedness. Yet even though Zen inherited these teachings from the sutras, it eventually fashioned its own unique and positively radical approach to them. Let us briefly interrupt this Zen odyssey in order to point out its originality.

Zen assigned top priority to the actual enlightenment experience, or *satori,* rather than the numerous scholastic commentaries surrounding it. No doubt the experience of enlightenment is the aim in all Buddhist schools. However, there is an important difference. Whereas the other schools, including the Mahayana, stress the primary need to rely upon and to seriously study the Buddhist texts, or sutras, Zen emphasizes the *direct experience of satori* itself as essential. What matters is the personal experience of awakening, not constructing an intellectual edifice of commentary and analysis about the experience.

Zen Buddhism in China (Ch'an Buddhism)

Buddhist teachings infiltrated China around the first century C.E. after they had already permeated much of India. And by the fourth century, this new religious philosophy had become highly developed. And Mahayana gained ascendancy partly because of certain affinities with Chinese Taoist teachings. This kinship with Taoism manifested itself in two ways. First, both stressed the need to be one with all of nature. This meant letting-things-be according to the natural Way, or Tao. Second, they emphasized the importance of meditation as an avenue to unify body and mind. Without a doubt, this communion with Taoism produced Zen's own unique style and flavor.

How did Zen find its way into China? To begin with, keep in mind the unique manner by which Zen teachings (called *Ch'an* in Chinese) were handed down. The heart of Zen teaching, referred to as the "seal of enlightenment," was passed on individually from the Zen master (Zen patriarch) to a selected student—the one most eligible due to his level of insight—who then became the next master.[4] The most famous figure in this transmission process was Bodhidharma (d. c. 534 C.E.), the twenty-eighth and last patriarch in India. He left India to travel to China and settled there as that country's first patriarch. Many legends surround his life. One account tells us that he sat in meditation for years in front of a wall until he finally reached his enlightenment, that is, until he experienced his true Buddha-nature. From the point of view of Zen, he is the historic bridge between India and China. In fact, some well-known *koans* (riddles utilized as a means to enlightenment) pose the question: What is the meaning of Bodhidharma's coming from the West? His coming from the West (that is, from India) to China symbolizes the meaning of Zen.

Moreover, the teachings of Bodhidharma resulted in the evolution of certain Zen precepts that represented a radical departure from orthodox Buddhism. These teachings can be listed as,

1. Transmission outside the scriptures
2. Not relying on letters
3. Pointing directly to one's mind
4. Attainment of Buddha-hood by seeing into one's Nature[5]

Transmission outside the scriptures. Keep in mind that numerous Buddhist schools debated with each other over interpretations of scriptures and texts that discussed the original awakening experience of the Buddha as well as his later teachings. Zen proposed that the essential aim is not intellectual understanding but a genuine *satori* experience. Trusting solely upon the intellect could actually impede the experience. Compared with the actual experience of awakening, intellectual knowledge is "like a small lamp under the shining sun."[6]

Not relying on letters. In like manner, the enlightenment experience, as with any experience, could never be captured in words. Words are like symbols; they ought not to be mistaken for the reality. Language describes an experience, and, in doing so, is like the finger that points to the moon. We, however, commit a fundamental error in confusing the finger that points to the moon with the moon itself. Zen teaches us that there is no better way to express the truth than to *live* it, to embody it in our actions.

Pointing directly to one's mind. This means that we have the power within us to free ourselves from our own minds. That is, our minds are usually fixed upon certain perspectives so that we are attached to particular points of reference, and we therefore discriminate. Only by detaching ourselves from our biases can we be genuinely free.

Attainment of Buddha-hood by seeing into one's Nature. There are two key terms here: "seeing" and "one's Nature." "Seeing" is more authentic than "knowing." Zen points out the critical importance of real experience rather than second-hand "experience," as found in ideas, concepts, and words. Moreover, our true "Nature" lies in our original Buddha-hood, and this constitutes a vital Zen precept. Our lifelong journey is to awaken to our true Nature, and the secret to this actually lies within us. However, we mistakenly think that it lies elsewhere, like the rider on a horse who travels from town to town, asking people, "Have you seen my horse?"

Bodhidharma. (Corbis/Sakamoto Photo Research Library)

Bodhidharma's successor was Hui-k'o (487–593), memorialized in Zen literature as an extreme paradigm for the vital importance of the master-student relationship. Another important figure in the development of Zen is Tao-hsin (580–651). He introduced a significant change in the lifestyle of Buddhist monks. Up until then, most monks were wanderers. Tao-hsin helped to change all this when he set up one of the first Zen communities for monks. In their novel, stable environment, Zen monks became self-sufficient. They also discovered a deep, spiritual meaning in their everyday chores, as well as in meditation. This lifestyle has retained its vitality to this day.

Eventually, a schism of far-reaching dimensions erupted. The patriarch Hung-jen was ready to pass on his Zen (or Ch'an) seal to his most deserving student. He requested that any willing student compose a *gatha,* or poem, on the meaning of Zen. Shen-hsiu, the monk considered most likely to inherit the patriarchate, wrote these verses and posted them on a wall:

The body is like the Bodhi tree,
The mind is like a clear mirror standing.
Take care to wipe it all the time,
Allow no grain of dust to cling.[7]

But a young boy of little education, Hui-neng (638–713), after hearing about the gatha (he could not read nor write), composed to himself the following response and had it written on the wall:

The Bodhi is not like a tree,
The clear mirror is nowhere standing.
Fundamentally not one thing exists;
Where, then, is a grain of dust to cling?[8]

Their respective gathas reveal a critical difference. Shen-hsiu's verses reflect duality and differentiation. In contrast, Hui-neng's gatha manifests nondualism, and it represents the doctrine of emptiness that lies at the core of Zen Buddhism.

The patriarch Hung-jen recognized that the young boy had captured the true essence of Zen in these verses. However, fearing that Shen-hsiu's resentment might bring harm to the boy, he transmitted the seal to the boy in private during the night and requested that he flee the monastery and journey south.[9] Consequently, two schools of Zen arose: the northern school headed by Shen-hsiu, and the southern school led by Hui-neng. The northern school emphasized a gradual approach to enlightenment, whereas the southern school stressed the sudden and instantaneous quality of enlightenment.

During the Golden Age of China (713–845), the predominant Zen masters were heirs to the southern school of Hui-neng. In the spirit of Hui-neng, they taught that since the mind already possesses enlightenment within itself, practices were not necessary. For instance, even though the Zen master

Te-shan (780–865) initially placed great trust in the inherent worth of the sutras as a guide to enlightenment, he later emphasized their worthlessness.

Despite the ensuing persecution of Buddhism under Emperor Wu-tsung, Zen managed to survive, and the period of the Five Dynasties (907–960) witnessed the evolution of these two schools into two official Zen sects, one headed by Ta'ao-tung (the earlier northern school) and the other by Lin-chi (the southern school). The Ta'ao-tung school emphasized the importance of quiet sitting in meditation (*zazen*) as a means to enlightenment. The Lin-chi school underscored the significance of a method known as *koan.*

The expansive hand of Zen upon Chinese culture is particularly prominent during the Sung period (Northern Sung dynasty 960–1126; Southern Sung dynasty, 1127–1279). Sung art is an outright expression of Zen teachings. Also, during this time, both "sitting meditation" (*zazen*) and the *koan* become standard methods in Zen practice. *Zazen* is a form of sitting meditation that requires strict discipline in maintaining proper bodily posture and proper breathing. It aims to empty, or pacify, the mind. In other words, its purpose is to quiet down mental commotion in order to restore the essential harmony between the physical and the mental. Emptying the mind enables us to shatter the illusion of a separate self and thereby to awaken to our true nature, the Buddha-nature, a nature that we share with all other beings.

The *koan,* on the other hand, is a "riddle" assigned to the Zen student, who then engages in an exhaustive intellectual effort to find a reasonable "answer" to the *koan* (emphasized more in the Lin-chi sect and later in the Rinzai sect in Japan). Here are some classic *koans:*

- What is the sound of one hand clapping?
- Wakuan said, "Why has the foreigner from the West no beard?" [Bodhidharma is the foreigner and is always portrayed with a bushy beard.]
- Goso said, "If you meet a man of Tao on the way, greet him neither with words nor with silence. Now tell me, how will you greet him?"[10]

The student's desire for a rational solution reflects his desire for stability and permanence. And there's the rub. There is no reasonable, intellectualized answer, and nothing is permanent. The *koan* demonstrates, therefore, the futility of intellect and aims to bring about a transformation in the way we view reality. The practice of the *koan* is designed to help us realize that there is no "answer" and that permanence as such does not exist, and this sets the condition for *satori,* the awakening to our true nature.

Zen Buddhism in Japan

When Buddhism entered Japan, it encountered the native backdrop of beliefs called Shinto, or "Way of the Gods." As in China, Buddhism did not at all displace indigenous tenets. Instead, it adapted itself to the needs of the people and eventually prevailed as the dominant religious force. Japan's Prince Regent

Shotoku Taishi (d. 621 C.E.) was one of Buddhism's most devout supporters. His unfailing trust in Hotoke, or Buddha, had a tremendous impact upon the people. The first Buddhist meditation hall was constructed about 653 C.E. at Nara.

Despite these hopeful beginnings, Zen did not become significantly popular until the Kamakura period (1185–1333). During this time, the famous monk Eisai (Zenko Kokushi, 1141–1215) carried the teachings of Lin-chi from China to Japan, and he founded the first Rinzai (the Japanese equivalent to Lin-chi) temple at Hakata in Kyushu in 1191. His energy and zeal for the spread of Zen attracted many devotees, and he is often regarded as the actual founder of Japanese Zen. In turn, Rinzai Zen permeated much of Japanese culture because of its endorsement by the Shogunate, a succession of military rulers.

During this same period, Dogen (1200–1253), one of the greatest figures in Japanese religious and intellectual history, founded the Soto school (Soto being the equivalent of Ta'ao-tung's school) and a Soto temple in Kyushu. He is famous for his *Shōbōgenzō* and for his emphasis upon *zazen*. He stressed the transitoriness of all things yet perceived the possibility of enlightenment in the most mundane matters in ordinary life.

The Kamakura period thus witnessed the blossoming of Zen in Japan. During this time, Zen had widespread appeal for both the nobility and the common people. The Zen teaching that everyone naturally possesses the Buddha-nature certainly impressed the common people. And for the warrior class, or *bushi,* Zen offered a means to achieve inner discipline as well as a dignified way to face death.

After a long period of internal strife and warfare, the Tokugawa period (1600–1868) unified Japan and placed its cultural and political life under strict control. The well-known Zen master Takuan (1573–1645) wrote a treatise on proper swordsmanship grounded upon Zen discipline. Another famous Zen teacher was Hakuin (1685–1768), who represented the Rinzai sect. Hakuin's *Orategama* emphasized the power of the *koan* as a means to enlightenment. As with all Zen teachings, he stressed the need for a radical detachment and a letting-go of passions and desires.

Up to the present day, both the Rinzai and Soto schools continue to influence the Japanese. At the same time, Zen remains steadfast in embodying the heart of Japanese culture. It touches nearly every pore of Japanese life and art, ranging from calligraphy, gardening, martial arts, sumi-e painting, and poetry to the tea ceremony.

Zen Buddhism as Moral Geometry

Does Zen have an ethic? If we take ethics in the Western sense of a systematic analysis of morality, the answer is a resounding No! Recall the four principles of Zen:

1. Transmission outside the scriptures
2. Not relying on letters

3. Pointing directly to one's mind

4. Attainment of Buddha-hood by seeing into one's Nature

We see here that Zen, in being almost utterly self-reliant, actually militates against depending upon intellectual and systematic analyses. There are no rules here, no methodical approach to principles and duties.

Nevertheless, even though there is no Zen ethics in the strict, systematic sense, Zen teachings certainly do have moral relevance. They comprise degrees of moral weight, a sort of "moral geometry" in that they help to carve out for us a proper disposition and lifestyle.[11]

As we have seen, the practice of Zen aims to bring about an enlightened state of mind, an awakening from our ordinary state of ignorance. Thus, Zen's goal is essentially transformative. And this transformative aim carries with it rich ethical dimensions. In Zen practice, the process of awakening requires a full awareness of being-with-others-in-the-world. And it helps us to cultivate an inner discipline and disposition to help us live in the best way we can in the world.

As a prelude to our next section, we can at least sketch the following features in Zen's moral geometry. First, there is a strong sense of "this worldliness" in Zen, that is, living fully in the present and being completely engaged in whatever we do. Zen teachings send us a wake-up call to the here-and-now. In this way, by focusing on each given task, we can cultivate a sincere inner disposition with which we can *integrate ourselves in our actions.* For example, the quality of a Japanese sword was assessed not only on the basis of its artisanship, but, in turn, upon the character and moral disposition of the swordsmith.

Waking up to the here-and-now also enables us to appreciate the meaning and beauty within the ordinary, whether we are quietly studying and working (as in the way of the monk), engaged in conflict (as in the way of the warrior), or immersed in creative expression (as in the way of the tea ceremony).

Next, Zen's moral geometry appreciates the interconnectedness of all things. This means that there are no isolated events. What occurs in Ethiopia touches everything and everyone. And there is no independent entity called "self" or "I". Therefore there are no grounds for my self-interest to be the center of my morality. Zen expands our "moral community" to encompass all being.

Another feature concerns the Buddhist notion of "emptiness," in the sense of uncluttering our minds. Zen teaches us that it is precisely our minds that hinder us from living fully and sincerely, with a pure heart. Yet we ourselves have the capacity to quiet and empty our minds, although the way to achieve this is exceedingly difficult. Nevertheless, we have the potential to live more focused and unassuming lives, that is, to live less superficially. *And this enables us to deal steadily and sensibly with moral conflicts.*

This inner capacity underscores the Zen teaching of *jiriki,* or self-effort. This means that I am ultimately responsible for my own destiny. My final accountability is to myself. Zen therefore urges the utmost in individual responsibility.

Jean-Paul Sartre, *Being and Nothingness*

[M]y freedom is the unique foundation of values and ... *nothing,* absolutely nothing, justifies me in adopting this or that particular scale of values. As a being by whom values exist, I am unjustifiable. My freedom is anguished at being the foundation of values while itself without foundation. . . .

. . . It is obvious that I remain free . . . to direct my attention on . . . values or to neglect them—exactly as it depends on me to look more closely at this table, my pen, or my package of tobacco. But whether they are the object of detailed attention or not, in any case, they *are.*

From Jean-Paul Sartre, *Being and Nothingness,* trans. Hazel E. Barnes (New York: Washington Square Press, 1966), pp. 76, 146.

The rest of the chapter examines this moral geometry in three figurative ways—the monk, the warrior, and the tea master. These are deliberately labeled "ways" in that Zen teachings show us ways that guide us in a clear moral direction. Furthermore, these "ways" speak to each one of us. They are not simply confined to the monk, warrior, or tea master. In a figurative sense, all of us are monks, warriors, and tea masters. And these ways or paths represent unique attitudes or dispositions that we can further cultivate. Thus, the way of the monk involves the path of study, prayer, and hard work. The way of the warrior embodies the path of action. And the way of the tea master symbolizes creativity. Each path emphasizes a principal, unique focus. At the same time, all three ways interact. For instance, the warrior works hard and studies, and the way of the tea master requires action and discipline. Indeed, all three ways are interrelated, and the secret to living is to keep all three in balance.

A WAY OF THE MONK: PRACTICE *IS* ATTAINMENT

Dogen's Question

One day a Zen master was fanning himself. At this, a monk was puzzled, so he asked the master:

> "The nature of wind is eternal and all-pervasive—why then do you use a fan?" The master said, "You only know the nature of wind is eternal, but do not yet know the principle of its omnipresence." The monk asked, "What is the principle of its omnipresence?" The master just fanned. The monk bowed.[12]

Dogen (1200–1253), the key spokesman for Zen Buddhism, alludes to this incident in his famous Zen treatise, *Shōbōgenzō*. The monk's inquiry is reminiscent of a question Dogen himself had once raised and with which he became thoroughly obsessed. Dogen's question was this: *If it is true, as Mahayana Buddhism asserts, that we are all originally enlightened since we all possess Buddha-nature, then why do we need to involve ourselves in various disciplined practices and methods in order to achieve enlightenment?* Why study the Buddhist sutras? Why invoke the name of Amida Buddha? The Tendai sect to which Dogen belonged stressed both of these as necessary means to enlightenment.

This question so overwhelmingly consumed Dogen that he eventually left the Tendai monastery and traveled to China to seek an answer. And when he finally settled down to study under the Ch'an Buddhist Master Ju-ching (1163–1228), he learned his most precious lesson—the practice of *zazen*, or "sitting meditation." As we mentioned earlier, *zazen*, along with the *koan* exercise, had become a mainstay in Ch'an Buddhist practice. Since its aim was to pacify the mind in order to restore harmony between the physical and the mental, it demanded a proper mental disposition and outlook. And since emptying the mind enables us to awaken to our true Buddha-nature, a nature that we share with all other sentient beings, ethically speaking, this involves an awakening to selflessness. In any case, while he was with Ju-ching, Dogen had his own enlightenment experience, his *satori*. And it was so utterly overpowering that it inspired in him the answer to his riddle.

Dogen's Resolution: Casting Off Body-Mind

How did Dogen resolve his question? First of all, he assigned the utmost importance to the practice of *zazen*. He maintained that the only true path to enlightenment, awakening to our Buddha-nature, lies in the practice of *zazen*. In fact, the Soto school of Zen, which he is credited with founding, is often referred to as *shikantaza*, or "*zazen* only."[13]

For Dogen, *zazen* demands a "casting off of the body-mind." This brings about a genuine liberation. Yet, what is this "body-mind," and what does it mean for me to cast it off? My "body-mind" is the impression I have that I am a separate, independent, autonomous self. Buddhists reject this belief. Yet they also claim that even though there are no empirical grounds for belief in my independent self, I still tend to cling to this "body-mind." However, it is precisely this "body-mind" that thwarts me from awakening to my true Buddha-nature.

Now what does it mean to "cast off body-mind"? Here is where the practice of *zazen* comes in, for the purpose of *zazen* is to free the mind through meditation. That is, to not allow our mental activity to interfere with a complete awareness of the present. This is what we mean by "casting off body-mind." How can we do this? Only through persistent, disciplined practice, a practice that typically requires years of proper training and attitude.

Let us be more clear. Usually, our minds are like train stations, with all sorts of commotion. And we mistakenly think that we are helpless victims of this—that armies of images, thoughts, feelings, and desires incessantly "invade" us. *Zazen* enables us to somehow curb this mental traffic. While meditating we can train ourselves to simply accept each thought as-it-is, in its suchness, without clinging to it. In this way, thoughts and feelings that "enter" our minds are neither resisted nor held on to. They are like clouds that simply come and go without effort. This is what we mean by casting off body-mind.

As for the scene presented previously, we can now understand why the Zen master fanning himself poses such a quandary for the monk. The monk is still attached to his body-mind, still tied to a view of himself as a separate self, and he therefore conceptualizes a strict difference between the nature of the wind and the singular action of the master, another separate self, using the fan. Therefore, although his challenge to the master appears on one level to be logically irrefutable, he still remains imprisoned in his intellect—he is still attached to *his* body-mind.

Because of this, the master chastises him for not truly understanding the nature of the wind, which is everywhere, and which thereby signifies reality. And when the monk seeks edification, the master gives no intellectual response. Instead, he simply continues to fan—no lecture, no dissertation, no resorting to intellectual analysis. In fanning, the master embodies the lesson: he *acts out* the wind's (that is, reality's) principle. It is *because* the wind is everywhere that the master fans himself. The master, in other words, is a manifestation of the wind's principle. The two are inseparable.

We now arrive at Dogen's resolution of the question that has defied his intellect, a question that presumes a conceptual difference between original enlightenment and the practice that leads to awakening. Dogen unravels the riddle *by casting off body-mind* through the practice of *zazen* and discovering the most profound and original insight in Zen Buddhism: *the oneness of practice and enlightenment.*

How do we reconcile original enlightenment with acquired awakening through practice? Dogen's answer: In essence, practice is not separate from enlightenment. Every step of the way in practice *is* enlightenment. Enlightenment does not lie at the end of practice, but lies *in* the practice.

How did Dogen arrive at this startling, unsurpassed notion? So long as he remained attached to his body-mind, his separate self, his question could not be resolved. This is because he still managed to reify both "enlightenment" and "practice," that is, to objectify them as if they were each separate, independent entities. By viewing them as separate, he split the means (practice) from the end (enlightenment).

However, by casting off his body-mind, he freed himself from the tyranny of his intellect, thus realizing that "enlightenment" and "practice" do not constitute separate entities. In reality, enlightenment naturally embraces practice and vice versa. In the same way, the end embraces the means to achieve it. The two are not separate. It is precisely *because* we are originally enlightened that we practice. (In like manner, it is because the wind is everywhere that the monk fans himself.) At the same time, each moment of practice, each moment of *zazen* is in itself enlightenment.

Ethical Dimensions

What are the ethical dimensions of all this? While Zen clearly does not have a systematic ethic, it still bears moral weight. Zen purports to bring about in us an enlightened state of being, and this naturally impacts upon our lifestyle. Furthermore, this enlightened state is not some final end or product but a constant process that requires an ongoing cultivation of the right disposition and attitudes necessary for good character. Let us elaborate further upon this.

The secret lies within us. First of all, Dogen continues to fully endorse the notion of our original enlightenment, along with that of all other sentient beings, because of our innate Buddha-nature. Therefore, in the most primal sense, we "instinctively" possess the means within us to awaken to this.

This is in contrast, for example, to Shinran, affiliated with the Jodo Pure Land sect of Buddhism, who asserts that our human natures are so driven by self-interest that, by ourselves, we are unable to cast off body-mind. According to Shinran, freedom is possible only through the efforts of someone other than ourselves (*tariki*), namely Amida Buddha, who responds favorably to our prayers and faith.

Instead, when Dogen claims that our enlightenment manifests itself in our *own* practice, what he means is that we can be free through our *own* efforts (*jiriki*), through a genuine self-awakening to our true nature and to the nature of all things. We ourselves can cast off our body-mind. Otherwise, by holding on to the body-mind, we imprison ourselves. Only we can free ourselves from our own chains.

What a heartening message in Dogen's teaching! We contain within ourselves the secret to our own freedom. We can awaken to our Buddha-nature through our own efforts. The key does not lie *outside* of us: not in any God, scripture, textbook, parent, teacher, peer, law, social custom, or social morality. The capacity to live according to our Buddha-nature lies within us. This means that we are ultimately responsible and accountable to ourselves.

Awakening to the Buddha-nature of all being: Self-other-nature. The beloved Zen monk Ikkyu (1394–1482), abbot of the Zen temple of Daitokuji in Kyoto, thoroughly disdained the arrogance of monks who considered themselves superior to laypeople. In his famous treatise called the "Skeleton," he writes:

> In bygone days, those whose hearts were awakened to faith entered the monasteries, but now they all forsake the temples. . . . With much satisfaction they glory in their monastic robes, and though they wear the habits of a monk they are only laymen in disguise. Let them put on cloaks and robes, and the robe becomes a rope which binds the body, while the cloak becomes an iron rod to torment it.[14]

Ikkyu once went out begging, wearing tattered clothes instead of the elaborate monk's robe that he wore as a mark of his office as abbot. When he came to the home of a wealthy landlord, a small coin of insignificant amount was left there by the door. Later, he revisited the same home, this time dressed in his monk's robe, and he was invited inside and offered a lavish meal, which he refused to eat. Instead, he stripped off his outer robe and placed it in front of the food, announcing that the meal belonged to the robe and not to him. In this way, Ikkyu reminds us that our common Buddha-nature bestows a common dignity.

Now Dogen goes even further and claims that *all being,* sentient and nonsentient, is Buddha-nature. This has even more radical ethical implications. It means that when I cast off my own body-mind and awaken to my Buddha-nature, I also awaken to that which is shared by all other being. Therefore, casting off my body-mind involves removing the body-mind of all being, an elimination of their separate existences.[15]

This has obvious moral relevance. Awakening to the Buddha-nature of all being entails shattering a fixed and rigid point of reference that is solely anthropocentric. It means sweeping away the viewpoint that values everything solely in terms of what is of interest to our own human species. Realizing the Buddha-nature of all being frees us from this anthropocentrism. And by acknowledging this interconnectedness, we, in effect, broaden the realm of what constitutes a "moral community." We can no longer restrict the moral community simply to ourselves as humans. The moral community now extends into the nonhuman and the natural domains as well. This Zen Buddhist view radically challenges our typical species-centered normative view.

Awakening to the Buddha-nature of all being sets in motion a unique moral starting point for an ecology that respects the status of all other beings—human and nonhuman, indeed, all of nature. When we are able to abandon the illusion of our separate selves, divorced and distinct from all other things, an ecological consciousness is born. Once we are able to cast off body-mind, we free ourselves from this illusion of separate selves. In turn, we naturally realize our essential oneness with all: other humans, all nonhumans, all aspects of nature. Although Zen Buddhism does not delineate more specifically this ecological consciousness, it nevertheless provides a strong basis.

Mary Midgley, *Beast and Man*

What we need here is to get rid of the language of means and ends, and use instead that of part and whole. Man needs to form part of a whole much greater than himself, one in which other members excel him in innumerable ways. He is adapted to live in one. Without it, he feels imprisoned; the lid of the ego presses down on him.

The world in which the kestrel [as Old World falcon] moves, the world that it sees, is, and will always be, entirely beyond us. That there are such worlds around us is an essential feature of our world. Calling the bird's existence "pointless" means only that it is not a device for any human end. It does not need that external point. It is in some sense—a sense that can certainly do with study—an end in itself. . . .

[W]e are receptive, imaginative beings, adapted to celebrate and rejoice in the existence, quite independent of ourselves, of the other beings on this planet.

From Mary Midgley, *Beast and Man: The Roots of Human Nature* (Ithaca, NY: Cornell University Press, 1978), pp. 359, 361.

Means and ends. Practice is enlightenment. This insight has clear implications in morality with respect to the relationship between means and ends. Indeed, the most vital question in ethical theory is: Do the ends justify the means? For instance, a utilitarian ethic seeks to achieve the greatest aggregate good by requiring that course of action that will in the long run produce the greatest good for the greatest number of people. A powerful advantage to this theory is that we are morally obliged to transcend self-interest in order to safeguard the interests of others. However, does it also lead us to embrace a dangerous proposition: that the ends do justify the means? May noble ends morally justify ignoble means to achieve them? We would intuitively respond no. But why? Because the means utilized to achieve an end have a way of coloring the quality of that same end. In other words, we cannot afford to readily separate means and ends.

If we take seriously Dogen's claim that the practice that aims for awakening is in essence the awakening itself, means and ends are thereby strongly interwoven. In fact, the means is the end. Each and every step of the way to the goal is ITSELF THE GOAL. This certainly challenges our usual view, whereby we tend to think of means as a process, a series of steps that will produce a goal after they have been accomplished. We conceptually disengage means and ends by viewing matters solely from either point of reference. If my point of reference is the end, I may justify any means so long as I consider the end to be legitimate. So I may justify cheating on my exam because my goal is to graduate successfully from college. Or my point of reference may be the means. I may determine that the cause to which any soldier is committed is noble because his own particular actions are themselves courageous. But we may overlook the end result of the soldier's actions. Whichever way we cut it, we still end up assuming a conceptual disparity between ends and means.

But separating present effort and future accomplishment fragments time and reality into static entities. The Japanese philosopher Masao Abe singles out some pernicious consequences of this ordinary view.[16] First of all, we assign meaning to the present only in terms of its usefulness for some future, not-yet event. We give no meaning to the present in itself. Second, this orientation toward the future causes us to experience a chronic sense of incompleteness or "restlessness." Third, this restlessness is all the more compounded because we abstract from the present experience, conceptualizing present and future, and therefore we are disconnected from the reality of the experience.[17]

For example, Dogen's resolution to his question strongly supports the inseparability of ends and means. Just as "enlightenment" *is* "practice," ends and means mutually define each other. Does the end justify the means? is the wrong question if it assumes a difference between the two. What Zen teaches us is that each moment of the means is itself the goal, so that what we do each step of the way continually colors, refines, and redefines what we set out as our end. This compels us to live both creatively and responsibly in each moment.

Thich Nhat Hanh and Interbeing

Indeed, all of this is the thrust behind the Order of Interbeing founded by the contemporary Vietnamese Zen Buddhist monk, Thich Nhat Hanh. He established his Order in the mid-1960s, when Vietnam was being ravaged by war and other violent expressions of factionalism. The Vietnamese words for the "Order of Interbeing" are *Tiep Hien. Tiep* refers to "being in touch with" and *hien* means "making it here and now." "Interbeing" is therefore Thich Nhat Hanh's way of reminding us that we are all, in essence, interconnected, just as Dogen also reminds us that all living beings share Buddha-nature. And Thich Nhat Hanh's example and guidance have become a remarkable source of inspiration not only for the Vietnamese but for people throughout the world.

Born in the mid-1920s, Thich Nhat Hanh became a monk at the age of sixteen. When his country became increasingly divided and various tensions erupted into ruthless conflicts, he based his lifestyle upon Buddhism's social ethical teachings. He and his fellow monks became thoroughly engaged in relieving those victimized by war. Moreover, they conducted overt, public demonstrations for peace.

Thich Nhat Hanh's was a gentle, yet firm and outspoken voice for the millions of oppressed Vietnamese torn apart by prevailing ideologies. And when he visited the United States in 1966 in an effort to extend global awareness of the plight of his suffering people, his forthright candor so daunted the

Vietnamese government that he could not return to his homeland without seriously imperiling his safety.

He established a Vietnamese Buddhist Peace Delegation in Paris in order to aid children victimized by the war. His group also made efforts to protect the refugees, called the "boat people," on the Gulf of Siam. Since then, he has lived in his retreat, Plum Village, in France. Yet he continues to lead retreats at various Zen centers throughout Europe and America.

His Order of Interbeing embodies Zen ethics, and the principles of the Order center on the previously described teachings regarding interdependence and the casting-off of the false notion of a separate self. All of this is expressed in the Order's Fourteen Mindfulness Trainings or Precepts. These precepts state in concrete fashion the ethical dimensions of Zen practice. Here are the Fourteen Mindfulness Trainings along with a brief commentary by Thich Nhat Hanh.

Thich Nhat Hanh

THE FOURTEEN MINDFULNESS TRAININGS

1

Aware of the suffering created by fanaticism and intolerance, we are determined not to be idolatrous about or bound to any doctrine, theory, or ideology, even Buddhist ones. Buddhist teachings are guiding means to help us learn to look deeply and to develop our understanding and compassion. They are not doctrines to fight, kill, or die for.

2

Aware of the suffering created by attachment to views and wrong perceptions, we are determined to avoid being narrow-minded and bound to present views. We shall learn and practice nonattachment from views in order to be open to others' insights and experiences. We are aware that the knowledge we presently possess is not changeless, absolute truth. Truth is found in life, and we will observe life within and around us in every moment, ready to learn throughout our lives.

3

Aware of the suffering brought about when we impose our views on others, we are committed not to force others, even our children, by any means whatsoever—such as authority, threat, money, propaganda, or indoctrination—to adopt our views. We will respect the right of others to be different and to choose what to believe and how to decide. We will, however, help others renounce fanaticism and narrowness through compassionate dialogue.

4

Aware that looking deeply at the nature of suffering can help us develop compassion and find ways out of suffering, we are determined not to avoid or close our eyes before suffering. We are committed to finding ways, including personal contact, images, and sounds, to be with those who suffer, so we can understand their situation deeply and help them transform their suffering into compassion, peace, and joy.

5

Aware that true happiness is rooted in peace, solidity, freedom, and compassion, and not in wealth or fame, we are determined not to take as the aim of our life fame, profit, wealth, or sensual pleasure, nor to accumulate wealth while millions are hungry and dying. We are committed to living simply and sharing our time, energy, and material resources with those in need. We will practice mindful consuming, not using alcohol, drugs, or any other products that bring toxins into our own and the collective body and consciousness.

6

Aware that anger blocks communication and creates suffering, we are determined to take care of the energy of anger when it arises and to recognize and transform the seeds of anger that lie deep in our consciousness. When anger comes up, we are determined not to do or say anything, but to practice mindful breathing or mindful walking and acknowledge, embrace, and look deeply into our anger. We will learn to look with the eyes of compassion at those we think are the cause of our anger.

7

Aware that life is available only in the present moment and that it is possible to live happily in the here and now, we are committed to training ourselves to live deeply each moment of daily life. We will try not to lose ourselves in dispersion or be carried away by regrets about the past, worries about the future, or craving, anger, or jealousy in the present.

We will practice mindful breathing to come back to what is happening in the present moment. We are determined to learn the art of mindful living by touching the wondrous, refreshing, and healing elements that are inside and around us, and by nourishing seeds of joy, peace, love, and understanding in ourselves, thus facilitating the work of transformation and healing in our consciousness.

8

Aware that the lack of communication always brings separation and suffering, we are committed to training ourselves in the practice of compassionate listening and loving speech. We will learn to listen deeply without judging or reacting and refrain from uttering words that can create discord or cause the community to break. We will make every effort to keep communications open and to reconcile and resolve all conflicts, however small.

9

Aware that words can create suffering or happiness, we are committed to learning to speak truthfully and constructively, using only words that inspire hope and confidence. We are determined not to say untruthful things for the sake of personal interest or to impress people, nor to utter words that might cause division or hatred. We will not spread news that we do not know to be certain nor criticize or condemn things of which we are not sure. We will do our best to speak out about situations of injustice, even when doing so may threaten our safety.

10

Aware that the essence and aim of a Sangha is the practice of under-standing and compassion, we are determined not to use the Buddhist community for personal gain or profit or transform our community into a political instrument. A spiritual community should, however, take a clear stand against oppression and injustice and should strive to change the situation without engaging in partisan conflicts.

11

Aware that great violence and injustice have been done to our environment and society, we are committed not to live with a vocation that is harm-ful to humans and nature. We will do our best to select a livelihood that helps realize our ideal of understanding and compassion. Aware of global economic, political and social realities, we will behave responsibly as consumers and as citizens, not investing in companies that deprive others of their chance to live.

12

Aware that much suffering is caused by war and conflict, we are determined to cultivate nonviolence, understanding, and compassion in our daily lives, to promote peace education, mindful mediation, and reconciliation within families, communities, nations, and in the world. We are determined not to kill and not to let others kill. We will diligently practice deep looking with our Sangha to discover better ways to protect life and prevent war.

13

Aware of the suffering caused by exploitation, social injustice, stealing, and oppression, we are committed to cultivating loving kindness and learning ways to work for the well-being of people, animals, plants, and minerals. We will practice generosity by sharing our time, energy, and material resources with those who are in need. We are determined not to steal and not to possess anything that should belong to others. We will respect the property of others, but will try to prevent others from profiting from human suffering or the suffering of other beings.

14

(For lay members): Aware that sexual relations motivated by craving cannot dissipate the feeling of loneliness but will create more suffering, frustration, and isolation, we are determined not to engage in sexual relations without mutual understanding, love, and a long-term commitment. In sexual relations, we must be aware of future suffering that may be caused. We know that to preserve the happiness of ourselves and others, we must respect the rights and commitments of ourselves and others. We will do everything in our power to protect children from sexual abuse and to protect couples and families from being broken by sexual misconduct. We will treat our bodies with respect and preserve our vital energies (sexual, breath, spirit) for the realization of our bodhisattva ideal. We will be fully aware of the responsibility of bringing new lives into the world, and will meditate on the world into which we are bringing new beings.

(For monastic members): Aware that the aspiration of a monk or a nun can only be realized when he or she wholly leaves behind the bonds of worldly love, we are committed to practicing chastity and to helping others protect themselves. We are aware that loneliness and suffering cannot be alleviated by the coming together of two bodies in a sexual relationship, but by the practice of true understanding and compassion. We know that a sexual relationship will destroy our life as a monk or a nun, will prevent us from realizing our ideal of serving living beings, and will harm others. We are determined not to suppress or mistreat our body or to look upon our body as only an instrument, but to learn to handle our body with respect. We are determined to preserve vital energies (sexual, breath, spirit) for the realization of our bodhisattva ideal.

Reprinted from *Teachings on Love* (1997) by Thich Nhat Hanh with permission of Parallax Press, Berkeley, California.

A WAY OF THE WARRIOR

We all face situations of conflict. How we deal with these situations will often rest upon our own disposition and values. Furthermore, our response in these situations will contribute in some form toward cultivating our character. For this reason, let us now look at Zen teachings regarding the conduct of the warrior. By highlighting some prominent figures and their ethical significance, we will see that their teachings are timeless in that they extend beyond matters of swordsmanship and the concerns of a warrior. Indeed, they provide us with a philosophy for handling conflict and confrontation in all situations.

Takuan Sōhō and the Undetained Mind

Two monks were traveling in the rain, the mud sloshing under their feet. As they passed a river crossing, they saw a beautiful woman, finely dressed, unable to cross because of the mud. Without a word, the older monk simply picked up the woman and carried her to the other side.

The younger monk, seemingly agitated for the rest of their journey, could not contain himself once they reached their destination. He exploded at the older monk, "How could you, a monk, even consider holding a woman in your arms, much less a young and beautiful one. It is against our teachings. It is dangerous."

"I put her down at the roadside," said the older monk. "Are you still carrying her?"[18]

According to the celebrated Zen monk Takuan Sōhō (1573–1645), we all tend to suffer from the same malaise as the young monk in the story: We tend to detain, or fix, our minds.

Takuan himself embodied the spirit of Zen in numerous ways: in his calligraphy, poetry, painting, gardening, and the art of the tea ceremony. At the extraordinarily young age of thirty-five, he became the abbot of Kyoto's Daitokuji Zen temple of the Rinzai sect. And besides acting as advisor to shoguns, or military rulers, he instructed two of Japan's most famed swordsmen, Yagyu Munenori and Miyamoto Musashi.

Here is the focal point of his advice to these warriors: *The real enemy is not your opponent but your own mind.* The moment your mind stops or is detained at some point, whether it be at your fear of dying, at your opponent's mind or sword, at your sword, at any parts of your opponent's movements, at your own movements, or at anything else, the result can be your death. It is of the utmost importance, therefore, to free yourself from your mind.

Consider Takuan's famous letter of instruction to the swordsman Yagyu Munenori, "The Mysterious Record of Immovable Wisdom" (*Fudōchishin-myōroku*). The monk spares no time warning Yagyu of the danger involved in detaining, or stopping the mind:

> [W]hen you first notice the sword that is moving to strike you, if you think of meeting that sword just as it is, your mind will stop at the sword in just that position, your own movements will be undone, and you will be cut down by your opponent. This is what *stopping* means.[19]

His advice is elementary: not to detain the mind in any one place. Even if we were to put the mind in a spot just below the navel, a technique apparently suggested by some rival schools of swordsmanship at that time, Takuan argues that the intention to center the mind in this way is in itself detaining the mind: "If you consider putting your mind below your navel and not letting it wander, your mind will be taken by the mind that thinks of this plan."[20] In other words, *deliberately* putting the mind *anywhere* is still *deliberate,* and results in *one-sidedness.* Thus, even the desire to free the mind, to undetain the mind, is itself a form of detaining.

For Takuan, the swordsman must not put the mind anywhere. Doing so will fix the mind, like a "tied-up cat."[21] Instead, he needs to relax the intent to fix the mind, and this, in effect, frees the body to respond:

> When a person does not think, "Where shall I put it?" the mind will extend throughout the entire body and move about to any place at all.[22]

Obviously, in the context of swordsmanship, achieving this freedom demands the utmost in mental training. For freedom only comes with discipline, in the same way that the pianist's freedom to execute a Bach fugue requires his training in technique. This is also similar to a *karateka* (student of karate) performing a *kata* (series of karate forms) effortlessly only after she has perfected the discipline: "The effort not to stop the mind in just one place—this is discipline."[23] As to this undetained, free mind, he tells us that "Put nowhere, it will be everywhere."[24]

Just before he died, Takuan instructed his students not to allow their minds to be detained even by his own death:

> Bury my body in the mountain behind the temple, cover it with dirt and go home. Read no sutras, hold no ceremony. Receive no gifts from either monk or laity. Let the monks wear their robes, eat their meals, and carry on as on normal days.[25]

Attentiveness from an uncluttered mind. In order for us to grasp the ethical relevance in this, let us first note that an undetained mind is an uncluttered mind, a necessary condition that enables us to be both fully attentive and free to act. This is especially so in situations of conflict, and even of potential conflict. Once, while the swordsman Munenori was peacefully admiring the cherry blossoms in his garden accompanied by his attendant (who was carrying his master's sword), he felt a sudden tinge of danger. But he looked around and saw no one other than his attendant. He was troubled over this, for he had learned to trust his senses. He later told his attendant:

> If I was the victim of an hallucination I cannot forgive myself. It is inexcusable. . . . I consider it to be the embodiment of swordsmanship to perceive the signs which occur before an opponent's actual movements.

At this the attendant confessed to his lord that while Munenori was admiring the cherry blossoms, a fleeting thought came to him:

> [I]f I were to strike at the lord with a sword from behind while he was lost in admiration of the cherry blossoms, even the lord, so renowned as an incomparable swordsman, might not be able to parry the attack.[26]

It was only due to Munenori's uncluttered mind that he was attentive enough to sense such covert danger. His admiration of the cherry blossoms did not disable his mind; he was not detained by them. He had complete presence of mind, fully attentive to his immediate surroundings, even to his attendant's fleeting thought.

Pure heart from an uncluttered mind. Furthermore, an undetained mind is a prerequisite for what is called a "pure heart." A pure heart encompasses a number of valued traits: freedom from considerations of self-interest, freedom from the tyranny of abstraction, and freedom from attachment to the consequences of our actions. Pure-heartedness often displays itself as an immediate response to a given situation, such as the response of the older monk who carried the woman across the mud.

For the warrior, his sword symbolizes his pure heart, made manifest through his honor, courage, and spirit of selflessness.

There is the story of Lord Akechi, whose castle was being attacked by General Hori Hidemasa. Sensing his imminent defeat, Lord Akechi sent Hori this message:

Japanese sword. (© Christies Images/PNI)

"My castle is burning, and soon I shall die. I have many excellent swords which I have treasured all my life, and am loath to have destroyed with me. . . . I will die happy, if you will stop your attack for a short while, so that I can have the swords sent out and presented to you." General Hori agreed, and fighting ceased while the swords were lowered out of the smoldering castle, wrapped in a mattress. Then it resumed, and the next day the castle fell and Lord Akechi died—presumably happy.[27]

Suzuki Shōsan: To Live Is to Die

In Akira Kurasawa's classic film *Ikiru* (*To Live*), Watanabe is a small-time bureaucrat who learns he has stomach cancer. He then undergoes bouts of depression, denial, and self-absorption. It is only when he confronts his impending death head-on that he experiences a catharsis. He comes face-to-face with death, accepts it, and then is free. Released from self-regard, he then commits himself totally to the task of building a park for children. Despite bureaucratic entanglements, he pursues this task relentlessly, but he dies before the park is built. Nevertheless, he triumphs because he faces death with equanimity, and throws himself totally into his commitment.

Here lies the integral message of the warrior turned Zen monk, Suzuki Shōsan: Only if we awaken ourselves to our own deaths can we truly begin to live. To die is to live.

Suzuki Shōsan (1579–1655), like Takuan, was born into a warrior family. Unlike Takuan, however, he took up the sword and was active as a samurai under the service of Tokugawa Ieyasu (1541–1616). He subsequently became a Zen monk at the age of forty-one, and he openly criticized monastic abuses. He severely reproached monks for escaping their worldly responsibilities and abdicating the supreme Buddhist virtue of compassion for all sentient beings. For him, the spirit of Zen applied to all four classes—warrior, farmers, artisans, and merchants. Therefore, he believed that the teachings of Buddhism cannot be divorced from everyday activities: "The World *Dharma* is the Buddha Dharma."[28]

Shosan's most intriguing idea, however, concerns our attitude toward death. He persistently instructs us to awaken to our deaths:

Put everything aside and only study death. Always study death, free yourself from it, and when death comes, you won't be flustered.[29]

Keeping death constantly before us frees us from clinging to life. It also frees us from clinging to the illusion of a separate self. On account of this, we can now live more fully and respond to the moment completely. To be sure, this must have inspired in the warrior the courage to throw himself completely into a life-and-death encounter. Furthermore, for Shosan, awakening to death releases a vital energy, *ki,* an immaterial force that pervades our being. And this enables us to live totally in the moment. So he advises all of us to "Make the character *death* the master in your heart, observing it and letting go of everything else."[30]

Indeed, in taking this "death awareness" to new heights, Shosan echoes an ongoing theme in both Zen and the warrior creed. Dogen, for instance, who was first impressed by life's impermanence when he viewed the smoke rising and vanishing from sticks of incense during his mother's funeral, held that each moment is the intersection of past, present, and future.[31] Each moment, therefore, contains in itself life and death.The classic manifesto of Bushido, or the Way of the Warrior, *Hagakure* (c. 1716), instructs us that "Bushido consists in dying—that is my conclusion." By having death always before him, and by being ready to die at any moment, the warrior is absolutely free to be fully attentive to the moment.

Detachment and courage. What moral message does this awakening to death send to us? First of all, it awakens us to the fact that impermanence fills every fiber of our existence, so that each moment undergoes birth and death. As Dogen cries out, "It is a mistake to assume that one moves *from* birth *to* death"[32] [italics mine]. Life and death constitute one inseparable flowing stream. Having realized this, we release ourselves from any need to control and possess, to seek permanence where there is none. Released from clinging to life, we are now genuinely detached.

This kind of detachment better enables us to cultivate the virtue of courage. We can now approach death with acceptance and resolve. Resolve means facing the predicament or conflict head-on and with determination. For instance, warriors (*bushi*) often signaled their resolve by girding their heads with a headband, or *hachimaki,* before putting on their helmet.[33] Resolve, or courage, does not require the absence of fear. It requires the overcoming of fear rather than being overcome by fear. Courage therefore means that one is not attached to the fear.

For instance, according to some Japanese perspectives, a test of courage is the composure one displays in the face of death, a mental attitude in Zen that is called *shugyo.* It has been historically demonstrated through acts of suicide, such as *seppuku,* a highly ritualized form of disembowelment.[34] Actually, it was not uncommon to perform *seppuku* in or near a Buddhist temple or garden.

All this brings us to one of the most penetrating insights in Zen. Our ultimate goal is not to conquer death. Death is not the enemy. Neither should we aim to abandon or escape from life, as if life is the enemy. Indeed, we can *free* ourselves from this stream of birth and death only by living WITHIN the stream of birth and death. In other words, we must avoid two extremes. We should neither *reject* this life-death stream nor *attach* ourselves to it. Otherwise, we still remain enslaved to the stream. We need to be totally free of attachment to this stream, including attachment to the desire to be free. This means accepting the stream for what it is. To illustrate, the Japanese observance of the anniversary of the day of someone's death, *meinichi,* contains two characters: one for "life," 命, and the other for "day," 日 . *Meinichi,* 命 日, therefore literally means "life day." Not only is it an occasion for the living to join together in commemorating the dead, it is also an opportunity to acknowledge that each moment gives witness to the interplay between life and death.[35]

Selflessness and compassion. Awakening to death further entails a dying to my self, a dying to my sense of a separate "I", so that I can no longer make my own individual, private interests the center of my morality. Indeed, the virtues that are uppermost are those that are other-directed, virtues that stress duty, loyalty, faith, and compassion.

This dying to my self is a self-emptying. In Zen Buddhism, it is the ground for genuine compassion. As stated by a contemporary Zen Buddhist:

> Most fundamentally, it [Zen practice] shatters the premise of separateness that has guided our behavior since infancy. And with this, mysteriously, a revolution of the heart begins, turning the Zen student from self-concern toward concern for the welfare of others, from concern for the small self toward concern for the Self in which there are no "others."[36]

As we see, this self-emptying forms the basis for compassion in the most authentic sense. Again, we turn to Thich Nhat Hanh who eloquently expresses the components of such compassion when he addresses the need for awareness in the fullest sense. He describes this compassionate awareness in his "Five Mindfulness Trainings."

Thich Nhat Hanh

THE FIVE MINDFULNESS TRAININGS

1. Aware of the suffering caused by the destruction of life, I am committed to cultivating compassion and learning ways to protect the lives of people, animals, plants, and minerals. I am determined not to kill, not to let others kill, and not to condone any act of killing in the world, in my thinking, and in my way of life.

2. Aware of the suffering caused by exploitation, social injustice, stealing, and oppression, I am committed to cultivating loving kindness and learning ways to work for the well-being of people, animals, plants, and minerals. I will practice generosity by sharing my time, energy, and material resources with those who are in real need. I am determined not to steal and not to possess anything that should belong to others. I will respect the property of others, but I will prevent others from profiting from human suffering or the suffering of other species on Earth.

3. *Aware of the suffering caused by sexual misconduct,* I am committed to cultivating responsibility and learning ways to protect the safety and integrity of individuals, couples, families, and society. I am determined not to engage in sexual relations without love and a long-term commitment. To preserve the happiness of myself and others, I am determined to respect my commitments and the commitments of others. I will do everything in my power to protect children from sexual abuse and to prevent couples and families from being broken by sexual misconduct.

4. *Aware of the suffering caused by unmindful speech and the inability to listen to others,* I am committed to cultivating loving speech and deep listening in order to bring joy and happiness to others and relieve others of their suffering. Knowing that words can create happiness or suffering, I am determined to speak truthfully, with words that inspire self-confidence, joy, and hope. I will not spread news that I do not know to be certain and will not criticize or condemn things of which I am not sure. I will refrain from uttering words that can cause division or discord, or that can cause the family or the community to break. I am determined to make all efforts to reconcile and resolve all conflicts, however small.

5. *Aware of the suffering caused by unmindful consumption,* I am committed to cultivating good health, both physical and mental, for myself, my family, and my society by practicing mindful eating, drinking, and consuming. I will ingest only items that preserve peace, well-being, and joy in my body, in my consciousness, and in the collective body and consciousness of my family and society. I am determined not to use alcohol or any other intoxicant or to ingest foods or other items that contain toxins, such as certain TV programs, magazines, books, films, and conversations. I am aware that to damage my body or my consciousness with these poisons is to betray my ancestors, my parents, my society, and future generations. I will work to transform violence, fear, anger, and confusion in myself and in society by practicing a diet for myself and for society. I understand that a proper diet is crucial for self-transformation and for the transformation of society.

Reprinted from *Teachings on Love* (1997) by Thich Nhat Hanh with permission of Parallax Press, Berkeley, California.

Through all of this, the supreme Buddhist virtue remains compassion because it is the purest expression of my dying to my self. Furthermore, it is the natural outcome of the Buddhist teaching concerning our fundamental interconnectedness with all sentient beings, and it underscores a fundamental Zen Buddhist notion: There is in reality no self opposed to some other; the "other" is not truly other.

Martin Buber, *I and Thou*

The relation to the *Thou* is direct. No systems of ideas, no foreknowledge, and no fancy intervene between *I* and *Thou*. The memory itself is transformed, as it plunges out of its isolation into the unity of the whole. No aim, no lust and no anticipation intervene between *I* and *Thou*. . . . Every means is an obstacle. Only when every means has collapsed does the meeting come about.

From Martin Buber, *I and Thou* (New York: Charles Scribner's Sons, 1958), pp. 11–12.

Miyamoto Musashi: An Island of Calm in the Storm

A master swordsman, who was also a practitioner of Zen, was about to retire from swordsmanship. Desiring to hand down his authority to the most deserving of his three sons, he put them to a test to see which one had learned the true art of the sword. He called each son at different times into his tent. Before doing so, he hid a soft pillow at the top of the entrance in such a way that upon opening the flap, the pillow would fall.

When the youngest son entered, the pillow fell. And just before it reached the ground, the youngest son had drawn out his sword and sliced it into pieces. Later, the father called in the second son. Again, another pillow fell, but this time the second son was able to slice it in half before it even reached his shoulders. Finally, the eldest son entered. Upon opening the tent flap a pillow dropped, and this eldest son caught it in his arms. He then gently placed the pillow back in its spot above the entrance. Which of the three sons had learned the true art of the sword?

We know very little of Miyamoto Musashi's life (1584–1645), other than what he recorded in his masterpiece, *The Book of Five Rings* (*Gorin no Sho*). We know that he was a masterless samurai, or *ronin,* devoted to the martial arts, and that he killed his first opponent when he was thirteen and his last when he was twenty-nine. During those sixteen years, he was unparalleled in the skill of swordsmanship, never having suffered a defeat. We also know that as he grew older, he realized that his victories had less to do with technical skill than with a state of mind. And, for the remainder of his life, he wholeheartedly devoted himself to instruct others in the art of the sword. His own school attracted students from all over Japan and was called the Individual School of Two Skies, or the School of Two Swords, because he perfected the unusual technique of fighting with two swords rather than one. We also know that, unlike Takuan and Shosan, he himself was not a Zen monk. Nevertheless, he was greatly influenced by the teachings of Zen Buddhism. Bear in mind that many samurai, or *bushi* (a more accurate term for warrior), often sought the guidance of Zen Buddhist monks in order to gain insight into the mental and spiritual discipline necessary to their occupation.[37]

Musashi is without a doubt the most celebrated of all Japanese warriors. His *Book of Five Rings* is an excellent treatise on proper physical techniques as well as on fighting strategy. Yet its real merit lies in its guidance on acquiring the proper mental disposition needed, not only for swordsmanship, but for all situations of conflict and confrontation in our lives. Throughout his work, Musashi emphasizes the need to maintain an inner calm and equilibrium in the midst of conflict.

In conflict situations, one's state of mind is quintessential. Inner calm and balance are crucial, for they transcend bodily technique and spell the difference between life and death. The mind cannot allow itself to be "dragged by the body" nor ruffled by circumstances. In his chapter called "Water Scroll," Musashi states:

> In the science of martial arts, the state of mind should remain the same as normal. In ordinary circumstances as well as when practicing martial arts, let there be no change at all—with the mind open and direct, neither tense nor lax, centering the mind so that there is no imbalance, calmly relax your mind, and savor this moment of ease thoroughly so that the relaxation does not stop its relaxation for even an instant.[38]

Notice here that a "relaxed" mind is not "lax." It avoids the extremes of agitation and indifference, each of which would result in carelessness.

The secret behind facing conflict of any kind lies in maintaining an unmoved mind. In the intensity of the struggle, we tend to be all the more excited. Yet if we can maintain our mental equilibrium, we will not be determined or overcome by the situation. Musashi describes this state of mind further:

> Let there be neither insufficiency nor excess in your mind. Even if superficially weakened, be inwardly stronghearted, and do not let others see into your mind. It is essential for those who are physically small to know what it is like to be large, and for those who are physically large to know what it is like to be small; whether you are physically large or small, *it is essential to keep your mind free from subjective biases.*[39] [italics mine]

In order to have a calm mind, we must not allow ourselves to become fixed on any one perspective or view. In a situation of conflict, or in the heat of argument and dissension, it is all the more imperative to sustain an impartial, nonbiased perspective. Otherwise, our subjectivity clouds our good judgment. Thus an uncluttered mind is an open mind. And genuine moral resolution through dialogue can occur only with an open mind, a state of being "unmoved in mind even in the heat of battle."[40]

Musashi's fellow swordsman, Yagyu Munenori, uses the metaphor of the "moon in the water" to describe this unmoved, relaxed mind. Our minds should be as the moon reflected in water, unmoved by the water's circumstances. Munenori instructs us in his *Book of Family Traditions on the Art of War:*

> People who have successfully managed to pacify their minds . . . are unstained even as they mingle with the dust in the world. Even if they are active all day, they are unmoved, just as the moon reflected in the water does not move even though thousands and tens of thousands of waves roll one after another. This is the state of people who have consummated Buddhism; I have recorded it here under the instruction of a teacher of that doctrine.[41]

A relaxed mind is uncluttered, undetained. It is completely present to the moment. The oldest son learned the secret of the sword: when NOT to use the sword. (This is the sword of no-sword.) He did not allow his mind to be "attacked" by the pillow. In being totally present to the situation, he immediately realizes that there is no need to draw his sword. Moreover, the eldest son appeared the most selfless in his actions. He had no need or desire to display his skills. The warrior's manual is entitled *Hagakure,* which literally means "hidden under the leaves," so that it describes being unpretentious and humble. The true warrior does not show off his skills because such a display of self-regard contradicts the spirit of the sword, as well as the spirit of Zen.

A WAY OF TEA: THE VIRTUE OF PRESENCE

In a beautifully moving scene near the end of *Thousand Cranes,* Fumiko visits Kikuji, and they behold a pair of tea bowls. One (a Shino bowl) had belonged to Fumiko's mother and the other (a Karatsu, of Korean origin) to Kikuji's father. These two people had been lovers.

Yasunari Kawabata

THOUSAND CRANES

They put the Shino and the Karatsu side by side. Their eyes met, and fell to the bowls.

"A man's and a woman's." Kikuji spoke in some confusion. "When you see them side by side."

Fumiko nodded, as if unable to speak.

> To Kikuji too the words had an odd ring.
>
> The Karatsu was undecorated, greenish with a touch of saffron and a touch too of carmine. It swelled powerfully toward the base.
>
> "A favorite your father took with him on trips. It's very much like your father."
>
> Fumiko seemed not to sense the danger in the remark.
>
> Kikuji could not bring himself to say that the Shino bowl was like her mother. But the two bowls before them were like the souls of his father and her mother.
>
> The tea bowls, three or four hundred years old, were sound and healthy, and they called up no morbid thoughts. Life seemed to stretch taut over them, however, in a way that was almost sensual.
>
> Seeing his father and Fumiko's mother in the bowls, Kikuji felt that they had raised two beautiful ghosts and placed them side by side.
>
> The tea bowls were here, present, and the present reality of Kikuji and Fumiko, facing across the bowls, seemed immaculate too.

They intensely gaze at the tea bowls and share a presence that intersects past, present, and future. As for the tea bowls, "Life seemed to stretch taut over them, however, in a way that was almost sensual." The bowls awaken the two to their parents' presence, and "The tea bowls were here, present, and the present reality of Kikuji and Fumiko, facing across the bowls, seemed immaculate too."

This "virtue" of presence, so wonderfully depicted by Kawabata, is a fundamental Zen attribute evoked in the art of tea, or *chanoyu*.[42] This presence is an awakening to the full reality of the moment. It is an awareness in the most complete sense: awareness of how diverse histories are actually linked together; awareness of my own connection to the tea and to those who have gone before me and to those yet to come. Presence therefore means BEING-THERE in the fullest sense.

Mono No Aware: A Sad Beauty

The cherry blossom, or *sakura,* blooms for less than one week out of the year. Just after reaching its peak of color and life, it dies, its delicate blossoms scattering in the breeze. And therein lies its beauty—in its transience. For the Japanese, the *sakura* reveals the solemn truth of life's impermanence. It also embodies a profound equation: Life's transience is its beauty.

All this evokes a deep-seated nostalgia, which the Japanese call *mono no aware,* meaning the "sadness of things," wherein life bears its own "sad beauty." Even though *mono no aware* predates Zen teachings in Japan, it still continues to find its expression in Zen and captures a Zen-like mood. Furthermore, this mood sets the background for the tea ceremony.

Plato, *Symposium*

And if, my dear Socrates, Diotima went on, man's life is ever worth the living, it is when he has attained this vision of the very soul of beauty. And once you have seen it, you will never be seduced again by the charm of gold, of dress. . . .

And remember, she said, that it is only when he discerns beauty itself through what makes it visible that a man will be quickened with the true, and not the seeming virtue—for it is virtue's self that quickens him, not virtue's semblance.

From Plato, *Symposium,* in Edith Hamilton and Huntington Cairns, *The Collected Dialogues of Plato* (Princeton, N.J.: Princeton University Press, Bollingen Series LXXI, 1961), sec. 221d, 212a, p. 563.

The truth of life's transience is a candid axiom in Zen. In the past, Japanese children often learned the phonetic syllables in their alphabet by memorizing a poem derived from the Nirvana Sutra:

Brightly coloured though the blossoms be,
All are doomed to scatter.
So, in this world of ours,
Who will last forever?
Today, having crossed the mountain recesses of Samskrita,
I shall be free of fleeting dreams,
Nor shall I be fuddled [by the pleasures of this world].[43]

Mono no aware fills the pages of Murasaki Shikibu's epic, *The Tale of Genji,* considered to be the world's first psychological novel.[44] Its characters grow weary of life's impermanence as they endure the passing of the seasons while suffering through the deaths of family and friends. No wonder they view their lives as unreal and dreamlike, and Lady Akashi asserts that "A night of endless dreams is my life."[45] And when Ukifune later becomes a nun, the priest encourages her:

For you . . . there remains only one thing—to pursue your devotions. Whether we are young or old, this is a world in which we can depend on nothing. You are quite right to regard it as an empty, fleeting place.[46]

We certainly see a strong Buddhist cast in the final book, "The Floating Bridge of Dreams." In this work, a bridge appears that links us from this life to the next, but it is actually a mirage. This bridge represents our existence, and so our world is a "floating world" and a "sad world" (*ukiyo*).[47]

Collective Karma

Mono no aware also ties in with the Buddhist teaching of karma, the moral law of cause and effect. By the tenth century, Japanese literature made frequent reference to karma in terms of "destiny" (*sukuse*). The historian George Sansom contends that "there can be no doubt that the adoption of this one idea [karma], which is entirely foreign and has no indigenous counterpart, brought about a truly revolutionary change in the moral outlook of the Japanese people."[48]

Karma, or destiny, is a further motif in *The Tale of Genji* as portrayed in the lives of the aristocrats during the Heian period. For example, the moral effect, or negative karma, of young Genji's transgressions may be the anguish he later undergoes upon discovering his wife's infidelity. Also, Ukifune's fate, particularly after she attempted suicide, is defined by her residue of karma. In much of Japanese literature, we see this pervading sense of near resignation to the "floating world" and to the power of karma. Thus both karma and transience fuse to evoke the mood of *mono no aware,* a sad awareness of things, a mood that finds eloquent expression in the tea ceremony.

The Zen Buddhist emphasis upon interdependence, or "interbeing," as Thich Nhat Hanh puts it, also compels us to view karma beyond simply the scope of individual actions. As we saw earlier, Kikuji and Fumiko share in a type of collective destiny, or collective karma. Our interconnectedness with all else makes us all the more aware of our sense of collective responsibility for all that happens, even though we as individuals may not be directly related to the events. The Zen scholar Christopher Ives puts it this way:

> All people affect the world and must take responsibility for it, but they exert different degrees of influence on different situations. For example, a white supremacist, a black coal miner, a New York gold trader, a baker in Melbourne and a boxer in Tokyo are all connected with the system of Apartheid, although in different ways and to markedly different degrees. . . .
> Cultivated in Zen practice, the discernment of the effects of actions heightens awareness of imbeddedness in the world and enhances one's sense of "responsibility" (in the causal and ethical senses, depending on the situation), but this does not exhaust the scope of the term. Zen can begin to formulate a social ethic by clarifying how the realisation of relationality and the consequent openness does, or may, lead to a greater "response ability," in that one can now begin to act responsibly and responsively.[49]

This notion of interconnectedness and collective responsibility is poignantly expressed in a poem written by Thich Nhat Hanh. He composed these verses in 1978 during his struggle to safeguard the "boat people," who were refugees fleeing Vietnam after the Vietnam War in dilapidated boats on the South China Sea:

Do not say that I'll depart tomorrow—
even today I still arrive.

Look deeply: every second I am arriving
to be a bud on a Spring branch,
to be a tiny bird in my new nest,
to be a caterpillar in the heart of a flower,
to be a jewel hiding itself in a stone.

I still arrive, in order to laugh and to cry,
to fear and to hope.
The rhythm of my heart is the birth and death of all that is alive.

I am a mayfly metamorphosing
on the surface of the river.
And I am the bird
that swoops down to swallow the mayfly.

I am a frog swimming happily
in the clear water of a pond.
And I am the grass-snake
that silently feeds on the frog.

I am the child in Uganda, all skin and bones,
my legs as thin as bamboo sticks.
And I am the arms merchant,
selling deadly weapons to Uganda.

I am the twelve-year-old girl,
refugee on a small boat,
who throws herself into the ocean
after being raped by a sea pirate.
And I am the pirate,
my heart not yet capable
of seeing and loving.

I am a member of the politburo,
with plenty of power in my hands.
And I am the man who has to pay
his "debt of blood" to my people
dying slowly in a forced-labor camp.

My joy is like Spring, so warm
it makes flowers bloom all over the Earth.
My pain is like a river of tears,
so vast it fills the four oceans.

Please call me by my true names,
so I can hear all my cries and laughter at once,
so I can see that my joy and pain are one.

Please call me by my true names,
So I can wake up
and the door of my heart
could be left open,
the door of compassion.[50]

Chanoyu: Tasting Beauty in the Ordinary

Two Zen-men were discussing Zen. One, named Chōkei [Ch'ang-ch'ing Hui'ling, 853–932], said "Even a fully enlightened arhat may be proclaimed to be still harboring something of the three poisonous passions [greed, anger, folly], but as to the Buddha, he never makes an equivocal statement. Whatever he asserts is absolute truth. What do you say to this?"

Hofuku [Pao-fu Ts'ung-chan, d. 928] asked, "What then is the Buddha's statement?"

Chōkei said, "The deaf cannot hear it."

This was criticized by Hofuku: "You are coming down onto a secondary level."

"What then is the Buddha's statement according to your judgement?"

"Have a cup of tea, O my brother-monk."[51]

The tea ceremony is an absorbing articulation of Zen. Originally practiced among Chinese monks who often sipped their tea before the image of Bodhidharma, it achieved its artistic peak under Japanese Zen monks. This was due to the efforts of Eisai (Zenkō Kokushi, 1141–1215), founder of the Rinzai Zen school; Murata Shukō (1422–1502), a student of the Zen master Ikkyū and regarded as the real founder of the tea ceremony; and Sen no Rikyu (1521–1591), undeniably the greatest tea master. Tea and Zen went hand-in-hand, as students learned that "the flavor of tea and the flavor of Zen are the same."[52]

How does tea relate to Zen? To begin with, consider the tea room (*sukiya*). The Zen scholar Daisetz Suzuki gives us a clear sketch.

Daisetz Teitaro Suzuki

ZEN AND JAPANESE CULTURE

The tearoom is symbolic of certain aspects of Eastern culture, especially of Japanese culture. In it we find in a most strongly and deeply concentrated form almost all the elements that go to make up what is characteristic of the Japanese mind statically viewed. As to its dynamic aspects, there are only a few signs betokening them in the tearoom, where even movements are so controlled as to add to the quietude generally prevailing here.

The room is small and the ceiling not at all high even for the stature of an average Japanese. It is devoid of decorations, except in the alcove (*tokonoma*),* where a *kakemono*† is hung and before which stands a flower vase containing perhaps a solitary flower not yet in full bloom. As I look around, in spite of its obvious simplicity the room betrays every mark of thoughtful designing: the windows are irregularly inserted; the ceiling is not of one pattern; the materials used, simple and unornamented, are of various kinds; the room is divided by a post obliquely setting off one corner for tea utensils; the floor has a small square opening as fireplace where hot water is boiling in an artistically-shaped iron kettle.

The papered *shōji* covering the windows admit only soft light, shutting off all the direct sunshine, which, when it is too strong for the teamen's sensibility, is further screened by a rustic *sudare* hanging just outside one of the windows. As I sit here quietly before the fireplace, I become conscious of the burning of incense. The odor is singularly nerve-soothing; the fragrant flower produces a contrary effect on the senses. The incense wood, I am told, comes from tropical countries, and is taken from old trees lying buried for a long time in water.

Thus composed in mind, I hear a soft breeze passing through the needle-leaves of the pine tree; the sound mingles with the trickling of water from a bamboo pipe into the stone basin. The flow and the breeze are rhythmical and soothing to the mind of the sitter inside the hut. In fact, they stimulate his meditative mood to move on to the bedrock of his being.

Tokonoma is a sort of alcove occupying a corner of the room where a *kakemono* is hung. The principal guest sits before this honored corner.
†A *kakemono* is a hanging scroll of either painting or calligraphy, which decorates the corner.

From D.T. Suzuki, *Zen and Japanese Culture.* Copyright © 1959 by Princeton University Press. Reprinted by permission of Princeton University Press.

Here, we detect the following Zen qualities: detachment, nondiscrimination, purifying the senses, uncluttering the mind, solitariness, and communion. In addition, *chanoyu* evokes a unique Zen-like aesthetic, namely the recognition of beauty in that which is ordinary, mundane, simple, incomplete, and asymmetrical. Each of these Zen qualities possess a definite "moral geometry" that sketches our relationship to all other things within the compass of being.[53]

Some examples illuminate these Zen attributes. The tea house itself is a small, modest cottage or hut. It reflects the purity and loneliness of simplicity. It depicts what Kakuzo Okakura, in his classic *The Book of Tea,* calls a "refined poverty."[54] The path that leads to the tea house as well as the tea garden (*roji*) marks our break from the outside world, and just before we enter the tea room we lay aside any weapons and baggage. In other words, we leave our conflicts, worries, concerns, and worldly affairs outside so that we can enjoy tea with a fresh, uncluttered mind. Thus, entering the tea room is similar to entering the warrior's dojo (training hall) or the monk's Zendo (meditation hall). For the tea room is a sanctuary, an abode of peace.

The spartanlike barrenness of the tea room represents our uncluttered mind. The room's only tenants are a solitary scroll (*kakemono*), which graces the alcove (*tokonoma*), perhaps a solitary flower not yet fully blossomed, a crude-looking kettle being heated by a fire in a small hole in the floor, and some unpretentious tea utensils. Actually modeled after a Zen chapel, the tea room embodies the elimination of the superfluous, inspiring the mind to attain a similar uncluttered state.[55]

And if our mind is uncluttered, we can be more fully attentive to *chanoyu*. We can purify our senses, as the warrior's text, *Hagakure,* describes in the following passage:

> A teamaster says: "The spirit of *cha-no-yu* is to cleanse the six senses from cont-amination. By seeing the *kakemono* in the *tokonoma* (alcove) and the flower in the vase, one's sense of smell is cleansed; by listening to the boiling of water in the iron kettle and to the dripping of water from the bamboo pipe, one's ears are cleansed; by tasting tea one's mouth is cleansed; and by handling the tea uten-sils one's sense of touch is cleansed. When thus all the sense organs are cleansed, the mind itself is cleansed of defilements. The art of tea is after all a spiritual disci-pline, and my aspiration for every hour of the day is not to depart from the spirit of the tea, which is by no means a matter of mere entertainment."[56]

Even warriors had time for tea. It offered a retreat from their turbulent world, an occasion to regain their energy through solitariness and quiet within the seclusion of the tea hut. In fact, tea is *the* drink of solitariness. The Zen poet Secchō describes the tea master:

> Standing by himself between heaven and earth,
> Facing infinitude of beings.[57]

Yet the solitariness of *chanoyu* is experienced in solidarity with others. *Chanoyu* involves those who embark upon the solitary venture of tea in communion with others. Despite any differences among the guests, they share a common bond in their tea. The ritual itself—bowing to the host and to others, serving the tea, the quiet conversation and the even quieter intervals—reveals this human intercourse. In this way, in his story Kawabata brilliantly unifies his diverse characters in the shared world of tea.

This common bond is conveyed in the way the tea room is constructed. Its entrance, not more than four feet high, is surely conducive to nondiscrim-ination. Whatever station the guest occupies, each is equal to the other, as his bending low to enter signifies humility. And this mirrors the Zen teaching of the Buddha-nature, which all sentient beings share.

Furthermore, virtually every aspect of the ceremony manifests an aesthetic that discovers beauty in things that are ordinary. It opposes ostentation and glitter and instead revels in that which is plain without slipping into banality. There is nothing ornate about the utensils. Their beauty lies in their ordinariness. Finding beauty in the ordinary is a vital feature in Zen and again reminds us of the fundamental equality of all things so that the ordinary is equal to the spiritual.

Even more important, the beauty and value of the tea utensils lie in their link to the past—their age, history, and previous owners, as we clearly see in *Thousand Cranes*. That is, they embody the character of their owners and blend together past and present. *Chanoyu* thereby signifies a reverence for tradition and for ancestry, an honest respect for heritage.

Beauty also consists in the incomplete, irregular, or asymmetrical. Like Zen, *chanoyu's* aesthetics militate against uniformity and order and view them as unnatural. Uniformity constitutes monotony and explains why tea cups of like color should be avoided. Okakura instructs us:

> If you have a living flower, a painting of flowers is not allowable. If you are using a round kettle, the water pitcher should be angular.[58]

By the same token, we cannot help but notice the irregularity and asymmetry of the stepping stones in the tea garden. In other words, the *possibility for completion* is more enticing than the finished product. Beauty lies in the process, not in any end, and this indeed reflects a singular quality in Zen teaching.

Tea Virtues

These Zen features together construct a moral geometry that places a supreme value on cultivating a proper inner disposition in *chanoyu*. Without a doubt, the most important ingredient in the tea ceremony is a harmonious temperament and good character:

> Once there was a master of wabi tea. All kinds of people, from noblemen to commoners, visited him. It was not that they all went to see his skilled preparation of tea, nor was it because they wanted to hear him speak, for he was well-informed of matters concerning chanoyu. People visited him not because he possessed famous calligraphy and tea containers that they wanted to see. Nor was it for an outing in a scenic place or because he served particularly high quality tea. *People went because they were impressed by the fact that his heart was honorable and wholly committed to the modesty and quietness of wabi. His dwelling was seasoned, and his aim was quiet simplicity.*[59] [italics mine]

Tranquillity. With honorable heart, the tea master was "committed to the modesty and quietness of wabi." What does *wabi* mean? *Wabi* is the core disposition in *chanoyu* and encompasses the following traits: inner harmony, gentleness, reverence, purity in heart, and simplicity. These can all be summed up in one word—*tranquillity*. Tranquillity reaches into the heart of tea and is the key to understanding *wabi* and its relation to Zen. In addition, tranquillity is actually a type of poverty.

A Chinese monk once said:
"In learning the Way of Zen one should first study poverty. Only after studying poverty and being poor will one become familiar with the Way."[60]

Poverty is indispensable in Zen. It does not simply mean material deprivation. Poverty also refers to a state of mind that is reduced to the bare essentials, simple, uncluttered, and detached. Poverty entails renouncing worldly things like fame, status, and affluence. Poverty is therefore detachment and in a genuinely moral sense is a vital condition for good character. The Chinese Zen poet Yung-chia Hsüan-chüeh writes:

I am a destitute follower of Buddha.
Although I may be called poor,
this is merely a material poverty.
I am not poor in the Way,
Because I am poor I dress in rags.
But in finding the Way
I bear a priceless jewel in my heart.[61]

Wabi is the gracious acceptance of this poverty. As the treatise on tea, *Zencharoku,* tells us:

Wabi is to lack material good, not to be able to satisfy one's desires, and to live in obscurity. Wabi is not to feel any need even if one is impoverished, not to feel want while lacking, and not to feel depression in manifold hardship. If a man suffers from poverty, grieves over scarcity, and complains of failure, he is truly poor and this is not wabi.[62]

Wabi is thus tranquillity within the context of poverty and simplicity. The celebrated tea master Shukō gives us a poignant illustration of this tranquillity. When asked about the real spirit of tea, he told the story of the Chinese poet who wrote the following verse:

In the woods over there deeply buried in snow,
Last night a few branches of the plum tree burst out in bloom.

The poet then shared the verse with his friend, who recommended that he modify the verse by changing "few branches" to "one branch." Thus *"one branch of the plum tree burst out in bloom"* in the woods *"deeply buried in snow."*[63] What a marvelous expression of tranquillity, "an inexpressible quiet joy deeply hidden beneath sheer poverty."[64]

Now this tranquillity calls for some crucial and morally relevant attitudes: sincerity (or pure heart), gentleness in demeanor, and respect and reverence for simplicity. Sōtan, the grandson of the great teamaster Rikyū, illustrates the moral significance of *wabi,* or tranquillity, in *chanoyu* by contrasting it with the ostentatious tea rooms constructed by those who are evidently wrapped up in their own self-worth:

> It is a great mistake, indeed, to make an ostentatious show of *wabi* while inwardly nothing is consonant with it. Such people construct a tearoom as far as appearances go with all that is needed for *wabi*; much gold and silver is wasted on the work; rare objects of art are purchased with the money realized by the sale of their farms—and this just to make a display before visitors. They think a life of *wabi* is here. But far from it. *Wabi* means insufficiency of things, inability to fulfill every desire one may cherish, generally a life of poverty and dejection.... But he does not brood over the situation. He has learned to be self-sufficient with insufficiency of things. He does not seek beyond his means.... If, however, he should still abide with the idea of the poverty, insufficiency, or general wretchedness of his condition, he would be no more a man of *wabi* but a poverty-stricken person.[65]

Sōtan then proceeds to underscore *wabi*'s full moral weight.

> Those who really know what *wabi* is are free from greed, violence, anger, indolence, uneasiness, and folly. Thus *wabi* corresponds to the Pāramitā of Morality as observed by the Buddhists.[66]

Presence. This all boils down to another related Zen "virtue," that of presence. As stated earlier, the virtue of presence simply means "being-there" in full awareness. After all, presence is a principal aim in Zen practice. For the Zen monk, the goal is to empty the mind in order to be fully attentive. For the warrior, "being-elsewhere" spells instant death. It is absolutely crucial to be totally present while facing an opponent who wields a four-foot "razor-blade" sword. As for *chanoyu,* presence means attentiveness to where one is and what one is doing—it is being-there in the most complete way, without distraction, with an uncluttered mind. As the tea text *Nampōroku* states:

> [O]nce host and guest have entered the roji and thatched hut, they sweep away the dust and rubbish [of worldly concerns] and engage in an encounter with mind open and entire.... *Chanoyu is just a matter of building a fire, boiling water, and drinking tea. There should be nothing else.*[67] [italics mine]

Keep in mind that for the tea ceremony to be pure, the character of the participants must also be pure. Here is where presence can help because "being-there" requires detachment, an uncluttered mind. Total presence also entails the abandonment of self-interest, and in turn this means that envy, greed, anger, and all matters of self-absorption have no place in *chanoyu* just as they have no place in Zen.

Now if this is what presence means—to "be-there," to be fully engaged in our daily business—nothing sounds simpler. Yet Zen argues that, in truth, this is our most difficult, lifelong task. Are we truly present in what we do? Can we be like Rikyū, who looked out over his tea garden and wrote:

> The court is left covered
> With the fallen leaves
> Of the pine tree;
> *No dust is stirred,*
> *And calm is my mind!*[68] [italics mine]

Can we be completely attentive to the present? Being-there in the spirit of tranquillity is an awakening to the beauty of the ordinary. This is an awareness that goes beyond simply seeing with our eyes and hearing with our ears. Can you imagine listening to a cold, mechanical rendition of Rachmaninov's *Rhapsody on a Theme from Paganini?* Just as the pianist must "live" the piece, the tea drinker must "taste" each sip. Thus Daitō Kokushi instructs us:

> If your ears see,
> And eyes hear,
> Not a doubt you'll cherish—
> How naturally the rain drips
> From the eaves![69]

REVIEW QUESTIONS

1. How do Zen teachings encompass an ethical dimension? Is there such a thing as a "Zen ethic"?
2. What is the significance of Dogen's question in the context of moral practice? How does his resolution entail an ethical dimension?
3. Dogen reminds us of the Buddha-nature of all beings. What is the ethical significance of this regarding the scope of our moral concern?
4. One can argue that Dogen, in his own way, puts forth a basis for an ecological awareness. How does an ecological consciousness relate to the idea of dependent origination?
5. According to Zen Buddhism (and to Buddhism in general), does the end justify the means?
6. How do the Fourteen Mindfulness Trainings reflect Zen teachings?
7. What is the ethical value behind having an uncluttered mind?
8. How do Thich Nhat Hanh's Five Mindfulness Trainings represent Zen thought?
9. According to Zen, what is the meaning behind the claim that "to live is to die"? To die to what? How is this morally relevant?

10. How can Zen teachings enable us to live better lives?

NOTES

1. Yasunari Kawabata, *Thousand Cranes,* trans. Edward G. Seidensticker (New York: G.P. Putnam's Sons, Perigee Books, 1959), pp. 19–20. Copyright © 1958 by Alfred A. Knopf, Inc. Reprinted by permission of the publisher.
2. Ibid., p. 108.
3. Ibid., p. 90.
4. Zen underwent a transmission through 28 patriarchs in India and 28 in China and 28 in Rinzai Zen before coming to America.
5. Zenkei Shibayama, *A Flower Does Not Talk,* trans. Sumiko Kudo (Rutland, VT: Charles E. Tuttle, 1970), p. 20.
6. Stated by the Zen master Enkan in *Dentoroku (The Transmission of the Lamp),* in Shibayama, *A Flower Does Not Talk,* p. 22.
7. Heinrich Dumoulin, S.J., *A History of Zen Buddhism,* trans. Paul Peachey (Boston: Beacon Press, 1969), pp. 81–82.
8. Ibid., p. 82.
9. Ibid.
10. The last two are from Zenkei Shibayama, *Zen Comments on the Mumonkan,* trans. Sumiko Kudo (New York: New American Library, Mentor Book, 1974), nos. 4, 36, pp. 50, 259.
11. Kakuzo Okakura uses the phrase "moral geometry" in his *The Book of Tea* to describe what he calls the "philosophy of tea," which is intimately related to Zen. This is not to identify tea with Zen. Zen may not be strictly identifiable with anything in particular, yet *chanoyu* does manage to convey a rich expression of Zen. See Kakuzo Okakura, *The Book of Tea* (New York: Dover, 1964), p. 1.
12. Thomas Cleary, trans., Genjōkoan (The Issue at Hand) in *Shōbōgenzō: Zen Essays by Dogen* (Honolulu: University of Hawaii Press, 1986), p. 35.
13. He did not entirely dismiss the significance of the *koan.* He simply believed that it was not primary. Here he differs from the Rinzai Zen school, which stresses the *koan* as all-important. For that matter, neither did he intend to downplay the serious study of the Buddhist sutras. For Dogen, practicing both *zazen* and the *koan* and studying the sutras are vital ways to cast off body-mind.
14. Cited in Dumoulin, *A History of Zen,* p. 185.
15. See Masao Abe, *A Study of Dogen: His Philosophy and Religion,* ed. by Steven Heine (Albany: SUNY Press, 1992), pp. 150–51.
16. Ibid., p. 31. Abe is a foremost representative of the Kyoto school of philosophy.
17. Ibid.

18. Miyamoto Musashi, *The Book of Five Rings,* trans. Nihon Services Corporation: B.J. Brown, Y. Kashiwagi, W.H. Barrett, and E. Sasagawa (New York: Bantam Books, 1982), pp. xxv–xxvi.
19. Takuan Soho, *The Unfettered Mind: Writings of the Zen Master to the Sword Master,* trans. William Scott Wilson (Tokyo: Kodansha International, 1986), p. 19.
20. Ibid., p. 30.
21. Ibid., p. 32.
22. Ibid., p. 31.
23. Ibid., p. 32.
24. Ibid.
25. Ibid., p. 12.
26. From Makoto Sugawara, *Lives of Master Swordsmen,* cited in Winston L. King, *Zen and the Way of the Sword: Arming the Samurai Psyche* (New York: Oxford University Press, 1993), p. 112.
27. From Noel Perrin, *Giving Up the Gun: Japan's Reversion to the Sword,* cited in King, *Zen and the Way of the Sword,* pp. 92–93.
28. Arthur Braverman, trans. and ed., *Warrior of Zen: The Diamond-hard Wisdom Mind of Suzuki Shosan* (New York: Kodansha America, 1994), p. 16.
29. Ibid.
30. Ibid., p. 61.
31. See Abe, *A Study of Dogen,* p. 111.
32. *Shobogenzo,* p. 122.
33. Certainly not all warriors were devotees of Zen. Nevertheless, it provides an example of resolve. We see a similar practice in World War II, when kamikaze pilots also wore *hachimaki* as they were prepared to meet death.
34. A recent case is the highly publicized *seppuku* of the accomplished writer Yukio Mishima. His suicide occurred after a failed attempt to take over government army headquarters by his right-wing band called the Shield Society. Another historic example is the suicide of the famous tea master Rikyu, which he performed only after he conducted one last tea ceremony for his friends.
35. The popular belief, derived from Buddhism, seems to be that the spirit of the deceased continues to live and will be appeased by such memorials.
36. N. Foster, "To Enter the Marketplace: The Politics of Prajna," in F. Eppsteiner, ed., *The Path of Compassion: Writings on Socially Engaged Buddhism* (Berkeley, CA: Parallax Press, 1988), p. 47.
37. At the same time, not all samurai associated with Zen, let alone lived up to its ideals.
38. Cleary, *Book of Five Rings,* p. 18.
39. Ibid.

40. Ibid.
41. Ibid., pp. 84–85.
42. *Chanoyu* literally means "hot water for tea" and is the usual term to express the tea ceremony. Another term is simply *chado,* or "way of tea."
43. In Ivan Morris, *The World of the Shining Prince: Court Life in Ancient Japan* (Middlesex, England: Peregrine Books, 1985), pp. 122–23.
44. The *Tale of Genji,* like *mono no aware,* predates Zen influence.
45. Cited in Morris, *The World of the Shining Prince,* p. 126.
46. Ibid., p. 131.
47. Ibid., p. 127.
48. George Sansom, *A History of Japan to 1334* (Stanford, CA: Stanford University Press, 1958), p. 220.
49. Christopher Ives, *Zen Awakening and Society* (Honolulu: University of Hawaii Press, 1992), pp. 119–20.
50. Thich Nhat Hanh, from "Call Me By My True Names," in *Teachings on Love* (Berkeley, CA: Parallax Press, 1997), pp. 174–76. Reprinted with permission of Parallax Press, Berkeley, California.
51. From Dentōroku, "Transmission of the Lamp," cited in Daisetz Teitaro Suzuki, *Zen and Japanese Culture* (Princeton, NJ: Princeton University Press, 1959), p. 294.
52. Haga Koshiro, "The *Wabi* Aesthetic through the Ages," in Nancy G. Hume, ed., *Japanese Aesthetics and Culture: A Reader* (Albany: SUNY Press, 1995), p. 271.
53. Kakuzo Okakura uses "moral geometry" in his *The Book of Tea* to refer to "our sense of proportion to the universe." See Okakura, p. 1.
54. Ibid., p. 31.
55. Kakuzo Okakura describes the Zen chapel in his *The Book of Tea,* p. 33:

   The room [Zen chapel] is bare except for a central alcove in which, behind the altar, is a statue of Bodhidharma, the founder of the sect, or of Sakyamuni attended by Kasyapa and Ananda, the two earliest Zen patriarchs. On the altar, flowers and incense are offered up in memory of the great contributions which these sages made to Zen. . . . [The altar of the Zen chapel was the prototype of the Tokonoma—the place of honour in a Japanese room where paintings and flowers are placed for the edification of the guests.

56. In Suzuki, *Zen and Japanese Culture,* p. 281.
57. Ibid., p. 298.
58. Okakura, *The Book of Tea,* p. 40.
59. "Seigan Zenji chaji jurokkujo, Chaji shuran," in Tetsuzo Tanikawa, "The Esthetics of Chanoyu, Part 4," in *Chanoyu Quarterly: Tea and the Arts of Japan* (1981), no. 27, pp. 46–47.
60. Alluded to by Dogen, in Hume, *Japanese Aesthetics,* p. 273.

61. Cited in ibid., pp. 274–75.
62. Tanikawa, *The Esthetics of Chanoyu,* p. 43.
63. In Suzuki, *Zen and Japanese Culture,* p. 285.
64. Ibid., p. 286.
65. Ibid., pp. 287–88.
66. Ibid., p. 288.
67. Tanikawa, *The Esthetics of Chanoyu,* p. 44.
68. Cited in Suzuki, *Zen and Japanese Culture,* p. 282.
69. Ibid., p. 300.

FOUR

Taoist Ethics

After Wang Ch'ung-yang reached his enlightenment and achieved his immortality, he made it his mission to help guide others to attain their spiritual goals as well. The first people he helped were Ma Tan-yang and Sun Pu-erh, husband and wife, a specially gifted couple. Though they were highly intelligent and in singular harmony with each other, their lives were still incomplete. They still needed to learn the secret of detachment. So, sensing Wang's exceptional insight, they invited him to be their instructor. And he began to teach them the most valuable lessons in attaining the Tao, such as cultivating their hearts and getting rid of ego and craving.

One day while Wang was in Ma Tan-yang's room instructing him, Sun Pu-erh was alone in her room meditating. Suddenly, Wang appeared before her and said:

> The Way of the Tao is intricate and mysterious. Although there are many methods, there is only one truth. The teachings of all sects draw from the origin. One must not be rigid. Practice naturally, and you will achieve effects. You have been sitting here all alone, thinking that there is only one way to cultivate the Tao. Do you know that *yin* cannot flourish without *yang?* Simply sitting will not balance the *yin* and *yang* in your body. If your *yin* and *yang* do not copulate, how can you become pregnant and give birth to a child? You don't understand this and you don't understand that. How can you cultivate the Tao?[1]

Sun felt insulted and disturbed. Not only was her privacy invaded, but Wang's words made little sense. She immediately left her room and ordered her servant to find her husband. When she told him about Wang's visit, he was perplexed since during this same time Master Wang was with him in his room. Upon hearing this, Sun Pu-erh became all the more confused and irritated.

A month went by, and again Master Wang was instructing Ma Tan-yang. And again Sun Pu-erh, alone in her room, was visited by Wang, who said:

> Know that in the Tao there is no division of male and female. If you separate *yin* and *yang* the Tao cannot be attained. . . . Your training has been unbalanced. Your "dead" sitting has made you irritable and inflexible. Know that male and female cannot exist without each other. *Yin* and *yang* must copulate. The Yellow Woman must act as the go-between so that the pair can unite.[2]

At this point Sun Pu-erh promptly left her room and locked the door, leaving Wang inside.

Now all this time Ma Tan-yang was in the meditation hall with Master Wang. Then Wang told him that someone was looking for him. As Ma Tan-yang stepped outside the hall, he ran into his wife who insisted that he come to her room. When they arrived at her room, she unlocked the door, and they both entered, finding no one there. Sun Pu-erh was baffled. Her husband comforted her:

> "There is nothing strange about all this. Your heart was not clear, and you fell to the prey of the monsters of illusion." Sun Pu-erh said, "I do not understand. I thought I was disciplined and focused in my training. How could I have strayed and hallucinated? . . ."
>
> When Sun Pu-erh had finished, Ma Tan-yang laughed and said, "You have always been smart, but this time you missed." Sun Pu-erh asked, "Where did I miss?" Ma Tan-yang replied, "Those who seek the Tao must be humble and patient and willing to learn. Otherwise you will not progress. The Tao is limitless. If you think you have learned everything about it, you have lost it. You were sitting in your room doing what you were instructed to do a long time ago. You thought that by gaining some progress you had completely mastered the methods of internal alchemy. Master Wang saw that you were stagnating to the point of losing what you had achieved. That was why he came to instruct you. His spirit left his body and came to your room. . . . By the union of male and female, Master Wang did not mean the physical relationship between man and woman. He was referring to the *yin* and *yang* energies in our body. If the two energies are isolated, your training will be unbalanced: you will have either too much *yang* or too much *yin*. *Yang* is fire in nature. Too much fire, and you will burn the herbs. *Yin* is water in nature. Too much water, and the herbs will rot. Either way, the Golden Pill cannot materialize. *Yang* is the clear, conceptualizing intelligence; *yin* is the receptive, intuiting quietude. *You have had too much yang in your training. You were analyzing too much at the expense of intuition.* The Yellow Woman is the true intention that can bring together the opposites and unite the *yin* and *yang*.[3] [italics mine]

This is one of many edifying stories from the Ming Dynasty (1368–1644) novel *Seven Taoist Masters*. Written around 1500, the book describes the adventures of Wang Ch'ung-yang and his seven disciples. It describes their personal paths to self-discovery and enlightenment. Representing the teachings of the most popular school of Taoism today, called the Singular Path (or Complete Perfection), the novel *Seven Taoist Masters* relates how the cultivation of the Tao can be reached only after developing the right attitudes. It recounts how each disciple overcomes his and her own personal flaw, the individual's own moral Achilles' heel, the biggest stumbling block to cultivating the Tao.

In the case of Sun Pu-erh, her major weakness was her attachment to her intellect. She suffered from "too much yang." This was her moral Achilles' heel. Because she confined learning strictly to the sphere of intellect, her attachment to her intelligence became her chief barrier to any further learning. Yet Taoism teaches us that "learning is limitless." Her enlightenment could come about only if she properly cultivates her yin—her powers of faith, trust, and intuition. She needed to strike this critical balance of yin and yang.

BACKGROUND

Chinese Cosmology

The early Chinese cosmology presents us with an initial context and starting point from which we can understand Taoist (as well as Confucian) teachings. The Chinese wrestled with the all-important question: How can we account for the fact of change and multiplicity in view of the need for some type of permanence and unity? Their solution provides a cosmological backdrop for all of Chinese thought, and it grips the imagination as well. They believed that *yin,* the principle of darkness, passivity, and femininity, mutually interacts with, complements, and influences *yang,* the principle of light, activity, and masculinity. These two forces act upon each other in an endless, mutual balance.

Moreover, the interaction of yin and yang manifests itself in the intermingling of the Five Phases or vital forces of water, fire, wood, metal, and earth. These interminglings produce the particular features that make up all the things in nature. Thus, Chinese cosmology, expressed in the classic text *I Ching,* or *Book of Changes,* views nature in terms of the ceaseless energy of yin and yang and these Five Phases.[4]

In view of this cosmology, the most pivotal Taoist ideas are *Tao* and *te. Tao,* literally meaning "road" or "way," was believed to be the all-pervading principle and underlying source of the universe, while *te* was the Tao's manifestation and power throughout the cosmos. Thus, the complementary interplay of yin and yang is the natural expression of the Tao.

Taoist Foundations: The *Lao Tzu* and the *Chuang Tzu*

The wellspring of Taoist thought clearly lies embedded in those teachings that made their mark during the time of fierce political and social upheaval known as the Warring States Period (403–221 B.C.E.). The devastation of the Chou capital and the assassination of its king in 771 B.C.E. set the tone for a lingering decline of order. This period of intense conflict also gave birth to two unparalleled works in all of Chinese literature: the *Lao Tzu,* more popularly known as the *Tao Te Ching,* and the *Chuang Tzu.* Their teachings were later organized and classified into the school officially known as Taoist.

This time of turmoil, which produced the most groundbreaking intellectual activity, is known as the Period of One Hundred Schools. Indeed, intellectual discussion flourished at this time, with all sorts of debates regarding human nature and the role of the state. The most prominent schools represented the Confucian, Taoist, Yin-Yang, and Legalist teachings. Needless to say, in this time of chaos there was an urgent need for meaning and for moral order.

This need for stability may have inspired the many tales surrounding the life of the legendary founder of Taoism, Lao Tzu. For example, according to Ssu-ma Ch'ien's *Records of the Historian,* it is said that Lao Tzu (or Lao Tan) composed his *Tao Te Ching* at the request of the gate keeper, Yin Hsi, who guarded the entry or Pass at Hsien-ku. The *Records* also claim that Lao Tzu's family name was Li, and that he watched over the imperial archives (the treasured records of the imperial families). They even allude to a visit by his younger contemporary Confucius. Whether or not any of this is true remains a matter for dispute. To be sure, Lao Tzu's real identity is still enveloped in speculation. Nevertheless, most scholars now believe that the *Tao Te Ching* was actually composed at a later date by various Taoists. In any case, the *Tao Te Ching,* a text that has generated more commentaries than any other work in Chinese thought, remains such a splendid fountain of wisdom that it is virtually impossible to savor Chinese philosophy without appreciating its teachings.

As for the *Chuang Tzu,* the life story of its alleged author with the same name is also shrouded in mystery. According to Ssu-ma Ch'ien, Chuang Tzu (or Chuang Chou, c. 399–c. 295 B.C.E.) was so renowned that he was offered an official position as prime minister of his region. Faithful to his own principles, however, he shunned the post and the status attached to it, and instead embraced individual freedom.

Chuang Tzu further refined the notions of Tao and *te.* He especially portrayed *te* in terms of the power of Tao interiorized within each entity. In other words, *te* empowers us to live the way we ought to live, beyond superficiality and social custom. Chuang Tzu's scathing indictment of social conventions and morality offers a glaring contrast to the more social orientation found in Confucianism.

Moreover, the *Chuang Tzu* is written in such an unconventional style that it positively requires the reader to give up any fixed notions about the customary ideas of, for example, life and death, or good and evil, before even beginning to comprehend its meaning.[5] The work has an abundance of paradox, hyperbole, and acrid wit. And it contains numerous lessons on a rich variety of themes with moral overtones such as freedom, equality, virtuous activity, and living naturally.

Chuang Tzu's teachings evoked searing criticisms from Confucians such as Hsün Tzu (fl. 298–238 B.C.E.) and the brilliant Neo-Confucian Chu Hsi (1130–1200 C.E.) for brandishing a dangerous form of quietism that advocated escaping from social responsibilities. Nevertheless, his far-reaching influence upon Taoism, as well as upon Ch'an Buddhism in China and Zen Buddhism in Japan, is indisputable.

Neo-Taoism

Rampant instability again resurfaced with the collapse of the Han Dynasty, followed by the era of the Three Kingdoms and Six Dynasties (220–589 C.E.). China was sundered into three separate kingdoms. Furthermore, the northern part of China soon gave way to foreign invasion. Political corruption accompanied incessant warfare. Periodic natural calamities such as famines and floods made matters worse.

In spite of all this, there was a renewed interest in the *Tao Te Ching* and the *Chuang Tzu.* For instance, some scholars regularly met in bamboo groves to freely discuss philosophical issues. They became known as the "Seven Sages of the Bamboo Grove." This reenergizing of Taoism, later named Neo-Taoism, had a twofold result. First, Taoist metaphysics were raised to another level. Second, Taoist morality was given more of a Confucian imprint with more overt social and political implications.

Two Neo-Taoists particularly stand out: Wang Pi (226–249) and Kuo Hsiang (d. 312). Wang Pi wrote an influential commentary on the *Lao Tzu,* while Kuo Hsiang is known for his commentary on the *Chuang Tzu.* Neo-Taoists stressed the active participation of the sage in social and political events. Instead of withdrawing into nature, the sage remains involved in human affairs. Inwardly, however, he remains detached. Therefore, for Neo-Taoists, Confucius was a true sage.

We thus see in Neo-Taoism an attempt to syncretize selected aspects of Taoist teachings with Confucianism. To keep matters in perspective, however, let us remember that this impulse to syncretize is evident throughout Chinese intellectual history. Nevertheless, Confucianism still maintained a virtual supremacy throughout most of Chinese history. Its key teachings therefore continued to influence the interpretations of both Taoism and Buddhism.

Religious Taoism

Another dimension to Taoism accompanied the philosophical movement of Neo-Taoism. In "religious Taoism" (*tao-chiao*) we witness the increasing divinization of the legendary sage Lao Tzu. Chang Tao-ling, generally regarded as the founder of religious Taoism, claimed to have experienced a vision of Lao-chün (the divinized Lao Tzu), who then conferred on him the title of

Heavenly Master (*T'ien-shih*). Chang then went on to establish a sect named the Way of Five Pecks, so-called because each follower had to contribute five pecks (or bushels) of rice. Eventually, there came about other sects led by alleged Heavenly Masters who claimed descendance from Chang. To this day, there are men who still claim to continue this lineage of Heavenly Masters.

We also see an emphasis upon longevity, along with techniques and medicinals to gain immortality such as elixirs, meditations, hygiene practices, and special diets. And the earlier notions of Tao and *te,* among others, were interpreted within a context that prioritized the quest for immortality. This all follows from the Taoist emphasis upon reestablishing harmony with the Tao. After all, this harmony is believed to be a healing relationship—healing our rupture from the Tao—so that healing, good health, and longevity became linked with cultivating the Tao. Thus the Taoist saint was also an immortal. And techniques for preserving life and enhancing health (*yang-sheng*) became part of the arsenal of Taoist training.

Another significant factor in the formation of religious Taoism had to do with Buddhist teachings, which reached China in the first century C.E. At first, Buddhist ideas were often erroneously associated with Taoism. In fact, quite a few Taoists even believed that the Buddha was actually Lao-Tzu, for he had supposedly journeyed west toward India.

Some Taoist sects had a jarring impact upon certain messianic movements that erupted in the early centuries, such as the famous Yellow Turban Revolt in 184, which predicted the downfall of the Han dynasty by announcing the era of T'ai-p'ing Tao, or the Great Peace Way. The inspiration behind this revolt was the *T'ai-ping ching,* the *Book of Great Peace,* a text that bolstered a divinized view of Taoist sages, underscored a vigorous ethic, and prescribed techniques for longevity. Although the revolt was brutally suppressed, the book was later incorporated into the Taoist canon.

As the Sung dynasty came to an end (in the 12th–13th centuries), accompanied by sporadic war and foreign occupation, certain groups would go on to have a lasting influence upon the development of Taoism. The most influential group or school was the Ch'üan-chen, the school of Complete Perfection, founded by Wang Ch'ung-yang (1113–1170). This is the same Master Wang in our opening story. After living in total seclusion for ten years, he shared his teachings and acquired a huge following. After his death, his seven devoted disciples (the Seven Taoist Masters) became the school's patriarchs. The school sought to syncretize elements of Taoism, Confucianism, and Buddhism. And it stressed meditation as a way to reconnect with one's true nature, thus having a definite Ch'an, or Zen-like aspect. This sect also maintained a religious Taoist flavor by insisting upon meditation as a means to longevity. Another school called Cheng-i (Official Unity), claimed to restore the lineage of Heavenly Masters described previously. These two are the most prominent Taoist schools today, with the school of Complete Perfection as the leading group. Other Taoist sects continue to have an abiding influence, such as the Wu-tang sect and the Shao-lin Temple, both dedicated to the practice of the martial art of *t'ai-chi-chüan*.

Moral Significance of Taoism

Although religious Taoism was in some ways distinct from the philosophical Taoism (*tao-chia*) of the ancient period, they both underscored the vital importance of living in accordance with the Tao. Only by cultivating the Tao could one develop a morally correct attitude and lifestyle. Religious Taoism emphasized morality within the context of living a healthier, longer life. For example, the Way of Five Pecks often interpreted illness as a consequence of immoral behavior. In this respect, many religious Taoists made a direct link between ethical activity and life span. They generally believed that immoral actions subtracted from what they postulated as our original allotment for our life span. On the other hand, virtuous deeds could lead to longevity, an extended life. The ideal was to achieve immortality. To illustrate, all seven of the Taoist masters in the school of Complete Perfection acquired their immortality only after they had perfectly cultivated the Tao by maintaining totally selfless and compassionate lives.

On the other hand, philosophical Taoism, as expressed in its classic texts, the *Tao Te Ching* and the *Chuang Tzu,* certainly possesses a distinct moral significance, though not as a means to attain immortality. For instance, the *Tao Te Ching* presents the sage as a paradigm of virtue because the sage quietly grasps the meaning behind the Tao and lives his life according to it. In this way, he lives in harmony with himself and is free from attachment.

Both the religious and philosophical aspects of Taoism concur that the key trouble lies with humans. According to all Taoists, we habitually breach our natural harmony with the Tao. As a result, we suffer from a false consciousness, isolated from the whole. We become fixed upon disparate aspects of existence, such as status, wealth, pleasures, and even "the good." As for "the good," we tend to confine ourselves within moral categories and labels that are socially contrived. The *Tao Te Ching,* the *Chuang Tzu,* and many other Taoist texts warn us that this counterfeit consciousness cuts us off from the flow of the Tao by creating false goals, goals that we need to abandon if we are to reconnect with our original nature.

Herein lies the Taoist moral imperative. We can liberate ourselves from this false consciousness only by reestablishing our harmony with the Tao. This effort to cultivate the Tao must come from within us. It consists in seeing through and rectifying our own chronic state of mind. It requires freeing ourselves from viewing matters of "right" and "wrong" from fixed perspectives. The moral significance is clear: Living in balance with ourselves, with others, and with nature can come about only if we live in balance with the Tao, the inexhaustible principle of all Nature.

On the surface, it appears that this Taoist emphasis upon inner, personal cultivation contradicts the Confucian emphasis upon social responsibility. Actually, these two streams complement each other. After all, we all have that public side wherein we need to be morally accountable to our families, friends, co-workers, and others. And, as we later see, Confucianism soberly reminds us of our public duties. At the same time, we remain private creatures, desiring sanctuary from our public lives. We have an incessant need to be in harmony with ourselves and with the unpretentious natural world. And here is where we find the wide appeal of Taoist thought.

Taoist Ethics or Ethos?

Before we introduce individual themes in Taoist ethics, perhaps it would help to sketch some of its more general traits. Indeed, we can assert from the start two unique attributes of Taoist ethics: its inward orientation and its ethos.

First, the orientation in Taoist ethics is primarily and unmistakably inward. In other words, it prompts us to cultivate our own inner harmony. Now this is in some respects distinct from how we usually approach ethics. To clarify, the center of concern in matters of ethics typically addresses the question: How ought I to live? Yet this generates two further questions: How should I be with others? How should I be with myself? Of the two, we tend to consider ethics in terms of our right behavior and interaction *with others,* so that it is more outer-directed. But Taoist teachings remind us that how we are with others ultimately stems from *our relationship with the Tao and how we are with ourselves.* This requires a painstaking audit of our own interior space—our fundamental disposition, attitudes, motives, and character. Taoist ethics, in its most fundamental sense, reveals a morality that is intensely intimate and not one that is solely derived from or defined by social convention, customs, and rules. Its most important question is, How should I live with myself? Its teachings, therefore, stress values that are crucial to developing the ideal personal disposition and attitude. The Taoist ethic principally aims to cultivate good character (here it is essentially similar to the Confucian ethic). It quietly prods us into realizing that how we interact with our environment, both natural and social, derives from the deepest core of who we are and whether we are in harmony with the Tao.

This takes us to the second feature of Taoist ethics. Taoist ideas are expressed in a manner far removed from any systematic analysis and ethical theory. In this sense, Taoism may lack an "ethic" in that there is no scrupulous attention to a strict method and rigorous argument. All the same, these teachings constitute a penetrating expression of Chinese beliefs and values. In this respect, Taoist teachings clearly furnish a basis for a Chinese "ethos" rather than a rigorous and methodic "ethic" in the manner many Western philosophers might tend to view as "ethics." By Taoist *ethos,* we mean a distinctive cultural disposition or pattern that manifests itself throughout Chinese thought and behavior.

So if we restrict our understanding of ethics to that which is analytic and systematized (and there are no real strong grounds for doing so), it would be hard to detect a Taoist "ethic" in the Western sense. Nevertheless, a Taoist ethos undeniably continues to nourish Chinese culture, sustain Chinese values, and breathe life into Chinese views as to proper conduct. We can therefore assert that Taoism, although it lacks a systematic formulation and may not even count as "ethics" in this rigorous sense, actually provides the underpinnings for ethical behavior. All of this, indeed, qualifies our notion of what constitutes Taoist ethics. Given these qualifiers, and on the grounds that there does exist a distinct Taoist ethic, let us now consider the most significant features of this ethic.

CULTIVATING THE TAO

Cultivating Our Original Nature

Consider the famous opening verses in the *Tao Te Ching (The Way and Its Power)*:

> Tao that can be spoken of,
> Is not the everlasting Tao.
> Name that can be named,
> Is not the everlasting name.
> Nameless, the origin of heaven and earth;
> Named, the mother of ten thousand things.
> Alternate . . .[6]

Here we confront an initial obstacle in attempting to describe the work's leading concept and without a doubt the most vital notion in all of Chinese philosophy—*Tao*.[7] Nevertheless, we know from its character, 道 , that it literally denotes "way," "path," or "road." And we can go on to refer to the Tao as the Way of all Reality, the principle and source of the universe, the origin of all that comes to exist as well as all that ceases to exist. Just as the Tao gives birth to the universe, the "ten thousand things," the Tao also brings about their transformation through death. In this most embryonic sense, the Tao is ultimately what is "great," the Great Principle that acts in a dynamic, pulsating fashion.

> I know not its name,
> I give its alias, Tao.
> If forced to picture it,
> I say it is "great."
> To say it is "great" is to say it is "moving away,"
> To say it is "moving away" is to say it is "far away,"
> To say it is "far away" is to say it is "returning."[8]

How does all of this impact upon Taoist morality and values? To begin with, the scholar Chad Hansen points out an interesting trait in the Chinese language in that the purpose behind the language is more prescriptive than it is descriptive. Surely the language goes about describing objects, persons, and events, but "the prescriptive function of language informs the Chinese view of language as the descriptive function informs ours."[9] In other words, the Chinese language especially intends to evoke from us congruent and appropriate decisions and actions; it helps us to guide our actions in the world.

Along these lines, Tao not only denotes the Way of the cosmos, but also suggests for us a prescription: We ought to cultivate the Tao; we ought to live in a manner essentially in harmony with the Tao, the Supreme Principle of Nature. And *living in harmony with the Tao is the basis for a Taoist ethos or ethics.* It sets the standard for determining what constitutes right behavior.[10]

In view of this, what then does it mean to cultivate the Tao? As a start, the *Tao Te Ching* gives us the metaphor of the innocence of an infant.

> In embracing the One with your soul,
>   Can you never forsake the Tao?
> In controlling your vital force to achieve gentleness,
>   Can you become like the new-born child?[11]

Here the newborn child represents our pristine innocence. The passage urges us to somehow reconnect with this original state, our original nature, by getting rid of those biases with which we have become adulterated and by which we evaluate and judge others. The ethical import is clear and profound. Essentially, wearing the heart of a newborn child entails freeing ourselves from our prejudices and preconceptions. In fact, it entails freeing ourselves from all forms of attachments. This is the state of original innocence.

Note this return to innocence echoed in the verse entitled "The Character of the Child":

> Who is rich in character
> Is like a child.
>   No poisonous insects sting him,
>   No wild beasts attack him,
>   And no birds of prey pounce upon him.
> His bones are soft, his sinews tender, yet his grip is strong.
> Not knowing the union of male and female, yet his organs are complete,
>   Which means his vigor is unspoiled.
> Crying the whole day, yet his voice never runs hoarse,
>   Which means his (natural) harmony is perfect.
> To know harmony is to be in accord with the eternal,
> (And) to know eternity is called discerning . . .
> And he who is against Tao perishes young.[12]

The first line, "Who is rich in character," sets forth the condition and consequence of morally sound behavior. These verses entreat us to cultivate our original natures. And by cultivating our original nature (sometimes described as our "uncarved block"), we set the condition for developing good character.[13]

The Chinese character for Tao. (Francis
Hogan/Electronic Publishing Services, Inc.)

Thus, the message is clear: Cultivating *the Tao* means cultivating our original
nature. And this in turn lays the groundwork for good character.

Cultivating Our True Heart

Wang Ch'ung-yang, certainly one of the most popular of Taoist sages, eventually perfected the art of cultivating the Tao only after a long period of training and undergoing many trials. In doing so he became an immortal.

His long road to enlightenment started when he took two beggars into
his home and fed them. Unbeknownst to him, these two beggars were immortals in disguise, and Wang envied their detachment from worldly concerns.
They were nicknamed "Gold-Is-Heavy" and "Empty-Mind." When the beggars
departed, Wang followed them across a mysterious bridge and up steep mountain slopes until they finally reached a crystal clear, tranquil lake high up on
the mountain. Here, Empty-Mind collected seven golden, fully blossomed lotus
flowers from the lake, handed them to Wang and instructed him:

> Take care of these flowers. They are the spirits of seven enlightened souls
> destined to be your disciples. Their karma is tied to yours. . . . We should meet
> again before too long, perhaps three months from now. Look for me by the
> bridge where our karmas are intertwined.[14]

The next thing Wang knew, he was back in his study. At first he thought this was all merely a dream. Soon, however, he realized that he had actually traveled with the two beggars and that these two beggars were in fact two famous immortals, Ch'ung-li Ch'uan and Lu Tung-pin.

After three months, Wang set out again and waited by the mystical bridge. Soon, the two beggars appeared. They suddenly transformed themselves into wearing brilliant garments, and Immortal Lu instructed Wang with the following lesson:

SEVEN TAOIST MASTERS

The real is that which is true and not false. Every person has a true heart. If the true heart strays, however, then it becomes untrue to its own nature. Every person has a true intention. But if the true intention strays, it becomes untrue to its own nature. Every person has a true feeling. When the true feeling strays from the original nature, it becomes untrue. An intention that originates from the true heart is true intention. The intention that is calculating and scheming is untrue. A feeling that originates from the true heart is true feeling. Feeling that has self-importance in it is untrue. What is the true heart? The true heart is original nature. The true heart tends toward goodness. Feeling and intention originate from the heart. If the heart is true, the feeling and intention will be true. Cultivating the true heart is cultivating original nature. Original nature is the manifestation of the natural way of Heaven. Many who claim to cultivate the Tao still possess egotistical thoughts. Where there is ego, the true heart cannot emerge. It is only in stillness and the absence of craving that original nature can be cultivated. Those who seek the Tao must begin with knowing the difference between true and untrue feeling, true and untrue intention. If you know the difference, then you will know the true heart. Intention and feeling can be known by observing the behavior in your daily life. If your actions are not sincere, then true feeling is absent. If your words are false, then true intention is absent. If you want to cultivate the Tao you must eradicate attachments that lead true intention and true feeling astray. Let original nature rather than your ego guide your actions. Do not waver in your pursuit of goodness. Then, your true heart, true feeling, and true intention will emerge and you will not be far from the Tao. These are the teachings of the real truth.

From *Seven Taoist Masters: A Folk Tale of China* translated by Eva Wong, © 1990. Reprinted by arrangement with Shambhala Publications, Inc., Boston.

We see from this passage that cultivating the Tao necessarily requires that we cultivate our original nature. Furthermore, this original nature is our true heart. Thus, acting in harmony with the Tao can come about only if we cultivate our hearts. And how do we cultivate our true heart? We do so by disentangling ourselves from our ego and by freeing ourselves from attachments.

Reconnecting with Our *Te*

The full title of the *Tao Te Ching—The Way and Its Power*—indicates that *te* is the "power" of the Tao.

> Tao gives birth,
> *Te* rears, Things shape,
> Circumstances complete.

> Therefore the ten thousand things,
> None do not respect Tao and treasure *te*.
> Tao is respected,
> *Te* is treasured,
> Not by decree,
> But by spontaneity.[15]

Te, the spontaneous expression of the Tao, manifests itself and permeates all of reality: "Such the scope of the All-pervading Power [*te*], That it alone can act through the Way."[16] Later, Neo-Taoists such as Kuo Hsiang devoted a good deal of attention to the idea of *te,* in that all things have their own principle of the Tao.

The scholar Arthur Waley points out an interesting link between *te* and the notion of "planting." *Te,* as the power of the Tao within us and all living things, conveys our own potency or "latent power." And there is no greater teacher of this than Nature. Through its rhythms and its seasons, Nature teaches us the most valuable lessons we need to learn in life. It also sets a splendid model for cultivating and living in harmony with the Tao.

> Man models himself after the Earth;
> The Earth models itself after Heaven;
> The Heaven models itself after Tao;
> Tao models itself after Nature.[17]

Te is also translated as "virtue," though not in the sense of a specific virtue or virtuous act. Still, it reveals somewhat of a moral overtone. Because *te* is the "power of Tao," cultivating *te* is in effect the consummate virtue for it also means cultivating the Tao.

This is why the Taoist ideal is personified by the two immortals who instructed Wang Ch'ung-yang, "Gold-Is-Heavy" and "Empty-Mind." They both cultivated the Tao by nourishing their *te,* their power of the Tao within. This led them to live lives of genuine simplicity and natural harmony, free from all worldly attachments. The following illustrations, one medical and the other dealing with the martial art of T'ai-chi, can help us further understand this deceptively simple equation: Harmony with *te* equals harmony with the Tao.

Nourishing Our *Ch'i*

Yen Guangzhen is a woman in her forties suffering from chronic fatigue, headaches, and depression, a condition labeled according to Chinese disease categories as neurasthenia. In order for us to discern the etiology of her condition, we need to discern the impact of certain events in her life story. Ever since the Cultural Revolution in the 1960s, her life has taken on a series of dislocations. She was one of the hundreds of millions of Chinese who were uprooted from their urban lifestyles to work on farms in rural communes. Her former life in the city was that of a serious and promising student. At the same time, she was also cut off from her natural family. In time, she became increasingly demoralized as her own natural talents were stifled. This led to a routine pattern of self-effacement persisting into her marriage. Disconnection lingered on in her life as she and her husband were forced to live separately, her two sons living with their father while she maintained custody of her daughter. That all-important natural family bond, acknowledged in Chinese culture as the most crucial and influential human relationship, was for Yen Guangzhen snapped in two.

Her most acute symptom of disassociation involved her strong feelings of guilt toward her daughter. She had not wanted another child, and she even attempted to terminate the pregnancy. Nevertheless, her daughter was born in all respects healthy and beautiful—except for a withered arm, and Yen blamed herself for the deformity. (Traditionally, the Chinese believed that during gestation the thoughts and feelings of the mother along with her behavior have an indelible effect upon the fetus.)

According to the Chinese doctor treating Yen, her diagnosis is straightforward: She suffers from a severe imbalance of *ch'i* (or *Qi,* or *Ki* in Japanese), a vital force that permeates our bodies, a life-giving energy. Moreover, *ch'i* is the tangible manifestation of the Tao. In turn, it is thereby an expression of *te,* the power of Tao. *Ch'i* appears in the form of breath and in the body's circulation. And illness results when the flow of ch'i throughout our body is disrupted.

On this account, we can now understand Yen's condition in view of her imbalance of *ch'i.* Her natural power or virtue, *te,* expressed itself in her talents and capacities. Yet her history of disconnectedness, through experiences that led her to thwart the expression of her own inner nature and capacities, consequently obstructed her flow of *ch'i.*[18] She was thus unable to reconnect with her *te,* her virtue and natural power. In the same fashion, we can say that she was not in harmony with the Tao.

Here we see the evident influence of Taoist teachings in Chinese medicine. The Tao naturally manifests its power, *te,* through the two universal principles of yin and yang, described earlier. Yin and yang interact in a universal symmetry. And *ch'i* is the life-giving energy that flows throughout our bodies in order to sustain this balance of yin and yang. The disruption of *ch'i* is an unnatural condition and results in illness.

When the natural power of Tao is obstructed in a person, her own inner harmony is hindered. Therefore Chinese medicine aims to revive our natural balance by restoring the flow of *ch'i* through measures such as diet, herbal medicines, acupuncture, and massage. In any case, the formula is clear: Lack of balance brings about illness. Such imbalance inevitably manifests itself in social relationships as well, and it carries with it moral consequences in terms of our behavior with others. In contrast, a condition of health, what some scholars call "orthopathy," reflects a proper balance with the Tao and *te* and manifests itself through equilibrium with nature and society.[19] Thus the prescription for sound health, physically and morally, lies in proper balance. It lies in cultivating the Tao.

Henri Bergson, *Creative Evolution*

So, from an immense reservoir of life, jets must be gushing out unceasingly, of which each, falling back, is a world. The evolution of living species within this world represents what subsists of the primitive direction of the original jet, and of an impulsion which continues itself in a direction the inverse of materiality. . . .

. . . There are no things, there are only actions. More particularly, if I consider the world in which we live, I find that the automatic and strictly determined evolution of this well-knit whole is action which is unmaking itself, and that the unforeseen forms which life cuts out in it, forms capable of being themselves prolonged into unforeseen movements, represent the action that is making itself. . . . In reality, life is a movement . . . we shut our eyes to the unity of the impulse which, passing through generations, links individuals with individuals, species with species, and makes of the whole series of the living one single immense wave flowing over matter . . .

From Henri Bergson, *Creative Evolution,* trans. Arthur Mitchell (New York: Modern Library, 1944), pp. 270–73.

As we see in Chinese medicine, a necessary link exists between *te* and *ch'i.* After all, *ch'i* is the tangible form of the Tao. Now let us take this one step further. Since *ch'i* flows through our bodies as energy, apparent through the visible activities of breathing and circulation, the way to maintain *chi*'s proper balance is through correct breathing. This is evident in the Asian martial arts, particularly the branch of Chinese "soft" martial arts. They are called "soft," as opposed to the more aggressive "hard" forms, because they are deliberately slower paced, appear more flowing and natural in character, and are more thoroughly Taoist in principle.

It has been said that some of the early Taoists withdrew from society to live as hermits in the mountains. They had a single-minded goal: to become aware of and to realize the power of the Tao. Yet living alone posed special dangers, particularly from wild animals. In order to protect themselves, they developed forms of self-defense. How? By observing animal habits.

Thus, what became the soft martial arts was based upon the natural movements of animals. For example, the art of *Hsing-i* is more of a defensive style that adopts the defensive forms (*hsing*) of animals (such as the tiger, bear, dragon, hawk, and chicken) in order to learn the real meaning or essence (*i*) *behind the form*. Acquiring skill in the technique is only part of the goal. Perfecting the form only comes once the student gains insight into the true meaning behind the form. And this insight requires a distinctive moral as well as physical and mental posture. That is, the ultimate aim in this and in all other martial arts is not only to perfect form but to cultivate proper character. Herein lies the moral purpose of martial arts training. It is a way to develop an unpretentious attitude and disposition of both confidence and humility.

The most widely practiced soft art is T'ai-chi. Every morning at dawn, millions of Chinese regularly practice this art form. T'ai-chi brings about numerous physical benefits: It enhances body toning, coordination, and control; it also allows the balanced flow of *ch'i* throughout the entire body by stressing the role of deliberate and proper breathing. Most important, T'ai-chi is a means whereby we can cultivate the Tao. For this reason, Chinese believe that precious medical benefits result from the practice of t'ai-chi, since the flow of *ch'i* helps to sustain vital organs such as the heart, liver, lungs, and kidneys. In addition, the practitioner learns to become properly centered through what is known as "sinking the *ch'i*." When *ch'i* is properly centered in a spot approximately three inches below the navel (called the *tan-tien*), it will flow in a balanced fashion through the rest of the body.

"Sinking the *chi*" enables the practitioner to be firmly rooted in a state of calm equilibrium.[20] Not only does it sharpen one's self-awareness, concentration, and alertness, but it also aims to bolster self-confidence, a necessary ingredient for character development. This is not a brash type of confidence, which is in fact contrary to the spirit of the martial arts. It is an unassuming trust in one's own ability to deal with all types of situations. The faithful exercise of T'ai-chi can lead to a state of mental calm and inner poise, which will enable the practitioner to deal with conflicts in a more balanced and morally appropriate manner.

T'ai-chi is performed in an exaggeratedly slow fashion, like the lingering motion of clouds. This is done in order to acquire a state of mind that is both relaxed and controlled, which can be exceptionally advantageous in life-threatening situations. If the adept student is about to be attacked, he or she should be able to respond almost instinctively and to execute the appropriate movements swiftly without a second thought. Moreover, the student ought to defend himself or herself by exerting just the sufficient amount of force. In other words, the student's defensive actions are morally fitting since they avoid the excessive use of force. This moral component accompanies our getting in touch with and following our *te,* our natural power, the power of Tao. It comes from cultivating the Tao.

At this point, we have stressed the importance of cultivating the Tao through practices such as cultivating our original nature and getting in touch with our *ch'i.* Let us examine further ways in which we can cultivate the Tao.

THE ART OF YIELDING *(WU-WEI)*

Which is more powerful: water or rock? Now imagine a waterfall. After centuries of steadily pursuing its natural course, the water has carved a path through solid rock. What accounts for its victory? Its constancy and its ability to yield:

> Nothing under heaven is softer or more yielding than water; but when it attacks things hard and resistant there is not one of them that can prevail. For they can find no way of altering it. That the yielding conquers the resistance and the soft conquers the hard is a fact known by all men, yet utilized by none.[21]

On one level, nothing is weaker than water since it naturally yields and gives way to what it comes into contact with. Yet it is precisely this fluidity that transforms its weakness into its greatest strength. It is the nature of water to yield, but its steadfast yielding eventually carves a path through solid rock to form the waterfall.

The waterfall conveys a hidden message that has profound moral over-tones. It gives us a valuable lesson in what it takes to cultivate good charac-ter. We learn that soft overcomes hard, that passivity can be a form of action, that yielding conquers aggressiveness, that flexibility wins out over rigidity, that constancy triumphs over impetuousness. This is the powerful meaning behind the Taoist concept of *wu-wei.*

Wu-wei literally means "nonaction" or "nondoing." However, *wu-wei* does not refer to total passivity or noneffort. Water is an exquisite metaphor for *wu-wei* because water simply follows its nature. Thus *wu-wei* means to act naturally by yielding to, instead of resisting, the natural flow of things. In this way, the water acts according to the Tao.

In like manner, the Tao is like water: It follows its natural course, and in doing so, it accomplishes all.

Waterfall detail. (Corbis/Burstein Collection, from "Landscape of the Four Seasons" by Shen Shih-ch'in)

Tao everlasting does not act,
And yet nothing is not done.
If kings and barons can abide by it,
The ten thousand things will transform by themselves.[22]

Note here that even rulers, "kings and barons," must learn the art of *wu-wei,* the moral relevance of which becomes especially evident in diplomacy. The art of ruling lies in the absence of aggressively imposing rule. According to the *Tao Te Ching,* the genuine ruler must be a sage, a paradigm of virtue. The sage acts as a model for morality because he lives by the principle of *wu-wei.* The following poem poignantly describes the sage-ruler's *wu-wei* conduct:

Win the world by doing nothing.
How do I know this?

Through this: —
    The more prohibitions there are, the poorer the people become.
The more sharp weapons there are,
    The greater the chaos in the state.
The more skills of technique,
    The more cunning things are produced.
The greater the number of statues,
    The greater the number of thieves and brigands.

Therefore the Sage says:
    I do nothing and the people are reformed of themselves.
    I love quietude and the people are righteous of themselves.
    I deal in no business and the people grow rich by themselves.
    I have no desires and the people are simple and honest by themselves.[23]

Thus the wise ruler is a paradigm of virtue who rules in the spirit of *wu-wei.* That is, he acts in accord with the Tao and is a model for his people, so that they too will grow to act in harmony with the Tao.

Indeed, this is an ideal state. It is also the moral ideal we should strive to achieve. Rather than meaning total inaction, *wu-wei* denotes action that is spontaneous and "appropriately" natural. In the same way, the "quietude" that the ruler seeks is not that of complete passivity or resignation. It is a letting-things-be according to their natural design.

Wu-wei and Detachment

When Wang Ch'ung-yang instructed his seven disciples (who eventually became immortals through cultivating the Tao and living selflessly), he never tired of emphasizing to them the critical need to rid themselves of all attachments. He continually reminded them that the root of ego, and the biggest obstacle to cultivating the Tao, lies in our human tendency to crave and desire. Craving and desire impede our ability to rediscover our original nature. He tells Ma Tan-yang and Sun Pu-erh:

> Everyone has original nature. We do not see it because it is often clouded by craving, desire, and evil thoughts. . . . We cannot see it because the ego has constructed a barrier. If we are able to dissolve the ego, then original nature, or the heart of the Tao, will emerge.[24]

How do we dissolve the ego? How do we get rid of craving? Wang's response echoes throughout the novel—by ridding ourselves of attachments. We need to cultivate our hearts so that our hearts become like a "still lake":

> Tame the heart [mind], and the intentions will not run wild. When the heart is emptied of desire, the cause of ill health will disappear. Cut the attachments externally, and the internal injuries will be healed. *Your heart should be clear and calm like a still lake reflecting the light of the moon.* If ripples appear on the water, then the image of the moon will be distorted and the Tao will never be realized in you.[25]

The heart as a "still lake"—therein lies the core meaning behind *wu-wei*. *Wu-wei* signifies a letting-go, taking-things-in-stride, allowing the natural course of things to occur without imposing our egos upon the situation. Thus practicing *wu-wei* is a necessary first step in "taming the heart," in cultivating the heart so that our hearts become like a "still lake."

The moral significance of *wu-wei* is now all the more clear. *Wu-wei* is not simply a spontaneous letting-go or letting-be. It also signifies a disinterested action, action that is free from the ego, action that is not driven by self-interest. In fact, the true spirit of detachment can come about only through *wu-wei*.

For instance, as we saw in our opening episode, Sun Pu-erh's chief character flaw was her attachment to her intellect. This prevented her from understanding the meaning behind Wang's message to her during his visitations. His message was that yang and yin must coexist in balance so that intellect and intuition are in harmony. Only in this way could she cultivate her heart and in turn cultivate the Tao. Yet she suffered from an excess of yang in that she was attached to her intellect and reason. Letting-go of these required *wu-wei,* which she finally realized after listening to her husband.

After that she devoted herself entirely to Wang's teachings. And to demonstrate her complete spirit of detachment, she even disfigured her face and sacrificed her physical beauty so that she would not herself be the object of desire. In this way, Sun Pu-erh went to extreme (perhaps even bizarre) lengths to show her total detachment.

For that matter, every one of Master Wang's seven disciples encountered trials for which they had to practice *wu-wei* and let go of their egos. Master Wang himself had once lived in abundant material comfort and security, enjoying elevated social prestige in his village. He gave up these advantages, letting go of any attachment he may have had to them in order to follow and learn from the two immortals disguised as beggars.

One of Wang's disciples, Ch'iu Ch'ang-ch'un, was even willing to sacrifice his own life to save another. In order to cultivate the Tao through practicing selflessness, he built a small hut by a river ford and made it his business to carry people across the river on his back, requesting nothing in return. On one stormy day, he was asked to carry three police captains across the river. They had just killed a wicked bandit and were bringing his head to the magistrate to be displayed. He carried the first two policemen across without any problem. However, the third captain slipped off Ch'iu's shoulders and fell into the water, and the bundle that contained the head was carried away by the torrent. Yet Ch'iu managed to pull the man to safety and brought him across. However, this man was distraught, saying "My life may have been saved for the time being, but the bundle with the bandit's head was swept away when I fell. If I do not present evidence to the magistrate that the bandit has been killed, I shall be beheaded." Ch'iu then offered his own head in place of the bandit's in order to save the captain's life. At that point, the three captains were transformed into the Lords of the Three Seasons and Keepers of Heaven, Earth, and Water. Moved by his willingness to sacrifice his own life, they assured him that he would himself one day become an immortal.[26]

A classic account of the importance of detachment is that of the famous ninth-century immortal, Lu Yan, more popularly known as Lu Dongbin (Cavernguest Lu). To this day, he continues to be venerated among Chinese. When Lu Yan was born, a patriarch sensed the child's exceptional destiny and proclaimed, "This child's bones are of no ordinary mortal. Extraordinary in character, he will hold aloof from worldly affairs."[27]

The turning point in his life came about when he met a Taoist priest, Master Cloudchamber. As they waited for a meal at an inn, Lu Yan fell asleep and had the most astonishing dream—a dream in which he accomplished all sorts of worldly success and acquired a vast sum of wealth. Yet in this same dream, all this wealth, power, and prestige worked to corrupt him. That was not all:

> Then suddenly, without warning, he was accused of a grave crime. His home and all his possessions were confiscated, his wife and children separated. He himself, a solitary outcast, was wandering toward his place of banishment beyond the mountains. He found his horse brought to a standstill in a snowstorm and was no longer able to continue the journey.[28]

At that point, Lu Yan awoke from his dream. To his astonishment, Master Cloudchamber knew of his dream. He then said to Lu Yan:

> In the dream that just came to you . . . you not only scaled the dizziest heights of splendor but also plumbed the uttermost depths of misery. Fifty years were

past and gone in the twinkling of an eye. *What you gained was not worth rejoic-ing over, what you lost was not worth grieving about. Only when people have a great awakening, they know that the world is but one big dream.*[29] [italics mine]

In the following reading, Master Cloudchamber then subjects Lu Yan (Lu Dongbin) to ten tests in order to ascertain his "inner stature." Each of the tests illustrates the critical weight given to detachment.

Lu Dongbin

LU DONGBIN IS TESTED

Master Cloudchamber duly subjected him to ten tests of his immortal stamina.

The first of these occurred when Dongbin returned home after a long journey to find his entire family dead from a mortal sickness. There was no feeling of vain sorrow in his heart. Instead he manfully set about making lavish preparations for the funeral, when—lo and behold!—they all rose up alive and well.

The second time Dongbin was put on trial he had sold some copper ware to a dealer who soon wanted to return the merchandise and asked for his money back. They sought out the market inspector, and Dongbin handed over the required sum without any ado. Another day, he was nego-tiating the sale of some of his belongings and had come to a definite agree-ment about the price. This notwithstanding, the dealer wished to cancel the bargain and pay only half the stipulated sum. Dongbin acquiesced and, handing over the goods, walked away without anger or engaging in dispute.

The third ordeal took place at the time of the New Year. As Dong-bin was leaving his house he was accosted by a beggar demanding alms. He handed over all he carried, cash and gifts in kind. But the beggar remained dissatisfied and threateningly demanded more, using the most abusive terms. Yet Dongbin kept a smiling face and again and again apol-ogized to him politely.

The fourth time he was put to the test, he was looking after some sheep in the mountains. A hungry tiger came upon them, with the result that the flock scattered in all directions. Dongbin interposed his own person between the tiger and the terrified sheep. The tiger gave up the chase and crept away.

In his fifth ordeal he had retired to a simple thatched hut in the mountains to study. One day a beautiful lady came to his door, graceful and lovely and radiant with such unearthly beauty that she was positively dazzling. She explained she was a newly married bride on the way to visit her parents but had become lost. Would he allow her to rest a short while in his hut? Dongbin granted her request. She then tried in a hundred different ways to snare him from the path of virtue, but he remained steadfast and unmoved to the end.

Dongbin's character was put to a test the sixth time when, on returning home from a walk in the country, he found that during his absence thieves had carried away all his goods and chattels, leaving the house bare. Not even then was his equanimity disturbed. He just set himself to earn a livelihood by tilling the ground. One day when at work with his hoe he unearthed gold pieces to the number of several score. Yet he took not a single one, but quickly covered them all up again.

In his seventh trial he again met Master Cloudchamber who told him, "In obedience to the summons of the Celestial Emperor, I am on the way to present myself before his throne. If you behave virtuously during your abode among humankind, thus acquiring merit, you will in time reach a place similar to mine."

"My aim," Dongbin replied with another deep bow, "is not to emulate you, sir, but to bring salvation to every living creature in this world. Only when this vow of mine has been fulfilled shall I ascend on high."

The eighth ordeal occurred when he bought some potent drugs from a crazy Taoist, who used to wander about selling them in the streets. He claimed that whoever partook of his wares would instantly die, but would attain the Tao in a future existence.

As Dongbin was about to buy the drug, the Taoist warned him, "The only thing for you to do now is to make speedy preparation for your death."

Yet Dongbin swallowed the stuff without batting an eyelid, and no harm befell him.

The ninth test Dongbin had to pass came in the spring when the entire country was flooded. Together with the rest of the local population, he was seeking safety in boats. Just as they reached the middle of the waters, a violent storm burst upon them. The waves rose high, lashed into fury by the wind. All were in a panic except Dongbin, who remained erect in his seat, calm and unconcerned.

On the tenth occasion, Dongbin was sitting alone in his house, when without warning there appeared to him an innumerable host of demons in weird and terrifying shapes, all seemingly determined to beat him to death. Yet he was not in the least afraid or dismayed. Then a sharp word of command came from the sky, and the whole crowd of devils vanished.

The voice was followed by a person who, descending from above, clapped his hands and laughed with delight. It was Master Cloudchamber.

"I have subjected you to ten tests," he said, "all of which have left you utterly unmoved. There can be no doubt you will succeed in attaining the Tao.

We see here the critical link between detachment and *wu-wei*. Developing the attitude of *wu-wei* is a necessary condition for detachment. Let us illustrate *wu-wei* further with ideas that are not from a Taoist text. Nevertheless, these ideas demonstrate how the principle behind *wu-wei* is made manifest in other Chinese traditions.

Seneca

To see a man fearless in danger,
Untainted by lust,
Happy in adversity,
Composed in turmoil,
And laughing at all those things
    which are either coveted or feared by others—
All men must acknowledge,
    that this can be nothing else but a beam of divinity animating a human body.

From Seneca, in Charles David, *Greek and Roman Stoicism* (Boston: Herbert B. Turner, 1903), p. 226.

To Subdue the Enemy Without Fighting

The forces of Wu and Ch'u were about to engage in a ferocious battle. Just before the clash, the general of the Wu armies lined up three thousand of his prisoners and criminals in front of his troops and in full view of the enemy. He then ordered all of them to cut their own throats. At the sight of this terrifying spectacle, the Ch'u forces retreated.[30]

Even if this account stretches the historical facts, one fact is clear. During the Warring States Period, warfare acquired a new type of savagery—it abandoned the earlier, more ritualistic codes of conduct that accompanied war. Cast aside were rules of honor and valor, such as the one-on-one duel between the most outstanding warriors as a prelude to battle. Abandoned was the unwritten rule that warfare was forbidden during certain seasons and special occasions, such as the period of mourning for deceased military and political leaders. Furthermore, it had been considered most dishonorable to attack cities and civilians, and forms of deceit against the enemy were viewed as vulgar.[31] After 500 B.C.E., however, all this changed, and warfare became brutish in all respects, violating former codes. There was a clear need to reinstate some semblance of order even into this most bitter of human conflicts. And to meet this need, Sun Tzu put together his *Art of War,* the first systematic exposition and manual of war.

Let us be clear. Sun Tzu was not a Taoist. Nevertheless, part of his treatise does seem to have a Taoist flavor. Namely, the most decisive factors in warfare have less to do with brute force and aggression, and more to do with the dispositions of the participants. Sun Tzu, therefore, proposed that knowledge properly applied along with a suitable moral disposition constitutes correct strategy.

In his opening chapter, Sun Tzu declares the five most necessary factors in waging a successful campaign:

> The first of these factors is moral influence [Tao]; the second, weather; the third, terrain; the fourth, command; and the fifth, doctrine.[32]

Note here that the translator added "Tao" to "moral influence." This suggests that the successful general must act in a way that is in accord with the Tao, and by doing so he exerts the necessary "moral influence" that will help to ensure victory. As Sun Tzu states:

> By moral influence I mean that which causes the people to be in harmony with their leaders, so that they will accompany them in life and unto death without fear of mortal peril.[33]

Sun Tzu further suggests another meaning behind "moral influence": *We ought not to pursue victory in war at any cost.* The leader with moral fiber will not permit the aim of victory to justify *any means whatsoever to achieve it.* And here we face the perennial question in ethics: *Does the end justify the means?* Underlying Sun Tzu's masterpiece in strategy is a critical premise— there is no clear-cut distinction between ends and means. That is, the means used to achieve an end have a way of affecting the quality of that same end. In fact, Sun Tzu's entire treatise is an exposition of what he considers to be the most appropriate avenues to reach the aim of victory.

In which case, we need to be more clear about the meaning of "victory." In what sense is victory the ultimate objective in war? According to Sun Tzu:

1. Generally in war the best policy is to take a state intact; to ruin it is inferior to this.
2. To capture the enemy's army is better than to destroy it; to take intact a battalion, a company or a five-man squad is better than to destroy them.

3. For to win one hundred victories in one hundred battles is not the acme of skill. *To subdue the enemy without fighting is the acme of skill.*

4. *Thus, what is of supreme importance in war is to attack the enemy's strategy.*[34] [italics mine]

Thus, true victory requires moral fiber in leadership as well as proper knowledge of climate and terrain. And it especially demands both knowing oneself and knowing one's enemy:

31. Therefore I say: Know the enemy and know yourself; in a hundred battles you will never be in peril.

32. When you are ignorant of the enemy but know yourself, your chances of winning or losing are equal.

33. If ignorant both of your enemy and of yourself, you are certain in every battle to be in peril.[35]

Given this, what more is needed "to subdue the enemy without fighting"? Though Sun Tzu is not a Taoist and does not use the term *wu-wei,* we can still detect in his work the idea behind *wu-wei,* a flexible and adaptable kind of yielding. For instance, the general must learn to yield a short-term benefit in order to gain a more permanent advantage. Moreover, Sun Tzu describes the ideal army by using the metaphor of water:

Now an army may be likened to water, for just as flowing water avoids the heights and hastens to the lowlands, so an army avoids strengths and strikes weaknesses.
And as water shapes its flow in accordance with the ground, so an army manages its victory in accordance with the situation of the enemy.
And as water has no constant form, there are in war no constant conditions.[36]

Such a strategy tells us that yielding (*wu-wei*) involves giving way to the strengths of the enemy and not assailing his strengths head-on. Strength against strength turns into a matter of sheer force and could bring about defeat, and this strategy certainly violates *wu-wei,* just as it would be unnatural for water to assault rock without accommodating itself to its form. The smart opponent refrains from directly confronting his adversary's strength. Instead, he patiently probes for, discovers, and then swiftly attacks his foe's weakness. And knowing the physical as well as mental terrain of the enemy is critical, so that one never allows himself to be lured into battle on the enemy's territory. Furthermore, the shrewd opponent lets go of consistent patterns. Predictability leads to defeat.

Subduing the enemy without resorting to arms further entails attacking the enemy's strategy rather than directly attacking the enemy: "The supreme excellence in war is to attack the enemy's plans," and as a result, "those skilled in war subdue the enemy's army without battle."[37] This, therefore, means being, as is water, adaptable enough to circumstances so that one can let go of fixation on one sole tactic. To illustrate, the military historian Li Ch'üan reports the following actual event:

> In the Later Han the Marquis of Tsan, Tsang Kung, surrounded the "Yao" rebels at Yüan Wu, but during a succession of months was unable to take the city. His officers and men were ill and covered with ulcers. The King of Tung Hai spoke to Tsang Kung, saying: "Now you have massed troops and encircled the enemy, who is determined to fight to the death. *This is no strategy!* You should lift the siege. Let them know that an escape route is open and they will flee and disperse. Then any village constable will be able to capture them!" Tsang Kung followed this advice and took Yüan Wu.[38]

Water is also able to overcome through persistence. Its steady flow is, in the long run, more powerful than a temporary outburst. In the same way, developing moral fiber requires maintaining a steady disposition. The display of unrestrained emotion, such as rage, could result in unnecessary harm. In a confrontation, such a display also glaringly trumpets a weak spot, which the astute and steady opponent will immediately recognize and attack. Sun Tzu warns:

> If the general is unable to control his impatience and orders his troops to swarm up the wall like ants, one-third of them will be killed without taking the city. Such is the calamity of these attacks.[39]

The ninth-century poet, Tu Mu, comments on this same passage with an historic anecdote:

> In the later Wei, the Emperor T'ai Wu led one hundred thousand troops to attack the Sung general Tsang Chih at Yu T'ai. The Emperor first asked Tsang Chih for some wine. [The exchange of gifts was a usual "preliminary to battle."] Tsang Chih sealed up a pot full of urine and sent it to him. T'ai Wu was transported with rage and immediately attacked the city, ordering his troops to scale the walls and engage in close combat. Corpses piled up to the top of the walls and after thirty days of this the dead exceeded half his force.[40]

T'ai Wu's uncontrolled rage was his undoing. He allowed his emotions to become extreme enough to enslave him, rather than simply accepting his feelings at face value and then letting them go. The message for us is clear: In a similar way, when faced with conflict and having to make a moral decision, we cannot afford to let our emotions get the better of us.

SPONTANEITY AS AWARENESS

The *Chuang Tzu* is indeed one of the most eccentric texts among the Chinese classics. While the *Chuang Tzu* contains a wealth of explicit expressions of

Tao, *te,* and *wu-wei,* it raises further issues, such as the relativity of aesthetic standards for determining beautiful and ugly:

> Men claim that Mao-ch'iang and Lady Li were beautiful, but if fish saw them they would dive to the bottom of the stream, if birds saw them they would fly away, and if deer saw them they would break into a run. Of these four, which knows how to fix the standard of beauty for the world?[41]

Yet don't be fooled by the apparently whimsical nature of this and many other passages. Underneath his wit, the author is deadly serious. Chuang Tzu's lessons are profound and penetrating. They involve freeing ourselves from those fixed and absolute standards that we, individually and collectively, have imposed upon ourselves. Indeed, this has sober implications. Thus, while we visit with Chuang Tzu, we are cautioned: Cast off our preconceptions about what is and is not, what should be and should not be, what we ought to do and ought not to do.

Spontaneity is an important idea in the *Chuang Tzu.* And within the work's context, what does spontaneity mean? For us, the term may conjure up images of behaving in a way that is impulsive, instinctive, and even irrational. Within the framework of the *Chuang Tzu,* however, it assumes a rather different interpretation: It means acting in harmony with our true natures and thereby acting in accord with the Tao by observing our *te.*

The Clear Mirror

A prime metaphor for spontaneity is the mirror. Note the following depiction of the ideal person:

> Embody to the fullest what has no end and wander where there is no trail. Hold on to all you have received from Heaven but do not think you have gotten anything. Be empty, that is all. The Perfect Man uses his mind like a mirror— going after nothing, welcoming nothing, responding but not storing. Therefore he can win over things and not hurt himself [them].[42]

The mirror simply reflects whatever comes before it. It reflects in a way that does not interpret, evaluate, measure, or judge. It simply reflects, always attentive. And it reflects in a way that is completely impartial; it does not highlight any particular object over any other.

Observe that the perfect person "uses his *mind* like a mirror" [italics mine]. This is called clear-mindedness. The mind is "empty" in the sense of having abandoned any attachment to a fixed point of view. And here we see its moral relevance. The mirror-mind does not assume any one privileged perspective or position. It therefore requires that we transcend self-interests in our pursuit of the most balanced ethical choice. Of course, we can never be absolutely impartial since we see events through our own eyes and filter them through our own minds. Nonetheless, we cannot presume that any one posture possesses a monopoly on moral truth. We therefore need to be as impartial as we possibly can. In this way, the clear mind acts spontaneously by being constantly attentive in the most lucid, impartial fashion.

Furthermore, the clear mind as mirror does not allow the dust of emotions to smear the mirror. It was T'ai Wu's blind rage that brought about needless carnage and his eventual downfall in battle. Clear-mindedness and spontaneity entail the absence or suppression of emotions so that we do not allow ourselves to be overcome and enslaved by our emotions. In a conversation between Hui Tzu and Chuang Tzu on the matter of emotions, Hui Tzu wonders how it is even possible for a person to be without feelings. Chuang Tzu responds:

> That's not what I mean by feelings. When I talk about feelings, I mean that a man *doesn't allow good or bad to get in and do him harm.* He just lets things be the way they are and doesn't try to help life along.[43] [italics mine]

The mirror-mind reflects all objects brought before it. Yet, just as the mirror impartially reflects objects, the mirror-mind also manages to remain free from becoming fixed and dominated by emotions.

Maurice Merleau-Ponty, *The Visible and the Invisible*

The visible about us seems to rest in itself. It is as though our vision were formed in the heart of the visible, or as though there were between it and us an intimacy as close as between the sea and the strand. And yet it is not possible that we blend into it, nor that it passes into us, for then the vision would vanish at the moment of formation, by disappearance of the seer or of the visible. What there is then are not things first identical with themselves, which would then offer themselves to the seer, nor is there a seer who is first empty and who, afterward, would open himself to them—but something to which we could not be closer than by palpating it with our look, things we could not dream of seeing "all naked" because the gaze itself envelops them, clothes them with its own flesh.

Maurice Merleau-Ponty, *The Visible and the Invisible*, ed. Claude Lefort, trans. Alphonso Lingis (Evanston, IL: Northwestern University Press, 1968), pp. 130–31.

This way of the mirror symbolizes spontaneity. Yet this is immensely difficult to accomplish and indicates all the more the radical nature of the message of spontaneity in the *Chuang Tzu*. At least on an attitudinal level, we need to make our minds more fully aware and attentive—aware of the "whole picture" and attentive to our own biases so that we do not project them onto our understanding.

The Wheelwright and the Cook

The renowned scholar A.C. Graham gives us one of the clearest explanations of the idea of spontaneity in the *Chuang Tzu*. He prefers to think of spontaneity as "awareness" in the most unaffected sense.[44] Furthermore, for Graham, "the Taoist ideal is a spontaneity disciplined by awareness of the objective."[45] Note the critical ingredients: *discipline, awareness,* and *objectivity*. A disciplined spontaneity resists a total lack of restraint.

The key lies in awareness. Genuine awareness is an awareness that is comprehensive, and therefore not marred by impulse or subjectivity. It is not riveted to any one standpoint as absolute. The principle of spontaneity, inspiring us to pursue our *te* and to be in accord with the Tao, simply means that we "respond with full awareness (of what is objectively so)."[46] As an example, the *Chuang Tzu* describes a wheelwright who responds naturally in the course of chiseling a wheel:

> Chisel the wheel too slow and it slides and does not grip, too fast and it jams and will not enter. Not too slow, not too fast; you feel it in the hand and respond from the heart, the mouth cannot say it, there is a knack in it somewhere which I cannot convey to my own son, which my own son cannot get from me.[47]

Here is a perfect example of "spontaneity disciplined by awareness of the objective." The training and discipline that go into chiseling a wheel are in total harmony with the wheelwright's full awareness. And the objective is perfectly clear: to make a good, strong, durable wheel. The wheelwright cannot afford to lose sight of his objective as he responds naturally to the surface of the wheel.

The same can be said for other crafts. Cook Ting was famous for his ability to carve meat, and everyone complimented his exceptional skills. But he claimed that his talent involved more than skill:

> What I care about is the Way, which goes beyond skill. When I first began cutting up oxen, all I could see was the ox itself. After three years I no longer saw the whole ox. And now—now I go at it by spirit and don't look with my eyes. Perception and understanding have come to a stop and spirit moves where it wants. I go along with the natural makeup, strike in the big hollows, guide the knife through the big openings, and follow things as they are. So I never touch the smallest ligament or tendon, much less a main joint.[48]

Cook Ting enjoys the true spirit of spontaneity, "disciplined by awareness of the objective." He does not lose sight of his purpose, and because of his discipline, he can transcend technique in order to allow his movement to respond naturally to the shape of each ox.

All of this is important because the *Chuang Tzu* is sometimes criticized for encouraging an extreme form of moral relativism, that is, for advocating the absence of any moral standards. What the *Chuang Tzu* teaches us is that in order to live according to the Tao, we need to respect the principle of spontaneity, a "spontaneity disciplined by awareness of the objective." We should not remain fixed on any one viewpoint. In fact (although this is not suggested by Chuang Tzu), we need to acquire the ability to perceive the matter from various perspectives.

In contrast to moral relativism, the *Chuang Tzu* and, for that matter, all of Taoism pose an ultimate standard—the standard of the Tao. In the final analysis, we must discipline ourselves to act in harmony with the Tao. This means acquiring the habit of spontaneity, or full awareness. Indeed, abandoning our customary attachment to one specific standpoint, almost always our own, is no easy task. Nevertheless, in the *Chuang Tzu,* this is our radical challenge, so that whatever we decide to do will be morally sound only if our decision and action do not derive from a fixed and rigid point of view. As Graham states,

> Whether the considerations that move me are prudential or moral, my whole understanding of the world . . . requires that in thought and imagination I am constantly shifting between and responding from different viewpoints, remembered or anticipated, individual or collective, my own or another's.[49]

FASTING OF THE MIND

Nan-jung Chu was alone when he visited Lao Tzu, intending to ask the revered sage about some personal concerns. However, when Lao Tzu saw him, he immediately asked his visitor, "Why did you come with all this crowd of people?" When Nan-jung Chu looked behind him to see who else was there, he saw no one.[50] What and where was this "crowd"? Nan-jung Chu carried within himself a crowd of preconceptions, ideas, and biases. This was his "crowd of people," the invisible throng by which his mind has become fixed. And this was the crowd from whom he must first free himself before he can learn from the sage.[51]

Here the *Chuang Tzu's* admonition against a fixation upon points of view is further described as a "fasting of the mind." Whereas a fasting of the body means forgoing food, a fasting of the mind requires abstaining from a self-centered attitude. It is, thereby, a deep-seated basis for a moral outlook. Moral action can begin only when we are able to go beyond the circle of self-interests. Thus our fundamental prescription for acting ethically demands transcending ego. It requires acting selflessly.

This prescription for selfless action is nowhere more apparent than in the Ten Precepts and Twelve Vows called the *Chishu yujue* ("Red Writings and Jade Instructions"), cited later. These precepts and vows indicate specific duties along the path toward cultivating the Tao. They specify concrete ways of directing moral conscience. Moreover, not only is the Taoist urged to cultivate the Tao for himself or herself, but to guide others along the way.

CHISHU YUJUE
(RED WRITINGS AND JADE INSTRUCTIONS)

The Ten Precepts

1. [2b] Don't harbor hatred or jealousy in your heart! Don't give rise to dark thieving thoughts! Be reserved in speech and wary of transgressions! Keep your thoughts on the Divine Law!

2. Maintain a kind heart and do not kill! Have pity for and support all living beings! Be compassionate and loving! Broadly reach out to bring universal redemption to all!

3. Maintain purity and be withdrawing in your social interactions! Be neither lascivious nor thieving, but constantly harbor good thoughts! Always take from yourself to aid others!

4. Don't set your mind on sex or give rise to passions! Be not licentious in your heart but remain pure and behave prudently! Make sure your actions are without blemish or stain!

5. Don't utter bad words! Don't use flowery and ornate language! Be straightforward within and without! Don't commit excesses of speech!

6. Don't take liquor! Moderate your behavior! Regulate and harmonize your energy and inner nature! Don't let your spirit be diminished! Don't commit any of the myriad evils!

7. Don't be envious if others are better than yourself! Don't contend for achievement and fame! [3a] Be retiring and modest in all things! Put yourself behind to serve the salvation of others!

8. Don't criticize or debate the scriptures and teachings! Don't revile or slander the saintly texts! Venerate the Divine Law with all your heart! Always act as if you were face to face with the gods!

9. Don't create disturbance through verbal argumentation! Don't criticize any believers, be they monks, nuns, male or female laity, or even heavenly beings! Remember, all censure and hate diminishes your spirit and energy!

10. Be equanimous and of whole heart in all of your actions! Make sure that all exchanges between humankind and the gods are proper and respectful!

The Twelve Vows

1. [3b] I will study the perfected scriptures that set forth the Divine Law and open the liberation and salvation of all. I will bring forth a strong determination of the Tao. I vow to rise to the status of a great sage in my lives to come.

2. I will constantly practice compassion. I vow that all will learn of the Divine Law and that salvation will extend universally, without hindrance or distortion.

3. I will delight in the scriptures and teachings. I will study them widely to let my understanding deepen and to make my determination firm and enlightened. I will liberate and transform all those in ignorance and darkness.

4. I will respectfully receive the instructions of my teacher. I will spread the wonderful teachings far and wide so that all living beings might enter the gate of the Divine Law and forever depart from their paths of blindness.

5. I will cause my faith to extend to the heights of mystery and wonder. I will venerate and honor the teachings and moral injunctions. I will recite the scriptures morning and night without being lazy or remiss.

6. I will not labor for glory and fancy ornaments but break the chain of worldly causations. I will maintain a steadfast heart and resolved determination, so that all I undertake will be within the Divine Law.

7. I will diligently recite the great scriptures. I vow that all beings shall find the bridge of release and that all future life will enjoy good karma.

8. I will always maintain a mind of friendliness, free from all perverseness or falsity. I will remain without envy and ill-will, without evil and jealousy.

9. I will represent the sages in all situations where things are given life. I will pass on the teachings of the Numinous Treasure uninterrupted and without lapse.

10. [4a] I will purify my body and keep the precepts. I will observe the fasts and establish merit. Thereby I will lead the myriad beings to salvation and complete liberation.

11. I will read broadly in my studies and deeply penetrate the law contained in the scriptures. Thus I will prepare the way for heavenly beings to save all.

12. I will be with an enlightened teacher life after life. I will receive the teachings and spread them so that innumerable living beings may be saved.

In another account of the *Seven Taoist Masters,* Ch'iu Ch'ang-ch'un sacrificed all sorts of material comfort to follow and learn from Master Wang. Nevertheless, his biggest character flaw was his restlessness and impatience to learn. He once visited a fortune teller who, by reading his face, told Ch'iu that he would die from hunger. Distraught, he believed that he needed to submissively resign himself to his pronounced destiny. However, impatient to acquiesce to this destiny, he became thoroughly consumed by the idea of dying from starvation to the point of contemplating suicide. Entirely despondent and obsessed with dying, he begged for enough coins to purchase a chain. With this chain, he climbed a tree and tied one end of the chain around his neck and looped the other end around a branch, ready to jump. At this point, a heavenly being, the Lord of the star T'ai-pai, assumed the guise of an herb gatherer who suddenly appeared under the tree. The account continues:

SEVEN TAOIST MASTERS

The herb gatherer called out to Ch'iu Ch'ang-ch'un, "Why are you trying to end your life? What have you done to deserve this ending?" Annoyed, Ch'iu Ch'ang-ch'un looked down and said, "What I do is none of your business." The herb gatherer said, "I am a follower of the Tao, and the life and death of sentient beings is my business. The Tao values the life of all things. Why don't you tell me why you wish to take your own life?" Ch'iu Ch'ang-ch'un said, "All right, I'll tell why I need to die. Some time ago I met a fortune-teller who told me that I was destined to die of hunger and that I should never attain enlightenment in this lifetime. My two attempts at starvation have failed. That is why I came here to hang myself. I wish to end my life now before anybody else interferes." The herb gatherer said, "So you wanted to die after listening to one man's words. Maybe another man's words will bring you back to your senses. Your mind is invaded by monsters, and your wisdom is clouded. Your folly has not only almost taken your life but also ruined your chances of becoming an immortal in this lifetime. Listen to what I have to say, and the monsters who have captured your mind will leave you." The herb gatherer sat down, motioned Ch'iu Ch'ang-ch'un to sit beside him, and said, "The lines of destiny written on your face are not true indicators of your destiny. For the true face is not your physical face but the face of your mind. And it is on the face of your mind that true destiny is written. Therefore, when the fortune-tellers say that a person has a kind disposition or a cruel disposition written on his or her face, they are merely referring to a minor determinant of destiny. The major determinant of destiny is in the heart. If a cruel heart is tamed, or a kind heart becomes cruel, the external features will change. Therefore, the facial appearance is merely an indicator of the destiny written on the internal face, which is your heart. Our destiny is determined by our own actions. People who were initially destined to die peacefully may end their lives in violence if they do evil deeds. People who were initially destined to die a violent death may die peacefully if they perform good deeds. Our destiny is in our own hands. Those who could not escape death by starvation were people who had hoarded grain, pillaged storage houses, or refused to alleviate famine. Retribution was inescapable. But as for you, you are supposed to be trained in the path of the Tao and yet you fell into the clutches of external forms and let your attachment to appearance ruin you. As a Taoist adept, you should know that immortality is within the reach of everyone and that it is up to our own efforts to make it a reality. You should know that it is not the 'destiny' written on your face that determines whether you will achieve enlightenment but the effort that you make."

The herb gatherer's words hit Ch'iu Ch'ang-ch'un like cold water. He felt as if he had been jolted out of a bad dream. Everything now made sense. He thought to himself, "How stupid of me! How could I have been so blind! From now on I shall throw off my preoccupation with death. I shall complete my training and attain the Tao."

From *Seven Taoist Masters: A Folk Tale of China,* translated by Eva Wong, © 1990. Reprinted by arrangement with Shambhala Publications, Inc., Boston.

Here we see that Ch'iu Ch'ang-ch'un was fixed upon his destiny, unaware that destiny itself is not really something that is immutable: "The major determinant of destiny is in the heart. . . . Our destiny is determined by our own actions." Therefore, we continually create our own destinies by what we do and by how we live. Only by learning the hard way, sinking into the depths of despondency, and by finally listening to the herb gatherer's message did Ch'iu realize the lesson behind fasting his mind.[52]

Fasting the mind means relaxing the mind so that no single perspective—like Ch'iu's unchanging destiny—is exaggerated at the expense of all others. Similar in spirit to *wu-wei,* this fasting of the mind is ultimately a letting-go of ego, the source of self-centeredness in which private interests maintain an absolute point of reference.

Consider the zookeeper who, about to feed his monkeys, explained to them that they would receive three acorns in the morning and four later in the evening. At this the monkeys were angry. So he placated them. He informed them that they would instead receive four acorns in the morning and three in the evening. Then they were satisfied.[53] In reality, there is no essential difference between both proposals. From the monkeys' standpoint, however, there is a vast difference. This is because they are fixed on a specific perspective   that of the morning. They lack the ability to shift between standpoints, what the *Chuang Tzu* calls "walking two roads."[54] They cannot permit their minds to fast.

This tale recalls one of the most familiar passages in the Chuang Tzu:

> Once Chuang Chou [Chuang Tzu] dreamt he was a butterfly, a butterfly flitting and fluttering around, happy with himself and doing as he pleased. He didn't know he was Chuang Chou. Suddenly he woke up and there he was, solid and unmistakable Chuang Chou. But he didn't know if he was Chuang Chou who had dreamt he was a butterfly, or a butterfly dreaming he was Chuang Chou. Between Chuang Chou and a butterfly there must be *some* distinction! This is called the Transformation of Things.[55]

Surely, on the level of action and daily behavior, it makes sense for Chuang Tzu to presume he is actually Chuang Tzu now that he is awake. Yet, at the same time, he is able to entertain a various set of viewpoints and to shift among them, not allowing himself to be stunted by attaching himself to one. This is what is meant by the fasting of the mind.

Fasting of the mind involves our capacity to realize that there are other viewpoints. Fasting of the mind allows us to become more spontaneous in the sense of becoming more fully aware of the whole picture. This is especially critical in making moral judgments, particularly as we recognize the real complexities within many moral conflicts. We will now see how we can further foster this awareness through the attitude of acceptance, an extraordinarily vital value in Taoist thought.

Acceptance and the Dream of the Skull

Without a doubt, acceptance, such as an acceptance of the uncertainties in life, is an indispensable disposition. It is a supreme ingredient in cultivating a proper attitude as a basis for sound moral character. Acceptance does not mean resignation or fatalism. It is close in meaning to *wu-wei,* a yielding, a letting-be, and a letting-go. As such it leads to a "true happiness."[56] It is an acceptance that induces a singular "purity" and "peace" through coming to terms with life: "The inaction [*wu-wei* as acceptance] of Heaven is its purity, the inaction of earth is its peace."[57] Thus, acceptance is not a passive but instead an active acceptance: "So I say, Heaven and earth do nothing and there is nothing that is not done."[58]

Marcus Aurelius, *Meditations*

With food and drinks and cunning magic arts/ Turning the channel's course to 'scape from death;/ The breeze which heaven has sent/ We must endure, and toil without complaining.

It is in thy power to live free from all compulsion in the greatest tranquility of mind, even if all the world cry out against thee as much as they choose, and even if wild beasts tear in pieces the members of this kneaded matter which has grown around thee. For what hinders the mind in the midst of all this from maintaining itself in tranquility, and in a just judgement of all surrounding things, and in a ready use of the objects which are presented to it, so that the judgement may say to the thing which falls under its observation: This thou art in substance [reality] though in men's opinion thou mayest appear to be of a different kind; and the use shall say to that which falls under the hand: Thou art the thing that I was seeking; for to me that which presents itself is always a material for virtue, both rational and political, and, in a word, for the exercise of art, which belongs to man and God. . . .

The perfection of moral character consists in this, in passing every day as the last, and in being neither violently excited, nor torpid, nor playing the hypocrite.

From *Meditations of Marcus Aurelius,* trans. George Long (Mount Vernon, NY: Peter Pauper Press, n.d.), VII, pp. 51, 68, 69, 106, 112, 113.

A decisive indicator of acceptance pertains to our attitudes toward death. There is a fictional account of how, when Chuang Tzu's wife had died, Hui Tzu visited Chuang Tzu to offer his respects. However, he was shocked when he found Chuang Tzu singing and playing music instead of grieving. Chuang Tzu explained to his friend that at first he naturally mourned for her and expressed his grief. But in time he also became aware that her death belonged to the nature of all things. Chuang Tzu declared:

> In the midst of the jumble of wonder and mystery a change took place and she had a spirit. Another change and she had a body. Another change and she was born. Now there's been another change and she's dead. It's just like the progression of the four seasons, spring, summer, fall, and winter.
> Now she's going to lie down peacefully in a vast room. If I were to follow after her bawling and sobbing, it would show that I don't understand anything about fate. So I stopped.[59]

It is crucial to keep in mind that this Taoist acceptance does not at all mean resignation or giving up. In this context, it demands that we *acknowledge* the nature of things and that we *embrace* the profound truth of our mortality in order to come to terms with it.

Michel De Montaigne, *Essays*

[T]his very felicity of our life, which depends upon the tranquility and contentment of a wellborn spirit and upon the resolution and assurance of a well-ordered soul, ought never to be attributed to any man until he has been seen to play the last, and doubtless the hardest, act of his comedy. There may be disguise in all the rest: either these fine philosophical discourses are only for the sake of appearance, or circumstances, not testing us to the quick, give us leisure to keep our countenance always calm. But in this last scene between death and ourselves there is no more counterfeiting. . . .

That is why all the actions of our life ought to be tried and tested by this last act. It is the master-day, it is the day that is judge of all the rest, "it is the day," says one of the ancients, "that must judge all my past years." To death do I refer the test of the fruit of all my studies. We shall then see whether my reasonings come only from my mouth or from my heart. . . .

In judging the life of another, I always observe how the end was borne; and one of the principal concerns of my own life is that the end be borne well, that is, calmly and insensibly.

From *Montaigne: Selected Essays,* trans. Charles Cotton, ed. W. Hazlitt (New York: Modern Library, 1949), pp. 11–13.

Acceptance also entails a fasting of the mind since it compels us to free ourselves from our own fixed, inflexible viewpoint, our false consciousness. Hui Tzu would have judged Chuang Tzu's outrageous actions to be immoral if Hui Tzu's viewpoint was defined solely by the customary Confucian mourning rituals.

This fixed standpoint can also be illustrated by the extreme vitalist belief that views death as the worst evil, so that staying alive at all costs is the highest good. In another story, while journeying to Ch'u, Chuang Tzu stumbles across an old skull on the road. He picks it up, closely studies it, and addresses it:

Sir, were you greedy for life and forgetful of reason, and so came to this? Was your state overthrown and did you bow beneath the ax and so came to this? Did you do some evil deed and were you ashamed to bring disgrace upon your parents and family, and so came to this? Was it through the pangs of cold and hunger that you came to this? Or did your springs and autumns pile up until they brought you to this?[60]

Here Chuang Tzu commiserates over the person's fate. Later on at night, he uses the skull as a pillow and falls asleep.

In the middle of the night, the skull came to him in a dream and said, "You chatter like a rhetorician and all your words betray the entanglements of a living man. The dead know nothing of these! Would you like to hear a lecture on the dead?"

"Indeed," said Chuang Tzu.

The skull said, "Among the dead there are no rulers above, no subjects below, and no chores of the four seasons. With nothing to do, our springs and autumns are as endless as heaven and earth. A king facing south on his throne could have no more happiness than this!"

Chuang Tzu couldn't believe this and said, "If I got the Arbiter of Fate to give you a body again, make you some bones and flesh, return you to your parents and family and your old home and friends, you would want that, wouldn't you?"

The skull frowned severely, wrinkling up its brow. "Why would I throw away more happiness than that of a king on a throne and take on the troubles of a human being again?" it said.[61]

In summary, all of these notions—spontaneity, fasting of the mind, and acceptance—are intricately interwoven. They are all features that form the basis for good character by living in harmony with the Tao and with the natural course of things. This constitutes the secret of living, the mastery of life:

He who has mastered the true nature of life does not labor over what life cannot do. He who has mastered the true nature of fate does not labor over what knowledge cannot change.[62]

This is called living "without entanglements."[63] This is true freedom, an emancipation from attachments and from self-centeredness.

Thus, cultivating the Tao in all of the ways previously shown underscores the need to live a life of balance. The secret of living lies in balance and in avoiding the extremes. T'ien K'ai-chih tried to explain this secret to Duke Wei of Chou by alluding to Shan Pao. Shan Pao lived as a hermit and fasted, drinking only water. He lived this way for seventy years until one day he was eaten by a tiger: "Shan Pao looked after what was on the inside and the tiger ate up his outside."[64] Although Shan Pao sought to develop his inner state, he neglected his physical needs.

On the other hand, Chang Yi lived the life of a profligate, constantly seeking material pleasure and gain. After living in this manner for forty years, he eventually died of a fever: "Chang Yi looked after what was on the outside and the sickness attacked him from the inside."[65] Chang Yi may have achieved material prosperity, but he did so by sacrificing interior well-being. The secret of living lies in being in accord with the Tao, and this ultimately means following a path of balance.

REVIEW QUESTIONS

1. Similar questions regarding whether or not there is a Zen ethic can be raised concerning Taoist ethics. In what respect can we consider Taoism to be a sort of ethic? What does it mean to claim that it possesses an "ethos"?

2. According to the immortal's teachings to Wang in the *Seven Taoist Masters,* what does it mean to cultivate our heart? How does this connect with cultivating the Tao?

3. What are the moral implications of sustaining our *ch'i?* In what way is this striking a balance?

4. *Wu-wei* is a crucial Taoist teaching. How does practicing *wu-wei* enable us to live more selflessly?

5. How does Lu Dongbin display detachment and *wu-wei* through each of his trials?

6. How can we subdue the enemy without fighting? In a deeper sense, who, or what, is our true enemy? What is the moral lesson in all this?

7. How is spontaneity a sort of awareness? Where is the balance in this?

8. What is the moral lesson that the herb-gatherer teaches Ch'iu? How does this story portray a "fasting of mind"?

9. In his dream, what moral lessons did Chuang Tzu learn from the skull?

10. What lessons can we learn from Taoism in order to live better lives?

NOTES

1. Eva Wong, trans., *Seven Taoist Masters: A Folk Tale of China* (Boston: Shambhala, 1990), p. 47. All excerpts © 1990. Reprinted by arrangement with Shambhala Publications, Inc., Boston.

2. Ibid., p. 49.

3. Ibid., pp. 51–52.

4. Originally used for purposes of divination, the *I Ching* relies upon an intricate reading of combinations of solid and broken lines fashioned into sixty-four hexagrams, each symbolizing various features of transformation within the cosmos.

5. Although Chuang Tzu may have contributed to the work, it appears to be the result of a number of different authors, put together at different periods.

6. Ellen M. Chen, trans., *The Tao Te Ching: A New Translation with Commentary* (New York: Paragon House, 1989), Ch. 1, 2, p. 51.

7. Ambiguities within the constructs of the Chinese language, different from Western languages which generally show a straightforward syntax and sentence structure, make this work all the more resistant to systematic analysis. The Chinese language particularly stresses the significance of contexts which provide the decisive clue as to the character's meaning.

8. Chen, Tao Te Ching, Ch. 25, cited in Daniel Bonevac and Stephen Phillips, eds., *Understanding Non-Western Philosophy* (Mountain View, CA: Mayfield Publishing Company, 1993), p. 268.

9. Chad Hansen, "Language in the Heart-mind," in Robert E. Allinson, ed., *Understanding the Chinese Mind: The Philosophical Roots* (Oxford: Oxford University Press, 1989), p. 84.

10. Here is where there are variations on this same moral theme on the part of Confucians and Taoists. As we uncover in the next chapter, Confucians predominately highlight *proper human interaction* within the human community as the right path to harmony with the Tao. This is consistent with their view of the Tao as the integrating principle of societal existence. On the other hand, Taoists construe the Tao as the supreme principle of the entire cosmos, of which the human community is but one aspect. Taoists therefore emphasize more of a harmony with the natural world.

11. Lin Yutang, trans., *The Wisdom of Laotse* (New York: Random House, Modern Library, 1948), Ch. 10, p. 83.

12. Ibid., Ch. 55, p. 252.

13. Arthur Waley, trans., *The Way and Its Power: A Study of the Tao Te Ching and Its Place in Chinese Thought* (New York: Grove Press, Evergreen Edition, 1958), Ch. LVII, p. 211.

14. Wong, *Seven Taoist Masters*, p. 5.

15. Chen, *Tao Te Ching*, Ch. 51, p. 175.

16. Waley, *The Way and Its Power*, Ch. XXI, p. 170.

17. Lin, *The Wisdom of Laotse*, Ch. 25, pp. 145–46.

18. In Arthur Kleinman, *The Illness Narratives: Suffering, Healing, and the Human Condition* (New York: Basic Books, 1988), pp. 100–10.

19. See the discussion in Manfred Porkert and Christian Ullmann, *Chinese Medicine*, trans. by Mark Howson (New York: Henry Holt, 1982), pp. 241–42.

20. Howard Reid and Michael Croucher, *The Way of the Warrior: The Paradox of the Martial Arts* (Woodstock, NY: The Overlook Press, 1983, 1995), pp. 107f.

21. Waley, *The Way and Its Power,* LXXVIII, p. 238.

22. Chen, *Tao Te Ching,* Ch. 37 cited in Bonevac and Phillips, *Understanding Non-Western Philosophy,* p. 269.

23. Lin, *The Wisdom of Laotse,* Ch. 57, pp. 265–66.

24. Wong, *Seven Taoist Masters,* p. 41.

25. Ibid., pp. 43–44.

26. Ibid., pp. 142–43.

27. From *Zengxian liexian zhuan* ("Illustrated Immortals' Biographies"), in Livia Kohn, *The Taoist Experience: An Anthology* (Albany: State University of New York Press, 1993), p. 127.

28. Ibid., p. 129.

29. Ibid.

30. Samuel B. Griffith, trans., *Sun Tzu: The Art of War* (London: Oxford University Press, Clarendon, 1963), p. 33. Griffith comments that, most likely, the criminals charged head-first into the enemy and were the first to die.

31. See discussion in ibid., pp. 30f.

32. Ibid., I,3, p. 63.

33. Ibid., I,4, p. 64.

34. Ibid., III, 1–4, p. 77.

35. Ibid., III, 31–33, p. 84.

36. Ibid., VI, 27–29, p. 101.

37. Ibid., p. 78, and III, 10, p. 79.

38. Ibid., p. 79.

39. Ibid., III, 9, pp. 78–79.

40. Ibid., p. 79.

41. Burton Watson, trans., *Chuang Tzu: Basic Writings* (New York: Columbia University Press, 1964), p. 41. All excerpts © 1964 Columbia University Press. Reprinted with the permission of the publisher.

42. Ibid., pp. 94–95. One reviewer pointed out that the term "himself" was a mistranslation by Watson.

43. Ibid., p. 72.

44. See A.C. Graham, *Taoist Spontaneity and the Dichotomy of "Is" and "Ought,"* in Victor H. Mair, ed., *Experimental Essays on Chuang-tzu* (Hawaii: University of Hawaii Press, 1983), pp. 3–23.

45. Ibid., p. 11.

46. Ibid.

47. From the Chuang Tzu, Ch. 36, v. 13, in Graham, p. 8.

48. Watson, Chuang Tzu, pp. 46–47.

49. Graham, "Taoist Spontaneity," p. 16. See discussion pp. 13–22.

50. Watson, Chuang Tzu, p. 4.

51. Ibid.
52. This lesson about destiny and action was something Ch'iu at least intellectually comprehended since he had previously instructed robbers about the meaning of karma and karmic retribution. Due to his advice to the robbers, they changed their ways.
53. Watson, Chuang Tzu, p. 36.
54. Ibid.
55. Ibid., p. 45.
56. Ibid., p. 112.
57. Ibid.
58. Ibid.
59. Ibid., p. 113.
60. Ibid., p. 114.
61. Ibid., pp. 114–115.
62. Ibid., p. 118.
63. Ibid.
64. Ibid., p. 123.
65. Ibid.

FIVE

Confucian Ethics

On an early snowy morning in December 1702, forty-six samurai of the late Lord Asano Naganori stole into a heavily guarded castle and assassinated its owner, Lord Kira Yoshinaka. They immediately carried his head to Sengakuji, the Buddhist temple where Asano was buried. To appease Asano's soul, they washed the head and offered it before his grave. In this way, they vindicated his death.

Two years earlier, Asano had been ordered by the ruling Tokugawa clan's strong-armed military government, the Bakufu, to commit *seppuku,* or ritual disembowelment, for boldly drawing his sword and injuring Kira inside Shogun Tsunayoshi's castle in Edo. Kira incited this reaction by first insulting Asano, yet he himself suffered no penalty. In the eyes of Asano's samurai, or retainers, justice was not fairly meted out. And from that time on, they secretly resolved to avenge their lord in due time.

After paying homage at the temple, they surrendered themselves to the authorities without a struggle. Following their detention, lasting nearly two years, all 46 *ronin,* or "masterless" samurai, were finally sentenced to commit *seppuku,* and their remains were buried at Sengakuji. To this day, their gravesite continues to be a place of visitation and veneration by countless Japanese.

News of the assassination of Kira sent shock waves among the people, most of whom approved the deed as fitting compensation for Asano's unjust execution. Moreover, they admired the *ronin* for their consummate loyalty to their lord, and for embodying the supreme virtue of duty in Bushido, the Code of the Warrior. However, among the official Confucian scholars who acted as consultants to the Bakufu in matters of law and morality, there was less consensus. The *ronin*'s vendetta stirred up heated debate. The law had been violated— that much was clear. Yet not all of the advisors denounced the *ronin*'s actions. According to Confucian teachings, loyalty to one's minister or lord was one of the highest virtues. And the *ronin*'s loyalty to Asano was an extension of the

Confucian virtue of filial piety, of showing respect to parents and other family members. Nevertheless, the *ronin* still breached the law, and it was urged that out of respect for the law, the law should prevail. Hence, the burning question: What would constitute a just penalty in dealing with these perpetrators?

And here enters Ogyū Sorai, one of the most influential Confucian scholars during the Tokugawa period. His own view of the affair was unique. Although the *ronin* displayed the Confucian and Bushido virtues of loyalty and duty, their act of vengeance was a private matter and conflicted with the public welfare. The settlement of private matters should not be permitted to jeopardize the well-being of the public as represented through its laws. In stating his case, Ogyū Sorai emphasized another vital Confucian idea: The good of the public overrides private interests. He therefore endorsed the execution of the *ronin*. At the same time, he opposed their execution by decapitation, the penalty for common criminals. Instead, in light of their sincere allegiance to the Confucian virtues of loyalty and filial piety along with the Bushido value of duty, he counseled that the *ronin* be allowed to die honorably as samurai, by their own hands through *seppuku*.

Remarkably, for centuries after their death, arguments pertaining to the proper interpretation and application of Confucian teachings persisted. Indeed, the whole affair attests to the far-reaching influence of Confucian thought before, during, and after the 200 years of Tokugawa rule. It also revealed the ascendancy and dominance of Confucian ethics outside of its birthplace in China. In fact, the *ronin*'s story produced an indelible imprint upon the Japanese literary imagination as expressed in its drama and Kabuki (traditional Japanese theater). Before we explore the principal motifs in Confucian ethics, which have permeated China, Korea, Japan, and other Asian countries, let us first travel lightly and take a brief historical and philosophical tour of the development of Confucian thought, a way of life that remains a monumental force in Asian values.

BACKGROUND

Confucianism took its first breath during electrifying times. The end of the Chou dynasty (1111–249 B.C.E.) was encountering such extreme social and political turmoil that it has been dubbed the Warring States Period (403–221 B.C.E.). To counter this unrest, eminent philosophers discussed and debated matters of morality, law, and human nature, sometimes even engaging in bitterly intense disputes. Confucians reproached Taoists for avoiding social responsibilities. Mohists rebuked Confucians for exaggerating the importance of ritual. Legalists criticized Confucians for their trust in the goodness of human nature. There was certainly enough fuel for debate: questions surrounding the role of law, the responsibilities of rulers, the relationship between the way of Heaven and the way of Earth, the essential character of human nature, and so on. This period of the "Hundred Schools" was no doubt intellectually passionate, and the schools that consequently prevailed—Confucian, Taoist, and Yin-Yang—generated a profound and permanent influence upon Chinese history and culture.

Confucius, Mencius, and Hsün Tzu

Chinese tradition credits Confucius (originally K'ung Fu Tzu, or Master K'ung, 551–479 B.C.E.) as its greatest teacher, yet his students are the ones responsible for recording his teachings in masterful works: the *Analects,* the *Great Learning,* and the *Doctrine of the Mean.* A durable cord binds them together: human-centeredness, a radical departure from the earlier Shang dynasty (1751–1112 B.C.E.) worldview underscoring spiritual forces.

Confucius' powerful humanism is apparent when he maintains that law is only meaningful if it sustains societal well-being. And his most penetrating articulation of humanism lies in his lifelong concern with moral cultivation and excellence. He asks, What standards determine moral character? How can we become a *chün-tzu,* a "superior person" of moral quality? Here, Confucius uncompromisingly sets strict standards: Moral excellence demands a proper balance of inner integrity and outer behavior. As his student Tsang comments:

> The doctrine of our master is to be true to the principles of our nature and the benevolent exercise of them to others—this and nothing more.[1]

How can we achieve this balance? Confucius' response is unmistakable—*through the practice of virtue.* And virtues have remained the heart of Confucian ethics for nearly 2,500 years. The supreme virtue of *jen,* meaning "humaneness" and "benevolence," enkindles the interrelated values of filial piety, respect, and loyalty. These are values that have helped to shape the vigorous collective and communal spirit of the Chinese. Another virtue is *li,* the exercise of propriety, good manners, and conduct. *Li* is the outward expression of *jen* and acts as the glue that connects the diverse elements within a society. It also means fulfilling our specific familial and social roles, what Confucius calls the "rectification of names." He spares no words in applying this especially to rulers and insists that rulers must be sages, embodying the virtue of *jen.* Only by being a *chün-tzu* can a ruler render service to his people in the right spirit. By his radical claim that the ruler must be a paragon of virtue, Confucius sets in motion the imperative notion of moral government. Moreover, he astounds the nobility all the more when he urges that education and moral cultivation be provided for all social classes and not solely for the elite.

Confucius' teachings survived especially through the labors of subsequent philosophers such as Mencius (Meng-tzu, c. 372–c. 298 B.C.E.) and Hsüntzu (c. 313–238 B.C.E.). Since we will later look more closely at their ethical teachings, here it is enough to acknowledge that Mencius clearly credited human nature as being inherently good, and therefore having the capacity for moral cultivation. Hsün-tzu, on the other hand, strongly disagreed, convinced that human nature was essentially corrupt. Indeed, as we will soon see, he apparently persuaded his most celebrated admirer, Han Fei Tzu, to agree. Despite this gulf in their views of human nature, Mencius and Hsün-tzu still managed to preserve Confucius' emphasis upon the need for moral cultivation through the practice of virtue, particularly the virtues of *jen* and *li*.

Challenges: Mo Tzu and Han Fei Tzu

Outstanding philosophies never grow in a vacuum. They mature in dialectical tension with other ideas. Throughout their history, Confucius' teachings faced constant challenges and reinterpretations. Early on, the most significant contender was Mo Tzu (c. 479–381 B.C.E.). He and his later school of Mohists severely chastised the Confucian emphasis upon ritual. For example, he heaped considerable scorn on the Confucians for squandering time and money on lavish funerals, money that could be better spent on the living. Mo Tzu was bluntly utilitarian in disposition. Beliefs and behavior were worthwhile only if they contributed to the overall benefit of society. In this spirit, he condemned warfare because in the long run it was detrimental to public welfare.[2]

His most lofty proposition was that of universal love (*chien ai*), meaning we ought to love everyone as an equal. Certainly Confucius espoused love, but on its own merit and on the basis of *jen*. But Mo Tzu encouraged universal love since it would more likely produce positive consequences for most people. This utilitarianism became especially militant when he upheld the belief in a supreme God who monitors human activity by rewarding the good and punishing the bad. Though this was different from the prevailing Confucian belief in the power of fate as an impersonal force, it was a powerful enough incentive to practice universal love.[3] Perhaps due to its harsh teachings, Mo Tzu's school survived for only a few centuries and was eventually overshadowed by the Confucians.

Another blistering challenge came from Han Fei Tzu (c. 280?–233 B.C.E.) and his Legalist school. Han Fei Tzu, influenced by Hsün Tzu, insisted, contrary to Confucius and Mencius, that our human natures are inherently corrupt, and therefore not inclined to practice virtue. Given this, he asks, Is it even possible to secure social and political order in this human jungle? He cautions us that such order is viable only through conscientious adherence to law rather than to virtue. Yet, if our natures are so depraved, how can we obey the law? Through strict and absolute rule. Han Fei Tzu argues that the ruler does not have to be a sage. Instead, he needs to deftly exert control with a heavy hand, using the "two handles" of reward and punishment. He states:

> These two handles are penalty and benevolence. What are penalty and benevolence? By penalty is meant capital punishment, and by benevolence is meant the

giving of rewards. Then subjects will stand in fear of punishment, and will receive benefit from reward.[4]

For Han Fei Tzu, this is the secret to governing: control through power and fear. These ideas helped spark the infamous Burning of the Books (213 B.C.E.) during the Ch'in dynasty in an attempt to stem the tide of teachings that could diminish the authority of the ruler. (Fortunately, many Confucian texts and teachings were put into hiding temporarily and survived.)

Neo-Confucianism

Confucianism evolved through further dialectical tension, as illustrated by the more syncretic type of Confucianism of Tung Chung-shu (176–104 B.C.E.), which incorporated Taoist and yin-yang elements. For instance, Tung Chung-shu's theory of correspondence depicted an astonishingly literal correlation between human conduct and the activity of Heaven, so that moral and immoral human behavior affects Nature. And, participating in a growing trend to divinize Confucius, he even raised the "Master" to the status of a spiritual ruler who mirrored Heaven's will.

Meanwhile, the rising popularity of Taoist and Buddhist teachings provoked other Confucians to reexamine primary Confucian texts, particularly the *Great Learning,* the *Doctrine of the Mean,* and the *Book of Changes.* In effect, it was the exegetical study of these books that rescued Confucian thought from syncretism and obscurity, and these same texts became the leading works spearheading the renewal of Confucianism in the movement known as Neo-Confucianism.

This revival of Confucian teachings centered on the fundamental notion of *li,* or "principle," which explains why the movement has also been called the "learning of nature and principle." *Li,* originally meaning "pattern or order," later referred to the principle for moral conduct. Now, in the minds of Neo-Confucians, *li* assumed a more metaphysical character and meant the hidden principle or essence in all things. Two other pivotal ideas were *T'ai-chi,* the Great Ultimate or source of principle, and *ch'i,* the material force that is a manifestation of *li.*

Two illustrious brothers stand out as precursors to this revival: Ch'eng Yi (1033–1108) and Ch'eng Hao (1032–1085). They both agreed that *li* is the same as *t'ien-li,* the Heavenly Principle, and therefore they identified Nature with the Heavenly Principle. And the principle, *li,* is intrinsically good, and therefore human nature is innately good since human nature embodies the principle. In this way, they embraced Mencius' postulate concerning the inborn goodness of human nature. Nevertheless, they disagreed as to the means to moral cultivation. Ch'eng Yi insisted on understanding *li,* or principle, through serious study and investigation of outward sources such as history and texts. Ch'eng Hao called for a more interior approach through self-examination in order to keep our minds pure as a "polished mirror."

These two helped pave the way for Chu Hsi (1130–1200), indisputably the greatest Neo-Confucian philosopher. In fact, Chu Hsi's school (named the school of Principle) is also called the Cheng-Chu school, due to similarities between the Ch'eng brothers (particularly Ch'eng Yi) and Chu Hsi. Chu Hsi's legacy is sweeping. He creatively synthesized the various directions in Neo-Confucian thought and placed the spotlight squarely on the interactive relationship between *li* and *ch'i,* principle and material force. He was also the preeminent interpreter and commentator on the classics. For nearly six centuries, his commentaries on the four classics—the *Analects,* the *Great Learning,* the *Doctrine of the Mean,* and the *Book of Changes (Meng-tzu)*—set the standard for interpretation and were required reading on examinations for government positions. Moreover, his reach extended significantly into Korea and Japan.

Chu Hsi did face some fiery opposition, however. Lu Hsiang-shan (1139–1193) reproached Chu Hsi for separating principle from mind, and in a series of dramatic debates at Goose Lake Monastery in 1175, he claimed that mind is identical to principle. This meant that moral cultivation did not require the investigation of things but rather an inner awareness of our inherent nobility.

Wang Yang-ming (1472–1529) took this an explosive step further during the Ming dynasty (1368–1644). His school of Mind stung the Cheng-Chu school of Principle by insisting that the strict identity of mind and principle was faithful to the classic texts of Confucius and Meng-tzu (Mencius). He accused Chu Hsi of inaccurately promoting external investigation instead of an interior "rectification" of mind requiring sincerity of will. Furthermore, Wang stunned the intellectual world with his original notion of the identity of knowledge and action: Genuine knowledge will naturally express itself in action, and authentic action constitutes true knowledge.

Despite Wang Yang-ming's onslaught and temporary dominance in Chinese thought, Chu Hsi's teachings regained preeminence when China came under Manchu rule in 1644. Chu Hsi's school, however, came under further attack from another corner, led by Tai Chen (1723–1777) and his Empirical school, also known as the Return to the Han Learning school. Tai Chen denounced what he regarded as the excessively abstract quality of Neo-Confucian thought and tended to conceive of *li* in more practical and concrete terms. In any case, regardless of their differences, all these schools sought to revitalize the genuine message of Confucius and Mencius.

As the nineteenth and twentieth centuries witnessed the collapse of Manchu rule, the ascendancy of Western influence, and the formation of the Chinese Republic (1912), Confucianism stepped down as the official ideology. Yet its spirit still thrives. Through the efforts of contemporary philosophers such as Fung Yu-lan (1895–1990) and Wing-Tsit Chan (1901–1994), Confucian teachings persist as the basis for moral guidance, weathering the storms following the Communist victory in 1949 and Mao Tse-tung's (1894–1976) Cultural Revolution in the 1960s. There is even now a renewed interest in Chu Hsi and

Wang Yang-ming. Throughout China, the heart of Confucian ethics—the values of *jen,* filial piety and loyalty—continues to prevail.

Confucianism in Korea and Japan

Outside of China, Confucian teachings have had a spectacular influence, especially in Korea and Japan. They gradually penetrated Korea in the early centuries C.E. and acquired a dominant force during the powerful Yi dynasty (1392–1910). By then, several academies entirely devoted themselves to the study of Confucian classics. In fact, it was a Confucian scholar, Kim Pu-sik, who in the twelfth century wrote the first history of the Korean dynasties, *Samguk sagi* (*Historical Record of the Three Kingdoms*). The Ch'eng-Chu school of Neo-Confucianism became so prominent that the Yi dynasty, serving social and political ends, grounded its government upon the moral teachings of Confucius.

The renowned Neo-Confucian Yi Hwang (1501–1570), also known as T'oegye, embraced Chu Hsi's emphasis upon *li,* extended its generative priority, and used it as a basis for his ethics. In opposition, Yi I (1536–1584), whose pen name was Yulgok, shattered the emphasis upon *li*'s priority by declaring material force, *ch'i,* as the real basis for living ethically. Intense debates as to the primacy of either principle or material force spawned questions pertaining to the essence of human nature and to whether *li* or *ch'i* is the source of moral activity.

The influence of Wang Yang-ming and Tai Chen eventually gained more prominence toward the eighteenth century and helped groom Korea for modernization. Nevertheless, as in China, despite efforts to modernize, an enclave of devoted intellectuals preserved Confucian teachings through their scholarship and lifestyles. For instance, Ch'oe Ik-hyon (1833–1906), imprisoned for resisting Japanese occupation, died of self-imposed starvation on the grounds of Confucian beliefs. And today, Confucianism still plays a vital role in Korean thought.

As for Japan, early records credit a Korean, Wani, for introducing the *Analects* into Japan in the third century C.E. And the official policies of Prince Shōtoku Taishi (573–621) partly reflected Confucian influence. Chu Hsi's teachings (called Shushi in Japan), initially overshadowed by Zen Buddhism, eventually secured autonomy and special recognition during the Tokugawa rule (1600–1868). Indeed, advisors to the Tokugawa military government (Bakufu), such as Hayashi Razan (1583–1657) and other renowned figures such as Yamazaki Ansai (1618–1682), were Neo-Confucian scholars, thus dispensing official sanction to Chu Hsi's ideas, particularly regarding his ethics.

At the same time, as in both China and Korea, Chu Hsi's interpretations did not go unchallenged. The Ancient Learning school, Kogaku, struck the deepest cut by exhorting a reliance upon the original texts of Confucius and Mencius rather than on Chu Hsi's commentaries. The astute Yamaga Sokō (1622–1685) applied these original teachings in a way that inspired the austere

code of Bushido or Way of the Warrior. Bushido became the principal standard of morality for samurai and other Japanese. Perhaps the most important
representative of the Kogaku was Ogyū Sorai (1666–1728), whom we recall
was the Confucian who counseled the shogun as to the fate of the 46 *ronin* in
1702. He argued that the original spirit of Confucius' teachings placed the
highest value upon public welfare rather than private acts of righteousness.

The onset of the Meiji Restoration in 1868 witnessed the loosening of
Confucianism's grip as a sovereign set of beliefs. At this time, there came
about a rough blend of some Confucian ideas with Shinto, along with a growing exposure of these philosophies to both modern and Western ideas. At the
same time, Wang Yang-ming's influence, called Yōmeigaku, surpassed that of
Chu Hsi. Nonetheless, Confucian ideals did not concede to the tide of events.
Actually, the Confucian values of duty, loyalty, filial piety, and collective
harmony became so ingrained in Japanese attitudes that they were consequently viewed as values characteristic to Japanese. In this fashion, Confucian
traits maintain their secure hold among the Japanese to this day.

LESSONS FROM THE *ANALECTS*

Balancing Personal Integrity and Social Harmony

There is the following curious passage in the *Analects:*

> The duke of Sheh informed Confucius, saying, "Among us here there are those
> who may be styled upright in their conduct. If their father has stolen a sheep, they
> will bear witness to the fact."
> Confucius said, "Among us, in our part of the country, those who are upright are
> different from this. *The father conceals the misconduct of the son, and the son conceals
> the misconduct of the father. Uprightness is to be found in this.*"[5] [italics mine]

Confucius' example of "uprightness" or righteousness (*chih*) is puzzling
because it confounds our ordinary sense of duty. In hiding the truth about our
father's theft, would we not be accessories to breaking the law?

Perhaps we can solve the puzzle if we read this passage on at least two
levels. Literally, the son is obviously caught between the horns of duty and
natural desire, between doing his civic duty and protecting his father from arrest.
On a deeper level, what is also at stake here is family harmony and equilibrium.
Obedience to the law conflicts with the son's heartfelt need to avoid further
rupture within the family. Reporting his father would almost certainly bring
disharmony to the family so that, in this particular instance, Confucius sanctions
concealment. To begin with, it is intuitive and natural to desire to safeguard the
father, and this expression of the heart is the genuine meaning of the virtue of
chih. Second, in some cases family harmony assumes priority even over the law.

Confucius does not mean to establish this latter point as an a priori rule.

Instead, he brings our attention to how matters of expediency can sometimes be a real, practical consideration. In other words, we have here an obvious conflict between two basic values: obeying the law and preserving family harmony. If the matter is slight (as perhaps stealing a sheep in this case appears), then legality gives way to the greater value of harmony. In contrast, the Duke of Sheh defines "uprightness" differently: It means adhering inflexibly to a principle, in this case the law, regardless of the circumstances.

Plato, *Euthyphro*

In Plato's dramatic dialogue *Euthyphro,* the main character, Euthyphro, is on his way to court, about to accuse his own father of murdering a slave. Euthyphro insists he is justified in this because he knows the meaning of piety, or goodness. Socrates persists in learning from Euthyphro more about the source of this moral knowledge. At one point, Euthyphro claims that his act of accusing his father is vindicated by the gods since they are the source of moral authority. The dialogue continues as Socrates then asks:

s: [L]et us assume, if you wish, that all the gods consider this [the murder of the slave] unjust and that they all hate it. However, is this the correction we are making in our discussion, that what the gods hate is impious, and what they love is pious, and that what some gods love and others hate is neither or both? Is that how you now wish us to define piety and impiety?

E: [I] would certainly say that the pious is what all the gods love, and the opposite, what all the gods hate, is the impious.

s: Then let us again examine whether that is a sound statement, or do we let it pass, and if one of us, or someone else, merely says that something is so, do we accept that it is so? Or should we examine what the speaker means?

E: We must examine it, but I certainly think that this is now a fine statement.

s: We shall soon know better whether it is. Consider this: Is the pious loved by the gods because it is pious, or is it pious because it is loved by the gods?

From G.M.A. Grube, trans., *Plato: Five Dialogues* (Indianapolis, IN: Hackett, 1981), p. 14.

Is Confucius suggesting that family harmony always and uncompromisingly assumes priority? In a well-known incident, the brothers of the Duke of Chou take part in a conspiracy to depose the duke and usurp the dynasty.

Upon his brothers' arrest, the duke faces a difficult choice. Instead of pardoning his brothers, he has them executed because of the serious threat they posed to the dynasty. Now Confucius openly holds the duke in high esteem, and he cites this incident to illustrate the uprightness of the duke.[6] In this case, the duke chooses law over family harmony. The circumstances seriously jeopardize public well-being. The duke's actions reveal that public welfare takes precedence over filial piety.

Note that Confucius does not teach in a systematic style or formality with deductive and inductive arguments. And there is no clearly outstanding dogma that Confucian ethics presents. Yet the lack of formal analysis has its merits and conveys that the true business of morality is of concern to everyone, not simply to academics.

In any case, what do these parables in the *Analects* reveal about Confucian ethics? As a start, Confucius constantly underscores the supreme necessity of moral practice. Furthermore, this moral cultivation requires the exercise of virtue. Yet the practice of virtue is not a strictly individual affair but occurs within the context of a dynamic and mutually defining relationship between the individual and the community. The identity of the sheep-stealing father is inseparable from his communal identity as father and citizen, and the identity of his son is inseparable from that of his relationship with his father and the state. In Chinese culture and thought, one's self is a web of relationships, originating within the family and extending outward into the wider community. So, regarding the duke who is a ruler as well as a brother, his first responsibility in this instance is to his constituency even if it results in his brothers' deaths.

Throughout the *Analects* this individual-communal dynamic provides the backdrop for moral cultivation. The exercise of virtue entails maintaining the right balance between self and society. And the underlying standard for acquiring this is clear: Collective well-being takes precedence over self-interests. The two previous instances also demonstrate that the understanding of this standard is initially nurtured and enhanced within the family. For this reason, throughout Chinese history and culture, family harmony is bestowed the highest honor and is a critical means to achieve social order.

With respect to this social order, moral cultivation also occurs by working within the parameters of our social roles and in congruence with our specific duties. Confucius calls this the "rectification of names" (*cheng ming*), and it compels a conscientious association between titles (such as "emperor," "minister," "noble," "father," and "son") and their respective obligations. For example, if one assumes the task of governing, then clarification of what it means to truly "govern" is absolutely essential to the political order. Otherwise, societal and political breakdown would result.

Confucius supplies us with a model for moral perfection—the "superior person," or *chün-tzu*.[7] However, he shocked the establishment by recasting its literal meaning, "son of the ruler." The term originally depicted a person of noble birth, so that only the elite were born as *chün-tzu*, regardless of moral conduct. In contrast, Confucius describes the superior person as a person of

moral excellence, committed to a lifelong practice of virtue, regardless of birth
and social station. The "superior person" cultivates the essential balance of
internal and external, of individual disposition and communal need, and
persons in all classes were capable of becoming *chün-tzu.*

All of this energizes Confucius' spotlight upon the proper cultivation of
moral character. For Confucius, as for his Greek counterpart Socrates, cultivating a life of virtue is our most important imperative, even if it demands the
sacrifice of one's life:

> The Master said, "Neither the knight who has truly the heart of a knight nor the
> man of good stock who has the qualities that belong to good stock will ever seek
> life at the expense of Goodness; and it may be that he has to give his life in order
> to achieve Goodness."[8]

But this challenge is not purely a private matter. Moral cultivation can never
be a segregated, autonomous process, but only transpires within the context
of the symbiotic relationship between the individual and the communal. In a
similar way, as we now look more closely at some key virtues, note that they
do not operate in isolation. Instead, they are intimately interrelated and
together form the basis for moral excellence.

Confucian Virtues

Jen. Without a doubt, *jen* is the cornerstone of the Confucian virtues. As the
highest virtue, it sets the foundation for striking a proper balance in individual-communal values. Though its precise meaning eludes us, Confucius often
describes it in the general sense of "virtue." For instance, he differentiates the
wise from the virtuous:

> The Master said, "Those who are without virtue [*jen*] cannot abide long either
> in a condition of poverty and hardship, or in a condition of enjoyment. The virtu-
> ous rest in virtue; the wise desire virtue."[9]

He then follows this up by assigning active and agitated attributes to the wise,
as opposed to peaceful and stable qualities in the virtuous:

> The Master said, "The wise find pleasure in water; the virtuous [*jen*] find plea-
> sure in hills. The wise are active; the virtuous tranquil. The wise are joyful; the
> virtuous are long-lived."[10]

Perhaps the Chinese ideogram for *jen* can lend a clue to its meaning in
that it actually combines two characters: One refers to the "individual human,"
and the other depicts "two." This clearly conveys interrelationship, necessitat-
ing a transcending of purely individual interests. Individual pursuits should
not trump the welfare of the community. Indeed, because individual and

Confucius. (FPG International)

communal interests need to be in proper harmony, *jen* can be meaningfully applied only within the context of relationships.

Apart from this general sense of *jen* as virtue, are there more precise meanings we can attach to it? The *Analects* go on to describe *jen* with an assortment of terms, such as "humanity," "humaneness," "human-heartedness," "goodness," "compassion," and "benevolence." And although there is no one exact meaning, each attribute constitutes a particular path to moral excellence within the nexus of the individual-communal relationship. Virtue can manifest itself only within the context of the reciprocity between the individual and the community.

In a famous passage, Chung-kung, a devoted student of Confucius, directly asks his teacher about the meaning of *jen*:

Chung-kung asked about perfect virtue [*jen*]. The Master said, "It is, when you go abroad, to behave to every one as if you were receiving a great guest; to employ the people as if you were assisting at a great sacrifice; not to do to others as you would not wish done to yourself; to have no murmuring against you in the country, and none in the family."[11]

What a remarkable message! As a guest in another country, we ought to treat everyone as if they were OUR guests; when asking for assistance, BE an assistant—a clear reversal of roles. Here we have Confucius' famous Golden Rule: *Jen* compels us to place ourselves in the situation of others. It requires sensitivity to our fundamental relationality, beginning within our family and extending into our wider social matrix.

In another passage, Confucius describes the practice of *jen* by way of correct or proper speech, referring to the virtuous person as a person "of principle":

The Master said, "The virtuous will be sure to speak correctly, but those whose speech is good may not always be virtuous. Men of principle are sure to be bold, but those who are bold may not always be men of principle."[12]

Here, what is especially critical is that *jen* as an internal attitude will always manifest itself outwardly in right behavior. By the same token, the external act in and of itself does not warrant that the person who acts necessarily possesses *jen*. For instance, what appears to be a courageous act does not necessarily mean that the one who does the act is him- or herself courageous. The virtue of courage requires the inner attitude of *jen*.

At another point, Confucius condenses the meaning of *jen* into five explicit traits:

Tzu-chang asked Master K'ung [Confucius] about Goodness [*jen*]. Master K'ung said, "He who could put the Five into practice everywhere under Heaven would be Good." Tzu-chang begged to hear what these were. The Master said, "Courtesy, breadth, good faith, diligence and clemency."[13]

These traits describe how *jen* must be extended to all others. Fan Ch'ih also asked Confucius about the meaning of *jen* as benevolence, and he replied, "It is to love all men."[14] However, as a critical caveat, this is not the same as Mo Tzu's universal love, which urges us to love everyone *as an equal*. Confucius is well aware that relationships are structured upon specific hierarchical roles, and these roles demand the fulfillment of reciprocal duties. Nowhere is this pattern of hierarchy better illustrated than in the Five Relationships that encompass the fundamental contexts within which a moral community can evolve:

- Ruler and government official
- Father and son
- Husband and wife

- Elder brother and younger brother
- Friend and friend

The vital importance attached to these relationships signifies all the more the Confucian emphasis upon achieving the right balance between individual and community, leading to what one scholar calls a "fiduciary community."[15] They also invoke the revered principle of filial piety, perhaps the longest-running moral undercurrent throughout the Confucian legacy. Not only does filial piety characterize the respect that children must demonstrate toward their parents, but it also carries itself into the wider social realm.

Although the meaning of *jen* is elusive, Confucius manages to describe *jen* in concrete terms in specific contexts. In doing so, he demonstrates to us that moral cultivation is a practical matter, a lifestyle, and not a topic confined to abstract analysis. Ethics is more a matter of conduct than of theoretical discussion.

Li. *Jen* cannot operate alone. It needs external expression in the form of *li*. Indeed, *li* is the other side of *jen*. As an exterior gauge for measuring moral excellence, *li* possesses multiple meanings including propriety, etiquette, proper ritual, and good conduct. Yet, its sense is unmistakable. Broadly, *li* refers to acting with discretion and propriety, that is, decently and with good manners. More narrowly, *li* denotes precise social rules and codes of behavior contingent upon the situation, as described in the classic text *Li Chi* (*Book of Rites*), where *li* is expressed in a wide range of activities, such as offerings, marriages, festivals, and funerals, as well as in rules of conduct within the family and other relational settings. Yet all these outward actions can be virtuous only if they spring from inner sincerity and human-heartedness—from *jen:*

> The Master said, "A man who is not Good [does not have *jen*], what can he have to do with ritual? A man who is not Good, what can he have to do with music?[16]

Proper ritual and etiquette without the appropriate inner disposition are counterfeit. Confucius tells us that "Fine words and an insinuating appearance are seldom associated with true virtue."[17] *Jen* and *li* work together, and one without the other is empty and directionless. The Confucian scholar Anthony Cua describes this aspect in Confucian ethics:

> A moral action, on this view, can be *completely* described only in terms of the satisfaction of both the internal *jen* criterion and external *li* criterion. What is thus a single description of moral action is, to the Western eye, a duality of logically independent descriptions: a description of an action as conforming to a moral standard or rule, and a description of the *style* or manner of performance.[18]

Thus *li* is not simply a formalized act. In this way, Confucian ethics appraises the character of the person performing the act as well as the act itself.

Why is Confucius so concerned with proper ritual, etiquette, and propriety?

There are at least two basic reasons. First, they help to foster personal moral development through discipline and socially appropriate rules: "It is by the Rules of Propriety that the character is established."[19] Second, personal discipline and right conduct sustain communal harmony. For instance, at the conclusion of the *Analects,* Confucius describes propriety in terms of restraint in the manner in which one speaks. Thus proper speech leads to good relations with others:

> Without an acquaintance with the rules of Propriety, it is impossible for the character to be established. Without knowing the force of words, it is impossible to know men.[20]

Moreover, social harmony derives from the harmony that needs to be maintained within the family. The family is the starting point for nurturing a sense of *li.* An awareness of the paramount value of *li* begins first and foremost within the family, primarily through the observance of filial piety. In the following excerpt, Meng I Tzu is a prominent official who inquires into the meaning of filial piety. Confucius responds by way of a vague description of *li.* Afterwards, discussing the matter with his student, he then offers more specific advice on the duties entailed in *li:*

> Meng I Tzu asked about the treatment of parents. The Master said, "Never disobey!" When Fan Ch'ih was driving his carriage for him, the Master said, "Meng asked me about the treatment of parents and I said, 'Never disobey!' " Fan Ch'ih said, "In what sense did you mean it?" The Master said, "While they are alive, serve them according to ritual. When they die, bury them according to ritual and sacrifice to them according to ritual."[21]

Chih. Of the key Confucian virtues, *chih,* or uprightness, is perhaps the most understated. *Chih* requires personal fidelity to our true nature and genuine feelings. If we act in a way that is harmonious with our essential nature, we are straightforward and upright. One of the finest examples lies in our earlier parable about the sheep-stealing father and the son's expedient concealment in order to safeguard family harmony. For the son to do otherwise would be to act contrary to his genuine feelings. Fung Yu-lan's description of *chih* as the "direct expression of one's heart" is perceptively accurate because *chih* does not mean simply catering to momentary whims and feelings.[22] Fung then comments on the alleged uprightness claimed by the Duke of Sheh:

> [T]he son bore witness to the fact that his father had appropriated a sheep. In this case the son either wished to get the name of uprightness through sacrificing his father, or lacked feeling toward his father. Hence this could not be true uprightness.[23]

Simply put, *chih* compels us to be true to ourselves, which in turn requires that we connect with our genuine feelings. Therefore, we must not place undue weight on the opinions of others. For instance, consider Confucius' comment about the man who is extremely popular either because he is liked or disliked:

> Tzu-kung asked, saying, "What would you feel about a man who was loved by all his fellow-villagers?" The Master said, "That is not enough."
> "What would you feel about a man who was hated by all his fellow-villagers?" The Master said, "That is not enough. Best of all would be that the good people in his village loved him and the bad hated him."[24]

The fact that a person is liked by everyone does not certify that he is upright and virtuous. Nor does public hatred mean that the object of that hatred is necessarily immoral. Surely, it is precarious to rely solely upon popular opinion as a standard for evaluating someone else or oneself.

As with all other virtues, *chih* does not work in isolation. It is properly actualized only through the exercise of *li*. After all, being true to one's genuine feelings needs to be complemented by appropriate order, discipline, and restraint:

> The Master said, "Respectfulness, without the rules of propriety, becomes laborious bustle; carefulness, without the rules of propriety, becomes timidity; boldness, without the rules of propriety, becomes insubordination; straightforwardness [*chih*], without the rules of propriety, becomes rudeness."[25]

Living in uprightness is serious business, so serious that without it, human life and dignity lose their center. Confucius solemnly underscores this:

> The Master said, "Man is born for uprightness [*chih*]. If a man lose his uprightness, and yet live, his escape *from death* is the effect of mere good fortune."[26]

HUMAN NATURE: IS IT ESSENTIALLY GOOD OR CORRUPT?

Mencius and the Four Beginnings

Starting out as seeds. Suppose you see a child sitting on the edge of a well. Suddenly, the child stumbles and is about to fall into the well. What would be your immediate response? Would you not feel anxious and therefore exert every effort to prevent the child from falling? Would you not rescue the child if he does fall? Why would you feel this way? Not because you seek the praise of the child's family or the compliments of your neighbors. You would feel this way because it is the natural way for you to react. We instinctively feel distressed and concerned for the child's safety because we inherently possess the capacity for compassion.

So states Mencius, Confucius' esteemed proponent. He renders this example to portray his conviction that at birth we are endowed with four capacities, or "four beginnings," that affirm our humanity. His is surely a profoundly optimistic message—we are all born with a propensity for goodness in four interconnected ways. These four beginnings are in effect four seeds that, if properly nourished, can actualize into four major virtues: *jen* (benevolence), *i* (righteousness), *li* (propriety), and *chih* (wisdom). In his powerfully clear and succinct style, Mencius briefly describes these seeds:

> The feeling of commiseration is the beginning of human-heartedness (*jen*). The feeling of shame and dislike is the beginning of righteousness (*i*). The feeling of modesty and yielding is the beginning of propriety (*li*). The sense of right and wrong is the beginning of wisdom (*chih*). Man has these four beginnings just as he has his four limbs.[27]

Heaven sows these four seeds in us, and they give witness to our natural nobility and our capacity for moral excellence, for "all things are already complete in oneself."[28]

But what accounts for the fact that many of us are corrupt? Surely the existence of these four capacities does not guarantee their actualization. These four beginnings are literally the *beginnings* we all inherit. We are all potential sages (*sheng*), the Confucian paradigm of moral excellence. We have the seeds for "sageliness within and kingliness without," but these need to be nurtured. This demands not only that we cultivate these seeds within ourselves, but also that we recognize and help to foster them in others. However, this is no easy task. Our lives undergo all shades of circumstances that obscure our genuine nature. Mencius sketches an example in his elegant allegory of Bull Mountain.

Mencius

BULL MOUNTAIN

The Bull Mountain was once covered with lovely trees. But it is near the capital of a great State. People came with their axes and choppers; they cut the woods down, and the mountain has lost its beauty. Yet even so, the day air and the night air came to it, rain and dew moistened it till here and there fresh sprouts began to grow. But soon cattle and sheep came along and browsed on them, and in the end the mountain became gaunt and bare, as it is now. And seeing it thus gaunt and bare people imagine that it was woodless from the start. Now just as the natural state of the mountain was quite different from what now appears, so too in every man (little though they may be apparent) there assuredly were once feelings of decency and kindness; and if these good feelings are no longer there, it is that they have been tampered with, hewn down with axe and bill. As each day dawns they are assailed anew. What chance then has our nature, any more than that mountain, of keeping its beauty? To us, too, comes the air of day, the air of night. Just at dawn, indeed, we have for a moment and in a certain degree a mood in which our promptings and aversions come near to being such as are proper to men. But something is sure to happen before the morning is over, by which these better feelings are ruffled or destroyed. And in the end, when they have been ruffled again and again, the night air is no longer able to preserve them, and soon our feelings are as near as may be to those of beasts and birds; so that anyone might make the same mistake about us as about the mountain, and think that there was never any good in us from the very start. Yet assuredly our present state of feeling is not what we begin with. Truly,

> 'If rightly tended, no creature but thrives;
> If left untended, no creature but pines away.'

Confucius said:

> 'Hold fast to it and you can keep it,
> Let go, and it will stray.
> For its comings and goings it has no time nor tide;
> None knows where it will bide.'

Arthur Waley, *Three Ways of Thought in Ancient China* (London: George Allen & Unwin Ltd., 1939), pp. 116–17.

Mencius' prescription is clear: We must work to enrich our original natures, our four seeds, and this involves a lifelong, continual process of nourishing and sustaining.

The greatest of these four seeds lies in our potential for *jen.* Moreover, Mencius gives *jen* the added meaning of "compassion." Our natural compassion evokes our spontaneous reaction to the child at the well. *Jen* enables us to commiserate with the sufferings of others. If we lack compassion, we lack the heart of moral cultivation. It is compassion that compels children to perform humane and decorous burial rituals for their deceased parents. Along with Confucius, Mencius emphasizes the proper observance of mourning because it is the natural expression of *jen.*

Immanuel Kant, *Lectures on Ethics*

Not self-favour but self-esteem should be the principle of our duties towards ourselves. This means that our actions must be in keeping with the worth of man. . . . Moral self-esteem, however, which is grounded in the worth of humanity, should not be derived from comparison with others, but from comparison with the moral law. . . . Moral humility, regarded as the curbing of our self-conceit in face of the moral law, can thus never rest upon a comparison of ourselves with others, but with the moral law. . . . If we deprecate the value of human virtues we do harm, because if we deny good intentions to the man who lives aright, where is the difference between him and the evil-doer? Each of us feels that at some time or other we have done a good action from a good disposition and that we are capable of doing so again. Though our actions are all very imperfect, and though we can never hope that they will attain to the standard of the moral law, yet they may approach ever nearer and nearer to it.

From Immanuel Kant, "Proper Self-Respect" and "Duties to Others" in *Lectures on Ethics,* trans. Louis Enfield (New York: Harper & Row, 1973), in Christina Sommers and Fred Sommers, *Vice and Virtue in Everyday Life,* 4th ed. (New York: Harcourt Brace, 1985), pp. 532–35.

Nourishing the seeds: Filial piety. Now as to the personal formation of virtues within the communal matrix, what could be more fitting and natural than the context of the family? Mencius states definitively that the "root of the empire is in the state, and the root of the state is in the family."[29] The family, particularly the relationship between parents and children, sets the stage for generating the growth of these beginning seeds of virtue: "The substantiation of benevolence begins with service to one's parents."[30] The love and respect for our parents is thereby innate and constitutes filial piety, the indisputable ground and cornerstone of Chinese society. Not only is devotion and service to parents the basis of all other human relationships, but it also constitutes the most concrete expression of the moral character.

The *Classic of Filial Piety* remains a pivotal text throughout Chinese culture and admonishes the reader, "Therefore to be without love of parents and to love other men [in their place] means to be a 'rebel against virtue'; to be without reverence for parents and to reverence other men means to be a 'rebel against sacred customs.' "[31] Service and reverence to parents incorporate various obligations not only while they are alive but also after they have died. For example, the length of the mourning period is traditionally set at 25 months and has no equal in other cultures. It has entailed abstaining from sexual relations, special foods, wine, and music. The long-standing practice of ancestor reverence (rather than worship) epitomizes the core value of filial piety (*hsiao*). At the same time, filial piety is not merely the mechanical expression of duties. It must be genuinely accompanied by the proper spirit and attitude.

Filial piety is the ground for all other relationships within the family, such as the sacred bond between husband and wife. Traditionally, their relationship is primarily to sustain the inviolability of family and ancestral lines.[32] This, in turn, imposes a special set of obligations toward one's children as well as toward each other. Filial respect is also the substratum for the mutual respect that siblings must display to each other, and the relationship between older and younger is especially important.

Though filial respect is anchored in the family, it does not end there:

> Treat with reverence the elders in your own family, so that the elders in other families shall be similarly treated; treat with kindness the young in your own family, so that the young in other families shall be similarly treated.[33]

Filial piety extends beyond the family, and colors all kinds of social duties and relationships with friends, co-workers, employers, and ministers. For this reason, persons who displayed filial respect to their parents and within their families were regarded as better qualified for public office.

In addition, the conscientious practice of filial piety results in good, morally responsive government, the "Kingly Way" (*Wang Tao*). Since the king holds the highest position, he must embody moral perfection. He is not great through the rule of force nor through popularity, but through the rule of his moral character. For instance, in alluding to the popularity of Kung-sun Yen and others, considered by many to be great, Mencius asks:

> What reason is there . . . to call them great men? . . . He who is at home in the great house of the world, stands firm in the highest place of the world, walks in the great highways of the world, if successful, lets the people have the benefit of his success, if unsuccessful, practises the Way all alone; he whom riches and honours cannot corrupt nor poverty and obscurity divert, whom neither threats nor violence itself can bend—he it is that I call a great man.[34]

The king's compassion, or *jen,* will permeate his own talent for ruling and allow him to rule in a fair and humane fashion. Mencius certainly surprises the elite when he defies the long-standing feudal structure by exhorting both king and nobles to fairly distribute land among their people and to ensure their material security. He further admonishes nobles to see to it that the public is educated. He boldly declares that state land is public land, and therefore its harvest should benefit everyone. At the same time, he insists upon clear and strict divisions of labor and duties within the state, thus reinforcing Confucius' rectification of names.

Hsün Tzu: Corrupt Beginnings

"The nature of man is evil; the good which it shows is factitious."[35] Consider the case of brothers who must divide among themselves their fair allotment of money and property. Left to their own devices, the end result is bickering and strife:

> Now to love gain and desire to get;—this is the natural feeling of men. Suppose the case that there is an amount of property or money to be divided among brothers, and let this natural feeling to love gain and to desire to get come into play;—why, then the brothers will be opposing, and snatching from one another. ...Thus it is that if they act in accordance with their natural feelings, brothers will quarrel together.[36]

This is Hsün Tzu's dire message: Our natures (*hsing*) are fundamentally corrupt, and at birth we are predisposed to evil. We are innately so self-centered that we are consumed by our natural desire to experience pleasures and to avoid pain.

What a dramatic contrast from Mencius, who claims that our natures are good since they originate from Heaven, which embraces the principle of good! Hsün Tzu views Heaven differently. Heaven may be the source of our natures, but it lacks a principle of goodness and is construed in merely mechanistic terms. The strong pull of our natural desires confines us in the prison of ego, leading to destruction on individual and social levels.

Hsün Tzu

THAT THE NATURE IS EVIL

The nature of man is evil; the good which it shows is factitious. There belongs to it, even at his birth, the love of gain, and as actions are in accordance with this, contentions and robberies grow up, and self-denial and yielding to others are not to be found; there belong to it envy and dislike, and as actions are in accordance with these, violence and injuries spring up, and self-devotedness and faith are not to be found; there belong to it the desires of the ears and the eyes, leading to the love of sounds and beauty, and as the actions are in accordance with these, lewdness and disorder spring up, and righteousness and propriety, with their various orderly displays, are not to be found. It thus appears, that to follow man's nature and yield obedience to its feelings will assuredly conduct to contentions and robberies, to the violation of the duties belonging to every one's lot, and the confounding of all distinctions, till the issue will be in a state of savagism; and that there must be the influence of teachers and laws, and the guidance of propriety and righteousness, from which will spring self-denial, yielding to others, and an observance of the well-ordered regulations of conduct, till the issue will be a state of good government.—From all this it is plain that the nature of man is evil; the good which it shows is factitious.

Hsün Tzu, in James Legge, trans., *The Chinese Classics,* Vol. II, cited in Michael Brannigan, *The Pulse of Wisdom* (Belmont, CA: Wadsworth, 1995), p. 293.

Behold one of the most devastating descriptions of human nature in Chinese literature. Note that the last line of the translation reads, "From all this it is plain that the nature of man is evil; *the good which it shows is factitious*" [italics mine]. The key word "factitious" denotes that it is artificially produced, and therefore unnatural. Nevertheless, good CAN come about. It is not fictitious, unreal, or imaginary. Despite our corrupt beginnings, we can still practice moral cultivation and become good, even achieve moral excellence.

"The man in the street can become a Yü," Yü being the sage-ruler celebrated for his virtue.[37] Hsün Tzu agrees with Confucius and Mencius that the king's successor must also be a sage, possessing wisdom and discrimination. However, given our fundamental weakness, he adds another requirement: The sage, besides possessing wisdom and discrimination, must be strong and able to wield strict power:

It was on this account, that anciently the sage kings, understanding that man's nature was bad, in a state of deflection and insecurity, instead of being correct; in a state of rebellious disorder, instead of one of happy rule, set up therefore the majesty of princes and governors to awe it; and set forth propriety and righteousness to change it; and framed laws and statutes of correctness to rule it; and *devised severe punishments* to restrain it: so that its outgoings might be under the dominion of rule, and in accordance with what is good.[38] [italics mine]

Thomas Hobbes, *De Cive*

[T]he conqueror may by right compel the conquered, or the strongest the weaker . . . to give caution of his future obedience. For since the right of protecting ourselves according to our own wills, proceeded from our danger, and our danger from our equality, it is more consonant to reason, and more certain for our conservation, using the present advantage to secure ourselves by taking caution, than when they shall be full grown and strong, and got out of our power, to endeavour to recover that power again by doubtful fight. And on the other side, nothing can be thought more absurd, than by discharging whom you already have weak in your power, to make him at once both an enemy and a strong one. From whence we may understand likewise as a corollary in the natural state of men, that, *a sure and irresistible power confers the right of dominion and ruling over those who cannot resist;* insomuch, as the right of all things that can be done, adheres essentially and immediately unto this omnipotence hence arising.

From Thomas Hobbes, "Of the State of Men without Civil Society," in *De Cive* (1642) in Christina Sommers and Fred Sommers, *Vice and Virtue in Everyday Life,* 4th ed. (New York: Harcourt Brace, 1985), pp. 470–71.

Yet as strict and absolute as a ruler's authority may be, it is still limited. It cannot be solely left up to the king-sage to enforce morality. And if we cannot be forced to be moral, then how can we become moral? Hsün Tzu responds: Only by transcending our natures. But how do we transcend our natures, especially since our desires are so powerful?

Challenged by the frequently irresistible power of our natural desires, moral cultivation is still possible because we have the use of reason and intellect. Through intellect, we can curb our desires and feelings—not annihilate them, but guide them in such a way that we can reasonably discern the consequences of our acts. And one way a proper balance of desires and reason is possible is through education in ethical awareness. We can model ourselves after the sage. Proper knowledge especially requires that we conduct our activities in the spirit of genuine sincerity (*ch'eng*), a consistency and unity of purpose. The key virtues of *jen, i, li,* and *chih* can be practiced only with this proper attitude. In these ways, through repeated practice, we can transcend our original natures.

Another way in which we can more practically acquire the balanced exercise of intellect as a guide for our desires is through the exercise of *li,* or propriety. Of all the Confucians, Hsün Tzu singularly elevates the status of *li.* Throughout, he stresses the "influence of teachers and laws, and the guidance of propriety and righteousness . . . and an observance of the well-ordered regulations of conduct."[39] Ranging from formal codes of conduct on special occasions and ceremonies to rules of behavior within various relationships, *li* plays a unique role as a means to moral excellence. Propriety and etiquette are indispensable for a stable society, a stability that would be impossible to achieve if we were left to the whims of our own natures.

Li therefore has two critical functions: It orders and it enhances. First, *li* induces order by restraining the pursuit of our desires. It regulates through prescribed rituals and conduct. *Li* tells us what to do and what not to do. Without these formal boundaries, the self-centered pursuit of our desires would lead to social decay. *Li* acts as a social harness, not intending to eradicate desires but to guide them. As Antonio Cua states:

> All those who maintain that desires must be got rid of before there can be orderly government fail to consider whether the desires can be guided. ... All those who maintain that desires must be lessened before there can be orderly government fail to consider whether desires can be controlled. ... Beings that possess desires and those that do not belong to two different categories—the living and the dead. But the possession or non-possession of desires has nothing to do with good government or bad.[40]

Our enemy does not lie with our desires but arises according to the degree to which we allow them to enslave us. The exercise of *li* allows us to still possess desires, rather than be possessed by them.

Li also works to transform our desires and enhance our lives in socially appropriate ways. Antonio Cua describes this activity of *li* as "ennobling."[41] For instance, refined expressions like painting, poetry, and music are displays of *li*. And meaningful rituals incorporate aesthetic elements that are morally enriching because they uplift and, in a sense, consecrate our natural desires. Our desires are not only channeled into socially acceptable avenues, but are creatively transformed. An example of this can be seen in the elegant performance of music. First of all, the needed discipline in playing music channels our natural desire for pleasure. This is *li*'s ordering function in that it civilizes our desires. Second, music is its own reward in a manner that creatively transports pleasure onto a higher plane. Here, *li* enhances by beautifying our desires. And the moral value attached to this lies precisely in the creative transformation of our natural state through *li*. Through these two functions, *li* enables us to achieve moral excellence by *transcending* our given natures, a claim intensely different from Mencius' belief that living virtuously requires living in *harmony* with our real natures.[42]

SEEKING THE RIGHT BALANCE
IN NEO-CONFUCIANISM

Chu Hsi's Pearl in the Mud

Imagine a pearl lying undiscovered in muddy water, that is until the water is cleared. With this metaphor, Chu Hsi envisions our natures. The principle of Heaven, also called the Supreme Ultimate, *T'ai-chi,* is like this pearl and rests within every one of us. It is our deepest, purest nature. Yet other aspects of our nature have a way of stirring up the water so that we habitually become unaware of our pearl. Here we have a metaphysical vision with profound ethi-

cal import. In fact, Chu Hsi's first concern lies less in a metaphysical recon-
struction of Confucian thought, and more in using it as a basis for moral cultivation. And in doing so, he breathes new life into Confucian ethics.

Nonetheless, let us review his metaphysics, which is clearly a synthesis of
three key notions: *T'ai-chi, li,* and *ch'i. T'ai-chi* is the ultimate principle, the
source as well as summation of all other principles of the universe. It manifests
itself as *li* (not the same as the *li* of propriety) so that all things that exist
contain its *li,* its principle, its essence, that without which it would not be what
it is. However, *li* needs to express itself, and *ch'i* enables it to manifest itself in
material form because *ch'i* is material energy or force.[43] Thus our physical
bodies are derived from material force, *ch'i* (also called Ether), and the human
being (along with all other beings) combines both *li* and *ch'i:*

> The creation of man depends simply upon the union of Principle with the Ether.
> Heavenly Principle (*t'ien li*) is, surely, vast and inexhaustible. Without the Ether,
> nevertheless, even though there be Principle, the latter will have no place to
> which to attach itself. Therefore the two Ethers (the *yin* and *yang*) must interact
> upon one another, condense, and thus create. . . . All men's capacity to speak,
> move, think, and act, is entirely (a product of) the Ether; and yet within this
> (Ether) Principle inheres."[44]

The entire material world as we know it comes about through the synthesis of
ch'i and *li. Ch'i,* material force, is the natural manifestation of *li,* principle. In
turn, *li* is the expression of the Supreme Ultimate, *T'ai-chi.*

What is the ethical significance of all this? To begin with, the Supreme
Ultimate, *T'ai-chi,* embraces the principle of Good. Therefore its ambassador
li is inherently good. Since *li* is naturally good and is our essence, then it follows
that our fundamental nature is good.

Given this, what then is the source of corruption? To start with, *ch'i* is
incomplete and imperfect, as opposed to *li,* which is complete in itself. Fung
Yu-lan gives the example of a circle. While we may be able to contemplate an
image of a perfect circle, once we attempt to actualize our idea and draw a
circle, whatever we draw will always remain imperfect. *Ch'i* carries within itself
its own corruptive elements and is the impediment to *li*'s perfect actualization. These impediments are represented by our feelings and desires, in themselves expressions of our material nature. And feelings and desires are often
a hindrance to our moral cultivation.

However, since *ch'i* is the material actualization of *li,* all things, including feelings, have their principle, their *li.* To illustrate, the feeling of empathy
toward another's suffering assumes the principle of the virtue of compassion,
or *jen.* In other words, *not all feelings obstruct.* Those desires that are selfish,
however, impede moral development. And because of these desires, we muddy
the water so that we find it difficult to recognize our genuine nature.

Can we discover our pearl? And if so, how? Here we uncover the thrust
of Chu Hsi's ethics. Chu Hsi claims that not only can we discover our pearl but,

"It is on this point alone that all one's efforts must be concentrated."[45] As to how, the answer is more involved. Clearing up the water involves two distinct yet interrelated conditions. First, we must instill in ourselves the habit of sincerity and seriousness (*ching*). Next, we must "extend our knowledge" through conscientious investigation and study:

> Man's nature is originally clear, but it is like a pearl immersed in impure water, where its luster cannot be seen. Being removed from the dirty water, however, it becomes lustrous of itself as before. If each person could himself realize that it is human desire that causes this obscuring, this would bring enlightenment (*ming*). It is on this point alone that all one's efforts must be concentrated.
>
> At the same time, however, one should pursue the "investigation of things." Today investigate one thing, and tomorrow investigate another. Then, just as when mobile troops storm a besieged city or capture a fortified spot, human desire will automatically be dissolved away.[46]

As to the first condition, Chu Hsi warns that seriousness, or earnestness, is "the first principle of the Confucian School. From the beginning to the end, it must not be interrupted for a single moment."[47] This means that one must be focused upon one's aim, and not be distracted by desires. Seriousness is the "mind being its own master" so that one's "mind will be tranquil and the Principle of nature will be perfectly clear to him."[48] Chu Hsi continues:

> [Seriousness] is merely to be apprehensive and careful and dare not give free rein to *oneself*. In this way both body and mind will be collected and concentrated as if one is apprehensive of something. If one can always be like this, his dispositions will naturally be changed. Only when one has succeeded in preserving this mind can he engage in study.[49] [italics mine]

The second prerequisite for moral cultivation is to "engage in study." Though this "extension of knowledge" through study was a vital teaching in the classic *Great Learning,* Chu Hsi became its most outstanding advocate. He maintains that study is a necessary condition for moral awareness. The investigation of things, if conducted properly through concentrated, serious effort, will lead to knowledge of the principle (*li*) of those things one studies. Furthermore, understanding the principle of things one studies will inspire an interest in learning the principle of other things. However, all principles are ultimately one in that they are reflections of the Supreme Ultimate. Therefore, through persistent and earnest inquiry, we will eventually discover our own principle, *li,* as well. Chu Hsi's message is clear: Comprehension of the external will eventually produce an awareness of the internal, that is, a liberating awareness of the Supreme Ultimate reality within all things. In this process, the natural virtues of *jen* (love), *i* (righteousness), *chih* (wisdom), and *li* (propriety) will grow.

Here we have an intimate connection between learning and moral cultivation. Genuine investigation does not simply mean being informed. It entails a genuine realization of the principle, *li,* or essence of the object of study. True learning is substantive and not superficial. Most important, the ultimate purpose of learning is ethical—learning must lead to moral cultivation. Chu Hsi instructs us on how to study:

> [T]he cultivation of the essential and the examination of the difference between the Principle of nature (*T'ien-li,* Principle of Heaven) and human selfish desires are things that must not be interrupted for a single movement in the course of our daily activities and movement and rest. If one understands this point clearly, he will naturally not get to the point where he will drift into the popular ways of success and profit and expedient schemes.[50]

Plato, *Republic*

[E]ducation is not what some declare it to be; they say that knowledge is not present in the soul and that they put it in, like putting sight into blind eyes. . . .

Our present argument shows . . . that the capacity to learn and the organ with which to do so are present in every person's soul. It is as if it were not possible to turn the eye from darkness to light without turning the whole body; so one must turn one's whole soul from the world of becoming until it can endure to contemplate reality, and the brightest of realities, which we say is the Good. . . .

Education then is the art of doing this very thing, this turning around, the knowledge of how the soul can most easily and most effectively be turned around; it is not the art of putting the capacity of sight into the soul; the soul possesses that already but it is not turned the right way or looking where it should. This is what education has to deal with.

From G.M.A. Grube, trans., *Plato's Republic* (Indianapolis, IN: Hackett, 1974), p. 171.

Wang Yang-ming's Polished Mirror

Consider a clear, untarnished mirror. It reflects any object placed before it in almost perfect clarity. Objects appear in the mirror just as they appear in reality. In like manner, the clear mind of the sage possesses the clarity of a polished mirror. The mind is clear because the mind *is* principle, or *li.*

Here Wang Yang-ming glaringly challenges Chu Hsi, who affirms a distinction between mind and principle since mind is both utilized to investigate and understand *li* and viewed as an aspect of *ch'i.* In direct opposition, Wang Yang-ming argues for the oneness of mind and *li:*

> The original mind is vacuous [devoid of selfish desires], intelligent, and not beclouded. All principles are contained therein and all events proceed from it. There is no principle outside the mind; there is no event outside the mind.[51]

By the same token, Wang Yang-ming fully agrees with Chu Hsi that *li* is in essence the same as Heavenly Principle. If this is so, since our minds are principle, then they possess an innate, intuitive knowledge of all things and their principles. Thus the metaphor of the mirror:

> The effort of the sage to extend his knowledge is characterized by utter sincerity and unceasingness. His intuitive knowledge is as brilliant as a clear mirror, unflecked by the slightest film.[52]

Elevating mind to this supreme level affects how Wang views the path to moral cultivation. In other words, because the mind *is* principle, and principle is good, we inherently know what is good. Wang astounds Neo-Confucians by arguing that there is no real need to investigate external things in order to discover their principle and eventually our own. Instead, we need to look inward. That is, genuine knowledge is intuitive; it is that "innate knowledge" that is the original state of mind; it is the condition for knowing right from wrong.

Furthermore, this self-examination requires a sincere will. Will plays a critical role: Not only does it motivate intuitive knowledge that in turn enables us to intuitively know what is good, but it also inspires in us the capacity to actualize what is good. Of course, Mencius earlier asserted our innate knowledge of virtue. But Wang takes an enormous leap beyond this by claiming our innate capacity to ACT virtuously. The force of will naturally leads to actualization.

This brings us to one of the most powerfully original ideas in Confucian ethics: *Genuine knowledge and action are identical.* They both form a unity— action completes knowledge, and knowledge automatically entails actions. Wang illustrates this through filial piety, when he states that the principle of filial piety *is* the mind since mind and principle are identical. And since the principle of filial piety is the mind, acting in harmony with that principle comes naturally. We naturally feel a love and respect toward our parents, and vice versa.

Yet, if this is so, why is it that many persons know of the principle of filial piety but do not fulfill it? So asks one of his students in Wang's *Instructions for Practical Life.*[53] Wang replies that self-centeredness has corrupted the "original substance" of this unity of knowledge and action:

> The knowledge and action you refer to are already separated by selfish desires and are no longer knowledge and action in their original substance. There have never been people who know but do not act. Those who are supposed to know but do not act *simply do not yet know.* . . . How can knowledge and action be

separated? This is the original substance of knowledge and action, which have not been separated by selfish desires. In teaching people, the Sage insisted that only this can be called knowledge. Otherwise, this is not yet knowledge. This is serious and practical business.[54] [italics mine]

Our innate knowledge of filial piety is like a polished mirror. Selfish desires have a way of clouding our intuitive knowledge. Wang also likens intuitive knowledge to the sun, and desires to clouds. The seven feelings—joy, grief, anger, fear, hate, love, desire—are distinct from intuitive knowledge but are still natural expressions of mind. These feelings are not in themselves good or evil. Corruption arises when we become attached to these feelings. Once this occurs, these feelings no longer pursue their natural course. This attachment clouds our natural state of mind and intuitive knowledge, just as a film of dust clings to the mirror. What separates the sage from others lies in the degree of attachment to these feelings. The sage does not possess his or her feelings, and his or her mind sustains its clarity, as in a clear mirror.

To grasp this knowledge-action unity perhaps more clearly, consider the perception of beautiful color:

> Seeing beautiful colors appertains to knowledge, while loving beautiful colors appertains to action. However, as soon as one sees that beautiful color, he has already loved it. It is not that he sees it first and then makes up his mind to love it.[55]

When we behold an object as beautiful, we already offer at the same time our response, or action, to that object. Our response accompanies our genuine intuitive knowledge. In the same way, our genuine, intuitive knowledge of the principle of filial piety will spontaneously include our response to that principle.

This is crucial: Genuine moral understanding necessarily entails an active response, and if it is obstructed by self-centeredness, it is not genuine. Wang characterizes moral understanding as a dynamic alternative to a more systematic and abstract approach to ethics. His knowledge-action unity is the result of his own personal reflection and painful experiences, the consequence of "a hundred deaths and a thousand sufferings."[56] And if one word can properly capture his ethics, it is "engagement," steady action that avoids the separation of knowledge and action.

Needless to say, this innovative thesis of the oneness of knowledge and action culled strong reactions. This was especially so after Wang wrote *Doctrines Reached by the Philosopher Chu in Later Life,* in which he claimed that Chu Hsi admitted his earlier errors and changed his views in accordance with those of Liu Hsiang-shan. Here is a selection from Wang's "Pulling Up the Root and Stopping Up the Source," regarded as the culmination of his ethics, along with the philosopher and translator Wing-tsit Chan's introduction.

Wang Yang-ming

INSTRUCTIONS FOR PRACTICAL LIVING

The special importance of the essay lies not only in these teachings themselves but also in their application to society and history. Elsewhere discussions on innate knowledge are by and large inclined to the individual, to the human mind, to what is common to all men, and to ethical problems. Here, however, the emphasis is on its relation to society, to one's talents and ability, to individual differences, and to social and political problems. With innate knowledge as the central theme, Wang vigorously attacks the four tendencies that had dominated the social and political scene for many years, namely, the stress on "hearing and seeing," the habit of "memorization and recitation," "the indulgence in flowery compositions," and the philosophy of "success and profit." He condemns especially the last, for he considers utilitarianism the wicked way of despots, and responsible for China's decline. His analysis of history is of course quite subjective, but there can be no mistake as to where his attention is directed. Wang still looks upon the past as the golden age and is confined to traditional Confucian concepts of value. But his spirit of challenge and his sense of responsibility, together with his powerful, direct, and sincere manner of expression, make the essay an inspiration.

142. If the doctrine of pulling up the root and stopping up the source does not clearly prevail in the world, people who study to become sages will be increasingly numerous and their task increasingly difficult. They will then degenerate into animals and barbarians and still think this degeneration is the way to study to become a sage. Though my doctrine may perhaps temporarily be made clear and prevail, the situation will ultimately be like that in which the cold abates in the west while the ice freezes in the east, and the fog dissipates in front while clouds rise in the rear. Though I keep on talking until I die in distress, I shall at the end not be the least help to the world.

The mind of a sage regards Heaven, Earth, and all things as one body. He looks upon all people of the world, whether inside or outside his family, or whether far or near, but all with blood and breath, as his brothers and children. He wants to secure, preserve, educate, and nourish all of them, so as to fulfill his desire of forming one body with all things. Now the mind of everybody is at first not different from that of the sage. Only because it is obstructed by selfishness and blocked by material desires, what was originally great becomes small and what was originally penetrating becomes obstructed. Everyone has his own selfish view, to the point where some regard their fathers, sons, and brothers as enemies. The Sage worried over this. He therefore extended his humanity which makes him form one body with Heaven, Earth, and all things, to teach the world, so as to enable the people to overcome their selfishness, remove their obstructions, and recover that which is common to the substance of the minds of all men.

The essentials of this teaching are what was successively transmitted by Yao, Shun, and Yü, and what is summed up in the saying, "The human mind is precarious [liable to make mistakes], the moral mind is subtle [follows the moral law]. Have absolute refinement and single-mindedness and hold fast the mean." Its details were given by Emperor Shun to Hsieh, namely, "between father and son there should be affection, between ruler and minister there should be righteousness, between husband and wife there should be attention to their separate functions, between old and young there should be a proper order, and between friends there should be faithfulness, that is all." At the time of Yao, Shun, and the Three Dynasties, teachers taught and students studied only this. At that time people did not have different opinions, nor did families have different practices. Those who practiced the teaching naturally and easily were called sages, and those who practiced it with effort and difficulty were called worthies, but those who violated it were considered degenerate even though they were as intelligent as Tan-chu. People of low station—those in villages and rural districts, farmers, artisans, and merchants—all received this teaching, which was devoted only to the perfection of virtue and conduct. How could this have been the case? Because there was no pursuit after the knowledge of seeing and hearing to confuse them, no memorization and recitation to hinder them, no writing of flowery compositions to indulge in, and no chasing after success and profit. They were taught only to be filially pious to their parents, brotherly to their elders, and faithful to their friends, so as to recover that which is common to the substance of the minds of all men. All this is inherent in our nature and does not depend on the outside. This being the case, who cannot do it?

The task of the school was solely to perfect virtue. However, people differed in capacity. Some excelled in ceremonies and music; others in government and education; and still others in public works and agriculture. Therefore, in accordance with their moral achievement, they were sent to school further to refine their abilities. When their virtue recommended them to government positions, they were enabled to serve in their positions throughout life without change. Those who employed them desired only to be united with them in one mind and one character to bring peace to the people. They considered whether the individual's ability was suitable, and did not regard a high or low position as important or unimportant, or a busy or leisurely job as good or bad. Those who served also desired only to be united with their superiors in one mind and one character to bring peace to the people. If their ability matched their positions, they served throughout life in busy and heavy work without regarding it as toilsome, and felt at ease with lowly work and odd jobs without regarding them as mean. At that time people were harmonious and contented. They regarded one another as belonging to one family. Those with inferior ability were contented with their positions as farmers, artisans, or merchants, all diligent in their various occupations, so as mutually to sustain and support the life of one another without any desire for exalted position or strife for external things. . . . Those with special ability like Kao, K'uei, Chi, and Hsieh, came forward and served with their ability, treating their work as their own family concern, some attending to the provision of clothing and food, some arranging for mutual help, and some providing utensils, planning and working together in order to fulfill their desires of serving their parents above and supporting their wives and children below. Their only concern was that those responsible for certain work might not be diligent in it and become a heavy burden to them. Therefore Chi worked hard in agriculture and did not feel ashamed that he was not a teacher but regarded Hsieh's expert teaching as his own. K'uei took charge of music and was not ashamed that he was not brilliant in ceremonies but regarded Po-i's understanding of ceremonies as his own. For the learning of their mind was pure and clear and had what was requisite to preserve the humanity that makes them and all things form one body. Consequently their spirit ran through and permeated all and their will prevailed and reached everywhere. There was no distinction between the self and the other, or between the self and things. It is like the body of a person. The eyes see, the ears hear, the hands hold, and the feet walk, all fulfilling the function of the body. The eyes are not ashamed of their not being able to hear. When the ears hear something, the eyes will direct their attention to it. The feet are not ashamed that they are not able to grasp. When a hand feels for something, the feet will move forward. For the original material force feels and is present in the entire body, and the blood and veins function smoothly. Therefore in feeling itchy and in breathing, their influence and the speedy response to it possess a mystery that can be understood without words. This is why the doctrine of the Sage is the easiest, the simplest, easy to know and easy to follow. The reason why the learning can easily be achieved and the ability easily perfected is precisely because the fundamentals of the doctrine consist only in recovering that which is common to our original minds, and are not concerned with any specific knowledge or skill.

143. As the Three Dynasties declined, the kingly way was stopped and the techniques of the despot flourished. After the passing of Confucius and Mencius, the doctrine of the Sage became obscure and perverse doctrines ran wild. Teachers no longer taught the doctrine of the Sage and students no longer studied it. Followers of despots stole and appropriated what seemed to be the teaching of ancient kings, and outwardly made a pretense of following it in order inwardly to satisfy their selfish desires. The whole world followed them in fashion. As a result the Way of the Sage was obstructed as though stopped by weeds. People imitated one another and every day searched for theories to acquire national wealth and power, for schemes to destroy and deceive, for plans to attack and invade, and for all sorts of tricks to cheat Heaven and entrap people and to get temporary advantages in order to reap fame or profit. There were numerous such people, like Kuan Chung [d. 645 B.C.], Shang Yang [d. 338 B.C.], Su Ch'in [d. 317 B.C.], and Chang I [d. 309 B.C.]. After a long time, the calamity of war and plundering became infinite. Thus people degenerated to the status of animals and barbarians, and even despotism itself could no longer operate. Confucian scholars of [Han] times were sad and distressed. They searched and collected the literature, documents, laws, and systems of ancient sage-kings and salvaged the remains left from the Burning of the Books and mended them. Their purpose was to restore the way of the ancient kings.

Since Confucian doctrines were discarded and the tradition of the technique of despotism had become strongly entrenched, even the virtuous and wise could not help being influenced by it. The doctrines elucidated and embellished in order to make them clear to the people, make them prevail, and restore them to the world, merely served to fortify the strongholds of despots. As a result, the door of Confucianism was blocked, and it was no longer to be seen. Therefore the learning of textual criticism developed and those perpetuating it were regarded as famous. The practice of memorization and recitation developed and those advocating it were regarded as extensively learned. The writing of flowery compositions developed and those indulging in it were regarded as elegant. Thus with great confusion and tremendous noise they set themselves up and competed with one another, and no one knew how many schools there were. Among tens of thousands of paths and thousands of tracks, none knew which to follow. Students of the world found themselves in a theater where a hundred plays were being presented, as it were. Actors cheered, jeered, hopped, and skipped. They emulated one another in novelty and in ingenuity. They forced smiles to please the audience and competed in appearing beautiful. All this rivalry appeared on all sides. The audience looked to the left and to the right and could not cope with the situation. Their ears and eyes became obscured and dizzy and their spirit dazed and confused. They drifted day and night and remained for a long time in this atmosphere as if they were insane and had lost their minds, and none had the self-realization to return to his family heritage [Confucianism]. Rulers of the time were also fooled and confounded by those doctrines and devoted their whole lives to useless superficialities without knowing what they meant. Occasionally some rulers realized the emptiness, falsehood, fragmentariness, and unnaturalness of their ways, and heroically roused themselves to great effort, which they wished to demonstrate in concrete action. But the most they could do was no more than to achieve national wealth, power, success, and profit, such as those of the Five Despots. Consequently the teachings of the Sage became more and more distant and obscured, while the current of success and profit ran deeper and deeper. Some students turned to Buddhism and Taoism and were deceived by them. But at bottom there was nothing in these systems that could overcome their desire for success and profit. Others sought to reconcile the conflicting doctrines within the Confucian school. But in the final analysis there was nothing in these doctrines that could destroy the view of success and profit. For up to the present time it has been several thousand years since the poison of the doctrine of success and profit has infected the innermost recesses of man's mind and has become his second nature. People have mutually boasted of their knowledge, crushed one another with power, rivaled each other for profit, mutually striven for superiority through skill, and attempted success through fame. . . . When they came forward to serve in the government, those in charge of the treasury wanted also to control the departments of military affairs and justice. Those in charge of ceremonies and music wanted also to have one foot in the important office of civil appointments. Magistrates and prefects aspired to the high office of a regional governor. And censors looked forward to the key position of the prime minister. Of course one could not take a concurrent position unless he could do the work and one could not expect any praise unless theories were advanced to justify the practice. Extensive memorization and recitation merely served to increase their pride, substantial and abundant knowledge merely served to help them do evil, enormous information merely served to help them indulge in argumentation, and wealth in flowery compositions merely served to cover up their artificiality. Thus that which Kao, K'uei, Chi, and Hsieh could not manage on the side young students of today want to justify in doctrine and to master in technique. Using slogans and borrowing labels, they say they want to work together with others to complete the work of the empire. In reality their purpose lies in their belief that unless they do so they cannot satisfy their selfishness and fulfill their desires.

Alas! on top of such affectation and such a motive, they preach such a doctrine! No wonder that when they hear the teachings of our

Sage they look upon them as useless and self-contradictory. It is inevitable that they consider innate knowledge as deficient and the doctrine of the Sage as useless. Alas! how can scholars living in this age still seek the doctrine of the Sage? How can they still discuss it? Is it not toilsome and difficult, is it not rugged and hazardous for scholars living in this age to devote themselves to study? Alas! how lamentable!

Fortunately, the Principle of Nature is inherent in the human mind and can never be destroyed and the intelligence of innate knowledge shines through eternity without variation. Therefore when they hear my doctrine of pulling up the root and stopping up the source, surely some will be pitifully distressed and compassionately pained, and will indignantly rise up, like a stream or a river which cannot be stopped, bursting its banks. To whom shall I look if not to heroic scholars who will rise up without further delay?

From *Instructions for Practical Living and Other Neo-Confucian Writings by Wang Yang-ming,* trans. Wing-tsit Chan. © 1963 Columbia University Press. Reprinted with the permission of the publisher.

A RETURN TO AKO:
JAPANESE NEO-CONFUCIANISM

In one of the most famous scenes in Japanese drama, Yuranosuke [who depicts Kuranosuke], head of the former retainers of Lord Enya [Asano], acts out a series of charades in order to safeguard a deadly secret. He, along with 45 other *ronin,* is plotting the assassination of Lord Moronao [Kira].

Earlier, Lord Moronao's insult to Enya came about in a skirmish, resulting in Enya slightly wounding Moronao. In turn, Enya was officially punished when he was required to commit *seppuku,* while his properties were confiscated and his retainers dispersed. Meanwhile, Moronao himself was not punished.

Now, Yuranosuke, pretending that he has succumbed to decadence by enjoying the company of prostitutes at the Ichiriki Teahouse, hides his real mission from other loyal samurai who come to meet him. He does this to trick a dangerous visitor, Kudayū, another former retainer of Enya whom Yuranosuke knows is in reality his enemy's spy. Kudayū has committed the supreme and unpardonable offense for a samurai: He has betrayed his lord. At the end of the scene, while Yuranosuke "privately" reads a personal letter from Lady Kaoyo, Kudayū lies hiding under the porch listening for the contents of the letter. In a split second, Yuranosuke unsheathes his sword and drives it through the porch and into Kudayū. The act closes with Yuranosuke instructing Heiemon, a low-ranking samurai, to hide Kudayū's body: "Heiemon—this customer has had too much to drink. Give him some watery gruel for his stomach in the Kamo River."[57]

This scene is from *Chūshingura*, subtitled *The Treasury of Loyal Retainers*, a classic in Japanese literature. It is a dramatic memorial of the famous Akō affair, better known as "The Tale of the Forty-Six *Ronin*."[58] Its protagonist is Yuranosuke, the leader of the *ronin;* and the play centers on the virtues of loyalty, duty, and righteousness. These virtues buttress the code of the warrior, Bushido, a code of honor that, since its inception during the Tokugawa period, continues to have a far-reaching effect upon Japanese values.

CHŪSHINGURA, ACT SEVEN

NARRATOR: If you would dally among flowers you will find in Gion a full range of colors. East, south, north, and west, with a glitter as bright as if Amida's Pure Land has been gilded anew, Gion sparkles with courtesans and geishas, so lovely as to steal away the senses of even the most jaded man, and leave him a raving fool.

KUDAYŪ: Is anybody here? Where's the master? Master!

MASTER: Rush, rush, rush! Who's there? Whom have I the pleasure of serving? Why, it's Master Ono Kudayū! How formal of you to ask to be shown in!

KUDAYŪ: I've brought a gentleman with me who's here for the first time. you seem awfully busy, but have you a room you can show this gentleman?

MASTER: Indeed I have, sir. Tonight that big spender Yuranosuke had the bright idea of gathering together all the best-known women of the Quarter. The downstairs rooms are full, but the detached wing is free.

KUDAYŪ: Full of cobwebs, no doubt.

MASTER: More of your usual sarcasm, sir?

KUDAYŪ: No, I'm just being careful not to get entangled at my age in a whore's cobweb.

MASTER: I'd never have guessed it. I can't accommodate you downstairs, then. I'll prepare an upstairs room.—Servants! Light the lamps and bring saké and tobacco.

NARRATOR: He calls out in a loud voice. Drums and samisens resound from the back rooms.

KUDAYŪ: What do you think, Bannai? Do you hear how Yuranosuke is carrying on?

BANNAI: He seems completely out of his head. Of course, we've had a series of private reports from you, Kudayū, but not even my master Moronao suspected how far gone Yuranosuke was. Moronao told me to come up to the capital and look over the situation. He said I should report anything suspicious. I'd never have believed it if I hadn't seen it with my own eyes. It's worse than I imagined. And what has become of his son, Rikiya?

KUDAYŪ: He comes here once in a while and the two of them have a wild time together. It's incredible that they don't feel any embarrassment in each other's presence. But tonight I've come with a plan for worming out the innermost secrets of Yuranosuke's heart. I'll tell you about it when we're alone. Let's go upstairs.

BANNAI: After you.

KUDAYŪ: Well, then, I'll lead the way.

NARRATOR: (*sings*):
　　　Though in truth your heart
　　　Has no thought for me,
　　　Your lips pretend you are in love,
　　　With great bewitchery—

JŪTARŌ: Yagorō and Kitahachi—this is the teahouse where Yuranosuke amuses himself. It's called Ichiriki. Oh, Heiemon, we'll call you when the time comes. Go wait in the kitchen.

HEIEMON: At your service, sir. Please do what you can for me.

JŪTARŌ: Is anyone there? I want to talk to somebody.

MAID: Yes, sir. Who is it, please?

JŪTARŌ: We've come on business with Yuranosuke. Go in and tell him that Yazama Jūtarō, Senzaki Yagorō, and Takemori Kitahachi are here. Several times we've sent a man to fetch him, but he never seems to leave this place. So the three of us have come to him. There's something we must discuss with him. We ask that he meet us. Be sure and tell him that.

MAID: I'm sorry to tell you, sir, but Yuranosuke has been drinking steadily for the past three days. You won't get much sense out of him, even if you see him. He's not himself.

JŪTARŌ: That may be, but please tell him what I said.

MAID: Yes, sir.

JŪTARŌ: Yagorō, did you hear her?

YAGORŌ: I did, and I'm amazed. At first I thought it was some trick of his to throw the enemy off the track. But he has abandoned himself to his pleasures more than convincingly. I simply don't understand it.

KITAHACHI: It's just as I said. He's not the same man in spirit. Our best plan would be to break in on him—

JŪTARŌ: No, first we'll have a heart-to-heart talk.

YAGORŌ: Very well, we'll wait for him here.

PROSTITUTE (*sings*): Come where my hands clap, hands clap, hands clap.
(*Yuranosuke enters. He is blindfolded.*)

YURANOSUKE: I'll catch you! I'll catch you!

PROSTITUTE: Come on, Yura the blind man! We're waiting!

YURANOSUKE: I'll catch you and make you drink.—Here!—Now I've got you! We'll have some saké! Bring on the saké! (*He grabs Jūtarō, taking him for his partner in blindman's buff.*)

JŪTARŌ: Come to yourself, Yuranosuke. I'm Yazama Jūtarō. What in the world are you doing?

YURANOSUKE: Good heavens! What an awful mistake!

PROSTITUTE: Oh, the kill-joys! Look at them, Sakae. Have you ever seen such sour-looking samurai? Are they all in the same party, do you think?

SAKAE: It certainly looks that way. They all have the same fierce look.

JŪTARŌ: Girls, we've come on business with Mr. Ōboshi. We'd appreciate it if you left the room for a while.

PROSTITUTES: We guessed as much. Yura, we'll be going to the back room. Come join us soon. This way, everybody.

JŪTARŌ: Yuranosuke, you remember me. I'm Yazama Jūtarō.

KITAHACHI: I'm Takemori Kitahachi.

YATARŌ: And I am Senzaki Yatarō. We've come here hoping to have a talk with you. I trust you're awake now?

YURANOSUKE: Thank you all for having come to see me. What have you in mind?

JŪTARŌ: When do we leave for Kamakura?

YURANOSUKE: That's a very important question you've asked me. There's a song in *Yosaku from Tamba** that goes, "When you leave for Edo, oh so far away. . . ." Ha, ha. Forgive me, gentlemen, I'm drunk.

THREE MEN: A man's character stays the same even when he's drunk, they say. If you're not in your right mind, the three of us will sober you up.

HEIEMON: Don't do anything rash, please. I hope you'll forgive me, gentlemen, but I'd like a word with him. Please hold off for a while before you start anything. Master Yuranosuke—I am Teraoka Heiemon. I am very glad to see you're in such good spirits.

YURANOSUKE: Teraoka Heiemon? Who might *you* be? Are you that fleet-footed foot soldier who was sent as a courier to the north?

HEIEMON: The same, sir. It was while I was in the north that I learned our master had commited *seppuku,* and I was dumbfounded. I started off for home, running so fast I all but flew through the air. On the way I was told that his lordship's mansion had been confiscated and his retainers dispersed. You can imagine what a shock that was. I served

---

*A famous play by Chikamatsu Monzaemon. Cf. Keene, trans., *Major Plays of Chikamatsu,* p. 94.

his lordship only as a foot soldier, but I am as much indebted to him as anyone. I went to Kamakura, intending to kill Moronao, our master's enemy. For three months I watched for my chance, disguising myself as a beggar, but our enemy is guarded so strongly I couldn't even get close to him. I felt I had no choice but to disembowel myself, but I thought then of my parents in the country, and I went back home, despondent though I was. But then—surely it was a heaven-sent revelation—I learned about the league you gentlemen have formed. How happy and thankful that made me! I didn't even bother to take my things with me, but went to call on these gentlemen at their lodgings. I begged with all my heart for them to intercede in my behalf. They praised me and called me a brave fellow, and promised to please for me with the chief. So I've come along with them here, encouraged by their assurances. Moronao's mansion—

YURANOSUKE: What's all this? You're not so much light of foot as exceedingly light of tongue. It's quite true that I felt a certain amount of indignation—about as big as a flea's head split by a hatchet—and tried forming a league of forty or fifty men, but what a crazy notion that was! I realized when I thought about it calmly that if we failed in our mission our heads would roll, and if we succeeded we'd have to commit *seppuku* afterwards. Either way, it was certain death. It was like taking expensive medicine, then hanging yourself afterwards because you couldn't pay for the cure. You're a foot soldier with a stipend of three *ryō* and an allowance of three men's rations. Now don't get angry—for you to throw away your life attacking the enemy, in return for a pittance suitable for a beggar priest, would be like putting on a performance of grand *kagura* to express your gratitude for some green *nori.*† My stipend was 1,500 *koku.*‡ Compared to you, I might take enemy heads by the bushel and still not do my share. And that's why I gave up the idea. Do you follow me? At any rate, this uncertain world (*sings*) is just that sort of place. *Tsuten Tsutsuten Tsutsuten.*§ Oh, when I hear the samisens playing like that I can't resist.

HEIEMON: I can't believe that is you speaking, Yuranosuke. Each man has only one life in this world, whether he's a wretch like myself with a bare income of three rations, or a rich man like you with 1,500

---

†*Kagura* is the sacred music and dance performed at Shinto shrines; by "grand *kagura*" is meant the especially exalted variety of the Great Shrine of Ise. Worshipers normally offered performances in return for blessings received, but a gift of *nori,* a kind of edible seaweed, would certainly not require such an elaborate display of thanks.

‡The stipends of samurai were calculated in *koku,* a measure of rice a little less than five bushels.

§Sounds intended to suggest the music of the samisen.

koku, and there is no high or low in the debt of gratitude we owe our master. But there's no disputing family lineage. I know it's presumptuous and rude for a miserable creature like myself to beg to join distinguished gentlemen who could have stood as deputies for our master. It's like a monkey imitating a man. But I want to go with you, even if it is only to carry your shoes or shoulder your baggage. Please take me with you. Sir, please listen to me, sir.—Oh, he seems to have fallen asleep.

KITAHACHI: Come, Heiemon. There's no point in wasting any more breath on him. Yuranosuke is as good as dead. Well, Yazama and Sensaki, have you see his true character? Shall we act as we agreed?

YAGORŌ: By all means, as a warning to the others in our league. Are you ready?

NARRATOR: They close in on Yuranosuke, but a cry from Heiemon stops them. With calming gestures he comes up beside them.

HEIEMON: It seems to me, as I turn things over in my mind, Yuranosuke has undergone many hardships in his efforts to avenge our master, ever since they were parted by death. He has had to worry, like a hunted man, over every noise and footfall, and stifle his resentment at people's abuse. He couldn't have survived this long if he hadn't taken so heavily to drink. Wait till he's sober before you deal with him.

NARRATOR: Forcibly restraining them, he leads them into the next room. Their shadows on the other side of the sliding door, cast by a light that illuminates the distinction between good and evil,* are blotted out as the moon sinks behind mountains.

Rikiya, Yuranosuke's son, having run the whole *ri* and a half from Yamashina, arrives breathless. He peeps inside and sees his father lying asleep. Afraid that people may hear, he goes up to his father's pillow and rattles his sword in its scabbard, instead of a horse's bit.¶ At the clink of the hilt Yuranosuke suddenly rises.

YURANOSUKE: Is that you, Rikiya? Has something urgent come up? Is that why you rattled the scabbard? Keep your voice low.

RIKIYA: An express courier just brought a secret letter from Lady Kaoyo [Enya's widow].

YURANOSUKE: Was there no verbal message besides?

RIKIYA: Our enemy Kō no Moronao's petition to return to his province has been granted and he will shortly start for home. Her ladyship said the details would be found in her letter.

---

*An obscure passage, perhaps intended to suggest that the light distinguishes these good men from the evil Kudayū, who is lurking in the next room. The phrase "moon sinks behind mountains" is used also to modify the place-name Yamashina in the next line.

¶Samurai dozing on horseback were said to awaken to the sound of the horse's bit.

YURANOSUKE: Very good. You return home and send a palanquin for me tonight. Be off now.

NARRATOR: Without a flicker of hesitation Rikiya sets off for Yamashina. Yuranosuke, worried about the contents of the letter, is about to cut the seal when a voice calls.

KUDAYŪ: Master Ōboshi! Master Yuranosuke! It's me, Ono Kudayū. I'd like a word with you.

YURANOSUKE: Well! I haven't seen you in a long time. How wrinkled you've become in the year since we last met. Have you come to this house to unfurrow those wrinkles? What an old lecher you are!

KUDAYŪ: Yura—they say little faults are overlooked in a great achievement. The fast life you've led here in the gay quarters, in defiance of people's criticism, will pave the foundation for your achievements. I consider you a hero, a man of great promise.

YURANOSUKE: Ha, ha. What a hard line you take! You've set up a perfect battery of catapults against me. But let's talk about something else.

KUDAYŪ: There's no point in pretending, Yuranosuke. Your dissipation is, in fact—

YURANOSUKE: You think it's a trick to enable me to attack the enemy?

KUDAYŪ: Of course I do.

YURANOSUKE: How you flatter me! I thought you'd laugh at me as a fool, a madman—over forty and still a slave to physical pleasure. But you tell me it's all a scheme to attack the enemy! Thank you, good Kudayū. You've made me happy.

KUDAYŪ: Then you have no intention of avenging our master Enya?

YURANOSUKE: Not in the least. I know that when we were about to turn over the house and the domain I said I would die fighting in the castle, but that was only to please her ladyship. I remember how you stalked out of the room at the time, saying that resistance would make us enemies of the shogun. But we continued our debate in deadly earnest. What idiots we were! In any case, our discussion got nowhere. We said we'd commit *seppuku* before his lordship's tomb, but one after another we stole out the back gate. I have you to thank for being able to enjoy these pleasures here, and I haven't forgotten our old friendship. Don't act so stiff! Relax with me.

KUDAYŪ: Yes, I see now, when I think back on the old days, that I used to be quite a fraud myself. Shall I show you my true nature and have a drink with you? How about it, Yuranosuke? The first cup we've shared in a long time.

YURANOSUKE: Are you going to ask for the cup back, as at a formal banquet?

KUDAYŪ: Pour the liquor and I'll drink.

YURANOSUKE: Drink up and I'll pour.

KUDAYŪ: Have a full cup. Here, I'll give you something to eat with it.

NARRATOR: He picks up in his chopsticks a piece of octopus that happens to be near him and holds it out to Yuranosuke.

YURANOSUKE: Putting out my hand, I accept an octopus foot. Thank you!

KUDAYŪ: Yuranosuke—tomorrow is the anniversary of the death of our master, Enya Hangan. The night before the anniversary is supposed to be especially important. Are you going to eat that octopus and think nothing of it?

YURANOSUKE: Of course I'll eat it. Or have you had word that Lord Enya has turned into an octopus? What foolish ideas you get into your head! You and I are *rōnin* now, thanks to Lord Hangan's recklessness. That's why I hold a grudge against him. I haven't the faintest intention of becoming a vegetarian for his sake, and I'm delighted to sample the fish you've so kindly provided.

NARRATOR: With the greatest aplomb he gulps down the fish in a single mouthful, a sight that stuns even the crafty Kudayū into silence.

YURANOSUKE: This fish is no good for drinking. We'll get them to wring a chicken's neck and give us chicken in the pot. Let's go to the back room. Come along, girls, and sing for us.

KUDAYŪ (*sings*):
> On uncertain legs he staggers off
> To the lively beat of the samisens
> *Tere tsuku teretsuku tsutsuten tsutsuten . . .*

YURANOSUKE (*to jesters*): Hey, you small fry! Do you expect to be let off without getting soused?

NARRATOR: Amid all the bustle he goes within. Sagisaka Bannai, who has been observing everything from beginning to end, comes down from the second floor.

BANNAI: I've kept close watch on him, Kudayū, and I can't believe a man so rotten at the core he'd even eat animal food on the anniversary of his master's death will ever attack his enemy. I intend to report this to my master Moronao, and to recommend that he relax his precautions and open his gates.

KUDAYŪ: You're right. Lord Moronao need not take such precautions any more.

BANNAI: Look here—he's forgotten his sword!

KUDAYŪ: Yes, that really proves what a nitwit he's become. Let's examine this symbol of his samurai spirit. Why, it's rusty as a red sardine!

BANNAI: Ha, ha, ha!

KUDAYŪ: This certainly shows us his true nature. your master can set his mind at rest. (*Calls.*) Where are my servants? I'm leaving. Bring my palanquin!

NARRATOR: With a shout they bring it forth.

KUDAYŪ: Now, Bannai, please get in.

BANNAI: No, sir, you're older than I. After you, please.

KUDAYŪ: In that case, by your leave.

NARRATOR: He gets in.

BANNAI: By the way, Kudayū, I hear that Kampei's wife is working in this place. Have you run into her here?

NARRATOR: Surprised not to receive a reply, he lifts the bamboo blinds of the palanquin and sees inside a fair-sized stone.

BANNAI: Good heavens! Kudayū has turned into a stone, like Lady Sayo of Matsuura!*

NARRATOR: He looks around him. A voice calls from under the veranda.

KUDAYŪ: Here I am, Bannai. I've played a trick and slipped out of the palanquin. I'm worried about the letter Rikiya brought a while ago. I'll watch what happens and let you know later on. Follow along beside the palanquin. Act as if we were leaving together.

BANNAI: I will.

NARRATOR: He nods in agreement and slowly walks beside the palanquin, pretending someone is inside.

Meanwhile, Kampei's wife Okaru is recovering in her upstairs room from intoxication; familiar now with the Quarter, she lets the blowing breezes dispel her sadness.

YURANOSUKE (*to women in back room*): I'll be back in a moment. Yuranosuke's supposed to be a samurai, but he's forgotten his precious sword. I'll go and fetch it. In the meantime, straighten the kakemono and put some charcoal on the stove.—Oh, I must be careful not to step on that samisen and break it. Well, that's a surprise! It looks as if Kudayū's gone. (*Sings.*)

He hears a tearful voice that cries,
"Father! Mother!" and to his surprise,
The words came from a parrot's beak:
His wife had taught the bird to speak!

NARRATOR: Yuranosuke looks around the room; then, standing under the light of a lantern hanging from the eaves, he reads the long letter from Lady Kaoyo describing in detail the enemy's situation. The letter is in woman's language, full of polite phrases, and not easy to follow.

---

*A famous legend, found as early as the *Manyōshū*, tells of this lady who waved her scarf at the ship carrying her husband to Korea. She waved so long she finally turned to stone. The name Matsuura is sometimes also read Matsura.

Okaru, envious of other people happily in love, tries to read the letter from upstairs, but it is dark and the letter far away and the writing indistinct. It occurs to her that by holding out her mirror to reflect the writing she can read the message. Under the veranda, by the light of the moon, Kudayū reads the letter as it unrolls and hangs, but Yuranosuke, being no god, is unaware of this. Okaru's hair ornament suddenly comes loose and falls. Yuranosuke looks up at the sound and hides the letter behind him. Kudayū, under the veranda, is still in smiles; Okaru in the upstairs room hides her mirror.

OKARU: Is that you, Yura?

YURANOSUKE: Oh, it's you, Okaru. What are you doing there?

OKARU: You got me completely drunk. It was so painful I've been cooling myself in the breeze, trying to sober up.

YURANOSUKE: You're lucky to have such a good breeze. But Okaru, there's a little matter I'd like to discuss with you. I can't talk from here, across the rooftops, like the two stars across the Milky Way— won't you come down here for a moment?

OKARU: Is this matter you'd like to discuss some favor you want to ask me?

YURANOSUKE: Yes, something like that.

OKARU: I'll go around and come down.

YURANOSUKE: No, if you go by the staircase some maid is sure to catch you and make you drink.

OKARU: What shall I do, then?

YURANOSUKE: Look—luckily there's a nine-runged ladder lying here. You can use it to come down.

NARRATOR: He leans the ladder against the eaves of the lower floor.

OKARU: What a funny ladder! Oh, I'm afraid! It feels dangerous somehow.

YURANOSUKE: Don't worry. You're way past the age for feeling afraid or in danger. You could come down three rungs at a time and still not open any new wounds.

OKARU: Don't be silly. I'm afraid. It feels like I'm on a boat.

YURANOSUKE: Of course it does. I can see your little boat god from here.

OKARU: Ohh—you mustn't peep!

YURANOSUKE: I'm admiring the autumn moon over Lake T'ung-t'ing.

OKARU: I won't come down if you're going to act that way.

YURANOSUKE: If you won't come down, I'll knock you up.

OKARU: There you go again with your awful language.

YURANOSUKE: You make such a fuss anybody would think you were a virgin. I'll take you from behind.

NARRATOR: He catches her in his arms from behind and sets her on the ground.

YURANOSUKE: Tell me, did you see anything?

OKARU: No, no, I didn't.

YURANOSUKE: I'm sure you did.

OKARU: It looked like a letter from a girl friend.

YURANOSUKE: Did you read the whole thing from up there?

OKARU: Why are you grilling me so?

YURANOSUKE: It's a matter of life and death.

OKARU: What in the world are you talking about?

YURANOSUKE: I mean—I know it's an old story, Okaru, but I've fallen for you. Will you be my wife?

OKARU: Now stop it! You're lying to me.

YURANOSUKE: The truth may have started as a lie, but if I didn't really mean it, I couldn't go through with it. Say yes, please.

OKARU: No, I won't.

YURANOSUKE: But why?

OKARU: Because what you say is not truth that started as a lie, but a lie that started as truth.

YURANOSUKE: Okaru, I'll redeem your contract.

OKARU: Will you?

YURANOSUKE: I'll prove to you I'm not lying. I'll buy out your contract tonight.

OKARU: No, I have a—

YURANOSUKE: If you have a lover, you can live with him.

OKARU: Do you really mean it?

YURANOSUKE: I swear, by the providence that made me a samurai. As long as I can keep you for three days, you are at liberty to do what you please afterwards.

OKARU: I'm sure you just want me to say how happy I am before you laugh at me.

YURANOSUKE: Absolutely not. I'll give the master the money at once and settle things here and now. You wait here and don't worry about anything.

OKARU: Then I'll wait for you. I promise.

YURANOSUKE: Don't move from the spot until I get back from paying the money. You're my wife now.

OKARU: And for just three days.

YURANOSUKE: Yes, I've agreed.

OKARU: I'm most grateful.

NARRATOR (*sings*):
> If ever woman was born
> Unlucky, I'm the one.
> How many pangs I've suffered
> For the man I love, alas.
> I cry alone with muffled notes
> Like a plover of the night.

Okaru, hearing this song from the back room, is sunk in thought as she feels how closely its words fit herself. At that moment Heiemon suddenly appears.

HEIEMON: Okaru—is that you?

OKARU: Heiemon! How shaming to meet you here!

NARRATOR: She hides her face.

HEIEMON: There's nothing to feel ashamed about. I stopped to see Mother on my way back from the East and she told me everything. It was noble of you to have sold yourself for your husband and our master. I'm proud of you.

OKARU: I am happy if you can think so kindly of me. But I have good news for you. Tonight, most unexpectedly, my contract is to be redeemed.

HEIEMON: No news could please me more. Whom have we to thank for this?

OKARU: Someone you know, Ōboshi Yuranosuke.

HEIEMON: What did you say? You contract is to be redeemed by Ōboshi Yuranosuke? Have you been intimate with him for a long time?

OKARU: How could I have been? I've occasionally, perhaps two or three times, drunk with him. He said that if I had a husband I could stay with him, and if I wanted to be free he would let me go. It's almost too good to be true.

HEIEMON: You mean, he doesn't know you're married to Hayano Kampei?

OKARU: No, he doesn't. How could I tell him, when my being here is a disgrace to my parents and my husband?

HEIEMON: It would seem, then, he's a libertine at heart. Obviously he has no intention of avenging our master.

OKARU: No, that's not so. He has, I know it. I can't say it aloud, but I'll whisper it. (*Whispers.*)

HEIEMON: Then you definitely saw what the letter said?

OKARU: I read every word. Then we happened to look each other in the face and he began to flirt with me. Finally he talked about redeeming me.

HEIEMON: This was after you read the whole letter?

OKARU: Yes.

HEIEMON: I understand everything, then. My sister, you're doomed. You can't escape. Let me take your life.

NARRATOR: He draws his sword and slashes at her, but she jumps nimbly aside.

OKARU: What is it, Heiemon? What have I done wrong? You're not free to kill me as you please. I have my husband Kampei and both my parents too. I've been looking forward so much to seeing my parents and my husband as soon as my contract is redeemed. Whatever my offense may be, I apologize. Please forgive me, pardon me.

NARRATOR: She clasps her hands in supplication. Heiemon flings down his naked sword and gives way to bitter tears.

HEIEMON: My poor dear sister. I see you know nothing of what happened. Our father, Yoichibei, was stabbed to death by a stranger on the night of the twenty-ninth of the sixth month.

OKARU: It's not possible!

HEIEMON: You haven't heard the worst. You say you want to join Kampei as soon as you're redeemed. But he committed *seppuku* and is dead.

OKARU: Oh, no! Is it true? Tell me!

NARRATOR: She clutches him and, with a cry, collapses in tears.

HEIEMON: I understand. No wonder you cry. But it would make too long a story to tell you everything. I feel sorriest for Mother. Every time she mentions what happened she weeps, every time she remembers she weeps again. She begged me not to tell you, saying you'd cry yourself to death if you knew. I made up my mind not to tell you, but you can't escape death now. Yuranosuke is singlemindedly, fanatically motivated by loyalty. He'd have had no reason to ransom you if he didn't know you were Kampei's wife. Certainly it wasn't because he's infatuated with you. The letter you saw was of the greatest importance. He will redeem your contract only to kill you. I'm sure that's what he has in mind. Even if you tell no one about the letter, the walls have ears, and any word of the plan leaking from somebody else is sure to be blamed on you. You were wrong to have peeped into a secret letter, and you must be killed for it. Rather than let you die at a stranger's hands, I will kill you with my own hands. I can't allow any woman with knowledge of the great secret to escape, even if she's my own sister. On the strength of having killed a person dangerous to our plot I shall ask to join the league and go with the others. The sad thing about being of the lower ranks is that unless you prove to the other samurai your spirit is better than theirs, they won't let you join them. Show you understand by giving me your life. Die for my sake, sister.

NARRATOR: Okaru sobs again and again as she listens to her brother's carefully reasoned words.

OKARU: I kept thinking all the while that the reason why he didn't write me was that he'd used the money I raised as the price of my body and started on his journey. I was resentful because he hadn't even come to say good-by. It's a dreadful thing for me to say, but though

Father met a horrible death he was, after all, an old man. But how sad and humiliating it must have been for Kampei to die when he was hardly thirty! I'm sure he must have wanted to see me. Why didn't anyone take me to him? What a terrible fate never even to have abstained from animal food in mourning for my husband and father. What reason have I to go on living? But if I died at your hands I'm sure Mother would hate you for it. I'll kill myself. After I'm dead, if my head or my body can bring you credit, please use it for that purpose. Now I must say farewell to you, my brother.

NARRATOR: She takes up the sword.

YURANOSUKE: Stop! Wait a moment!

NARRATOR: Yuranosuke restrains her. Heiemon jumps in astonishment. Okaru cries out.

OKARU: Let me go! Let me die!

NARRATOR: Yuranosuke holds her back and she struggles, impatient for death.

YURANOSUKE: You are an admirable brother and sister. All my doubts have been resolved. Heiemon, you may join us on our eastward journey. You, Okaru, must live on so you can offer prayers for the future repose of his soul.

OKARU: I'll pray for him by going with him to the afterworld.

NARRATOR: Yuranosuke holds firmly the sword he has twisted from her grasp.

YURANOSUKE: We admitted your husband Kampei to our league, but he was never able to kill a single enemy. What excuse will he be able to offer our master when he meets him in the afterworld? This may serve as his apology!

NARRATOR: He drives the sword hard between the mats. Underneath the floor Kudayū, his shoulder run through, writhes in agony.

YURANOSUKE: Drag him out!

NARRATOR: Even before the command leaves Yuranosuke's mouth, Heiemon leaps from the veranda and resolutely drags out Kudayū, dripping with blood.

HEIEMON: Kudayū! It serves you right!

NARRATOR: He hauls him up and throws him before Yuranosuke, who grabs Kudayū by the topknot, not letting him rise, and pulls him over.

YURANOSUKE: The worm that feeds on the lion's body—that's you! You received a large stipend from our master and benefited by innumerable other kindnesses, and yet you became a spy for his enemy Moronao and secretly informed him of everything, true and false alike. The forty and more of us have left our parents and separated from our children, and have even forced our wives, who should have been our lifelong companions, to work as prostitutes, all out of the desire to avenge our late master. As soon as we wake up in the morning, then all through the day, we think about how he committed *seppuku,* and the remembrances arouse tears of impotent rage. We have racked ourselves with pain, mind and body. Tonight especially, the night before our master's anniversary, I spoke vile words of every sort, but in my heart I was practicing the most profound abstention. How dared you thrust fish before my face? What anguish I felt in my heart, not being able to accept or refuse. And how do you think I felt on the night before the anniversary of a master whose family my family has served for three generations, when the fish passed my throat? My whole body seemed to crumble to pieces all at once, and my bones felt as though they were breaking. Ahh—you fiend, you diabolical monster!

NARRATOR: He rubs and twists Kudayū's body into the ground, then breaks into tears of despair.

YURANOSUKE: Heiemon, I forgot my rusty sword a while ago. It was a sign I was meant to torture him to death with it. Make him suffer, but don't kill him.

HEIEMON: Yes, sir.

NARRATOR: He unsheathes his sword and at once leaps and pounces on Kudayū, slashing him again and again, though the wounds are superficial. He scores Kudayū's body until no part is left unscathed.

KUDAYŪ: Heiemon, Okaru, please intercede for me!

NARRATOR: He joins his hands in entreaty. What a repulsive sight— Kudayū, who always despised Teraoka as a lowly foot soldier, and refused to favor him with so much as a glance, now prostrates himself humbly.

YURANOSUKE: If we kill him here we'll have trouble explaining it. Pretend he's drunk and take him home.

NARRATOR: He throws his cloak over Kudayū to hide the wounds. Yazama, Senzaki, and Takemori, who have been listening in secret, fling open the sliding doors.

THREE MEN: Yuranosuke, we humbly apologize.

YURANOSUKE: Heiemon—this customer has had too much to drink. Give him some watery gruel for his stomach in the Kamo River.

HEIEMON: Yes, sir.

YURANOSUKE: Go!

From *Chūshingura: The Treasury of Loyal Retainers: A Puppet Play,* trans. Donald Keene. © 1971 Columbia University Press. Reprinted with the permission of the publisher.

Though earlier records such as the *Gunki Monogatori* underscored the importance of loyalty, duty, and honor, these virtues were codified during the Tokugawa period because of the influence of Confucian scholars, known as *jusha*, in particular Nakae Tōju (1608–1648) and Yamaga Sokō.[59]

Nakae highly esteems the virtues of filial piety and loyalty, and he makes a special case for extending filial piety to one's lord. His emphasis neatly fits into the strict class system that existed in the Tokugawa era in Japan. So strict is this class system that Heiemon, in *Chūshingura,* because he is a samurai of lower rank, cannot be admitted into the entourage of the avenging *ronin* even though he displays great loyalty. In any case, loyalty becomes the core principle in the samurai's code of honor:

> The samurai must give single-hearted obedience; forsaking self, he must serve his master, he must be well-versed in his duties, must be faithful to friends, careful of his words, seeking to do right in all things, and in time of danger be prepared to do his lord efficient service.[60]

Influenced by Nakae, Yamaga Sokō elevates all this by codifying the ethics of the samurai (*bushi*) in his Bushido. And although Bushido includes Buddhist as well as Shinto elements, the Confucian influence in Yamaga's construction of the code is profound. For instance, the principal idea in the code is the imperative of duty (*giri* in Japanese), a fundamental Confucian idea that also means "righteousness": "For a samurai, nothing is more important than duty."[61] Duty to one's lord is not only the supreme virtue for samurai, but it also reflects an extension of the Confucian principle of filial piety. In addition, as part of their training along with the martial arts, samurai are required to study the classic Confucian works, especially those of Confucius and Mencius. Therefore, it was of the utmost importance for samurai to practice the Confucian virtues of benevolence, propriety, righteousness, wisdom, and uprightness.

Despite the display of duty and absolute loyalty by Yuranosuke and his *ronin,* all of whom proved their filiality to their lord by vindicating his unjust death and by their final act of self-sacrifice, for centuries after the incident scholars have continued to debate the *ronin*'s degree of moral culpability. From a legal standpoint, it was a clear-cut case. On a number of counts, the *ronin* had violated the law. First, they conspired in private to assassinate Kira. Thus Yuranosuke maintains his ruse in order to prevent their secret from being discovered. Moreover, such clandestine gatherings were illegal. In matters of private disputes, the parties in the dispute were required to petition an official resolution, and any other outsiders were absolutely forbidden to participate in the matter. This explains further why Yuranosuke puts up a front, not wanting to involve well-intending outsiders, since this would place them in danger through guilt by association. Next, Yuranosuke and all the other *ronin* were determined to commit suicide as a group (known as *junshi*) if their plot did not succeed. Since the establishment of the Tokugawa rule, such acts were discouraged and considered illegal.[62] Finally, the assassination itself was obviously an affront to the law.

Nonetheless, *jusha* (Confucian scholars) were requested to provide their counsel, and there was clearly no consensus about the ethics of the *ronin*'s act. Muro Kyūsō of the Chu Hsi school showered praise upon the *ronin* in his *Akō gijin roku*. He claimed they displayed the Bushido virtue of righteousness at a time when traditional Confucian values were diminishing because of an increasing interest in commercial and material profit rather than in traditional virtues. Hayashi Nobuatsu, leader of the official Confucian university at the time, and another follower of the Chu Hsi school, publicly praised the *ronin* in his eulogy for them. He cited instances in Chinese history of comparable loyalty and righteousness. In his official report, however, Hayashi pointed out the distinction between acting out of personal motives, even though they may be righteous, and acting in a way that weakens the law and the state.

This viewpoint approaches the position of Ogyu Sorai, the renowned *jusha* who represented the Kogaku, a school criticizing Chu Hsi and urging a return to the original classical teachings of Confucius and Mencius. For Sorai, the vendetta of the *ronin* was a righteous act in view of their loyalty, filial piety, and the Confucian teaching that "no man could live under the same heaven as his father's murderer."[63] However, he considered their righteous act a strictly private affair:

> Although that act was righteous since it was in accordance with the way of making oneself pure, it was in the last analysis an act based on private and selfish considerations, because it was a matter that was limited to that faction. . . . If we let public considerations be hurt by private considerations, it will later be impossible to set up laws for the world.[64]

Through all of this, Confucian scholars attempt to resolve an obvious tension between Bushido principles, which Confucian virtues both support and reinforce, and the Bakufu law. At the same time, what is of vital importance is that Sorai appeals further to Confucian teachings in his assessment. Namely he cites the precept that collective harmony and public well-being override individual, personal interests.[65] The samurai may have been righteous in their vendetta, and they have certainly demonstrated the virtues of loyalty and filial piety, and for this reason, they should be allowed to die honorably as samurai. Nevertheless, they must not be acquitted. Their execution sends a signal that public welfare remains the uppermost concern in Confucian teachings.

In this historic case, we see the deep influence that Confucian teachings have had upon Japanese values. To this day, the story of the 46 *ronin* continues to capture the Japanese imagination as it is repeated, embellished, and memorialized with each new generation.

The 46 *ronin* deliver the head of Lord Moronao to the grave of their master, Enya, at Sengakuji Temple. (The Spencer Museum, Scene XI from *Chūshingura*)

CAPITALISM AND HUMAN RIGHTS

Confucianism and Capitalism

An intriguing recent issue concerns the incredible surge in economic growth in China and in other countries whose populations continue to practice Confucianism. For instance, the economic "miracles" of free-market enterprise wrought by Hong Kong, Singapore, Taiwan, and South Korea seem to be solid evidence of capitalism's firm hold in these countries despite more recent signs of recession. How can these developments be explained in view of their strong Confucian tradition?

First of all, keep in mind that Hong Kong, Singapore, and Taiwan were among the first of the Confucian societies to be placed under foreign control, in this case that of Britain and the United States. Contact with these Western powers led to the assimilation of various types of capitalist development. Indeed, as a result of such economic and cultural interchange, much of Asia is presently under at least the modest spell of capitalism. Japan and South Korea, especially, have developed strong capitalist economies. Aside from western influences, are there any other factors that play a role in these developments? Where does Confucianism enter in?

Francis Fukuyama, an analyst for the RAND corporation, gives us an

insightful analysis of this phenomenon.[66] He asserts that the economic growth
in Confucian societies can be better understood by considering certain cultural
traits that have been sustained through Confucian teachings. Essentially, these
traits have to do with ideas pertaining to the centrality of family and lineage
in Chinese society.

When the Chinese Communists took over the government of China in
1949, they made a concerted effort to weaken the power of the Chinese family.
After all, the family was the leading societal group, and all other social connec-
tions in China, including government were secondary. Communists perceived
the traditional patrilineal family as an obstacle to progress. Perhaps the most
clear-cut example of the Communists' attempt to reduce the role of the family
was their family planning policy, which limited family size to two parents and
just one child.

Nonetheless, the new government underestimated the powerful cornerstone of Confucian teachings and the family persevered as China's vital, core
component of society. And the principle of filial piety (as we have seen, a leading Confucian doctrine) continued to perpetuate the authority of the family
by maintaining habitual deference toward parents. Because of assumed obligations within the family, particularly between sons and fathers, filial piety
strengthened the family's central role.

Moreover, as witnessed throughout Chinese history, this centrality of the
family resulted in families constituting their own independent unit. This familial autonomy included the need for economic self-sufficiency, and, therefore,
matters of business were essentially managed within kinship ties. And this, in
turn, led to economic competition *among families rather than among separate
individuals.* With the influence of Western values, including capitalism, the
competition at times grew intense.

A corollary of this drive toward familial economic self-sufficiency was
that only family members could be entrusted to conduct proper economic
behavior, whereas those outside of the family structure could not be trusted.
Fukuyama points out that this inherent distrust of people outside one's
family is a critical ingredient in understanding the makeup of the Chinese
economy.

To begin with, the Confucian concept of family is intergenerational, with
members of the family of all ages living together. The joint family, in which
families of male descendants live together, was also viewed as ideal. And even
though in reality these arrangements are less practicable and hardly frequent
in contemporary China, the importance given in theory to this ideal type of
"family" has remained.

As a result, the Chinese also value wider circles of kinship called
lineages, "a *corporate* group which celebrates *ritual unity* and is based on
demonstrated descent from a common ancestor."[67] And because of the familial need for economic self-sufficiency, and the perceived competition from
other families, these lineages have developed into enormously critical

economic entities. For these lineages not only extended the area of what constitutes "family," but they also expanded the sphere of kinship and of those who could be trusted.

Fukuyama asserts that these lineages have played a decisive role in recent economic progress. For example, Chinese communities in Singapore and Taiwan were linked through lineage ties to families in mainland China. This produced a mutual exchange of personal capital in the form of both intensive labor and talent:

> Much of the economic development that has taken place in Fujian and Guang-dong [Chinese provinces in the south] in the past decade consists of expatriate Chinese capital ramifying backward into its hinterland along family—and lineage based—networks. This is particularly true of Hong Kong and its New Territories.[68]

In view of all of this, along with China's lingering contact with the West and its acceptance of the idea of free enterprise, the centrality of the Chinese family continued in the face of Communist efforts to displace it. This served to counter the Communist ideology by fostering a particular brand of capitalism in these countries—a capitalism in which intense competition occurs not among individuals, but among family-run enterprises.[69] In any case, prolonged contact with Western powers and the emphasis upon Chinese lineage ties, which have their root in imbedded Confucian teachings regarding family and filial piety, have worked together to sustain a more capitalist orientation.

Confucianism and Human Rights

This chapter would be incomplete without some reference to the ongoing allegations of human rights abuses in China. These cover a broad range of accusations, from hindering free speech to curbing religious expression and oppressing women. In particular, these claims have strained the political and diplomatic ties between China and the United States. How does all this square with Confucian teachings?

One of the most edifying commentaries on this issue is that of the respected scholar of Chinese studies Roger Ames.[70] To begin with, Ames points out that the idea of "human rights" as some universal, abstract principle is quite foreign to the Chinese. As we have seen throughout this chapter, teachings that are central to Confucianism such as *jen, li,* and filial piety make sense within specific concrete contexts. They do not in themselves represent abstract, universal, and formal principles. Confucian moral teachings are socially and culturally bound and find their meaning within empirical, social contexts.

Therefore, not only is "human rights" as an abstraction difficult for the Chinese to grasp, but the idea of "equality" is just as abstract. Confucianism recognizes individual differences, talents, dispositions, and merit. Instead of an abstract principle of equality, it emphasizes a kind of equity that entails a harmonious working together by acknowledging natural differences.

Moreover, this whole matter concerns deep-rooted and fundamental cultural differences and presuppositions between East and West. As Ames puts it:

> [T]he rhetoric of rights which dominates Western political discussion is still very foreign in popular Chinese culture. This Chinese resistance to the notion of human rights is due to factors far more fundamental than bad translation. Rights as defined in the classical Western tradition entail assumptions that are in many ways incompatible with Chinese social considerations.[71]

Let us elaborate. According to Ames, the notion of human rights evolved in Western thought because of an inevitable conflict between the "small familial community" and the "modern nation-state." The idea of individual human rights evolved in order to rectify this conflict, that is, as a protective measure against the more impersonal, state-induced injustices.

This makes sense, especially in societies such as the United States that place enormous weight on cultivating individuality. However, whereas Americans place a high premium upon the awareness and exercise of individual autonomy or self-determination, the Chinese generally make no such assumptions.

Confucian teachings have steadily maintained that there exists a necessary, symbiotic relationship between the individual and the community, with the state as a formal expression of the community. Individual and community exist in a mutually defining, constantly interacting and interweaving relationship. More important, there is no assumption of an adversarial contest between the state and the individual, for such a contest assumes two separate entities—state and individual—whose interests will inevitably be at odds.

As far as the state goes, even Chinese constitutional law does not presume an adversarial relationship:

> Because the constitution is primarily a compact of cooperation formulated on a premise of trust between person and community, rather than a contract between potential adversaries, there are no independent provisions for the formal enforcement of rights claims against the state. The assumption is that order will be effected and guaranteed by informal community pressures that are more immediate to the circumstances and allow greater popular participation.[72]

Thus the ideal is to resolve conflict through peaceful, communal pressures. Resorting to litigation to solve conflict is actually viewed as demeaning and embarrassing, for it signals the failure of the community. Furthermore, this means that within the Confucian context "rights are socially derived *proprieties* rather than individual *properties*."[73]

In light of all this, Ames maintains that the Confucian virtue of *li* is absolutely critical. As we saw earlier, *li* refers to forms of propriety such as ritual action and etiquette, and its constant practice in effect constructs social and cultural patterns. *Li* is the "determinative fabric of Chinese culture and, further, defines the sociopolitical order."[74] Engagement in ritual actions, for example, is a concrete way of sustaining social order and harmony. This is their ultimate purpose. They achieve what Ames calls a "social syntax" in which individualism, as conceived in the West, has no proper place.

The practice of *li* reinforces the Confucian view of "self" as a dynamic network of human interrelationships. In this regard, Mencius, especially, pointed out the dynamic character of each person, each person as a "kind of doing" rather than a static "sort of being."[75] This human "doing" takes place within concentric circles of relationships, with the family at the center. Confucian teachings, therefore, do not at all support an isolated, privatized sense of self.

To conclude, it is the practice of *li* that provides the undercurrent of a moral society and not the abstract notion of human rights. Yet, this is not to deny that the alleged abuses have no foundation in fact. Indeed, although *jen,* or benevolence, is a Confucian virtue, the teaching of *jen* does not guarantee its practice.

What all this means is that whatever abuses may occur, we need to judiciously assess these violations in a balanced perspective and not solely on our own terms. In the same spirit, neither does this preclude us from formulating some type of judgment. But it enables a more fitting judgment, one secured after wearing the lens of the Chinese (and any other culture) in a genuine effort to both understand the Chinese and enrich our vision.

REVIEW QUESTIONS

1. Do you agree with the official verdict to have the 46 *ronin* commit suicide? Whether or not you agree, what are your reasons?

2. Why does Confucius defend the son for not turning in his sheep-stealing father? According to Confucian teachings, how do we balance matters of personal integrity with those of social harmony? And does familial harmony always take precedence over the state?

3. Discuss the Confucian virtues of *jen, li,* and *chih.* How can practicing them lead to a balanced life?

4. Using the Bull Mountain metaphor, according to Mencius, how does our innate goodness manifest itself in filial piety?

5. Contrast Mencius's view of human nature with that of Hsun Tzu.

6. How do Chu Hsi and Wang Yang-ming elaborate further on Mencius's idea of natural goodness? What is the essential difference between Chu Hsi and Wang Yang-ming? Is this a crucial moral difference?

7. Discuss the debate among Japanese Confucians concerning the act of vengeance by the 46 *ronin.*

8. What is one way to explain the rise of capitalism in certain Confucian cultures? Do you think that Confucian teachings are incompatible with capitalism?
9. How can we begin to address the violation of human rights in some Confucian cultures?
10. What are the essential moral lessons we can learn from Confucianism?

NOTES

1. James Legge, trans., Analects IV, 15 in *Confucius: Confucian Analects, The Great Learning, and the Doctrine of the Mean* (Oxford: Clarendon Press, 1893; New York: Dover, 1971), p. 170.
2. He had his own group of loyal followers, similar to the *hsieh,* or knights, but their goal was to prevent and alleviate conflict.
3. This was a strong belief of the religious community founded upon Mo Tzu's teachings and organized after his death.
4. From *Han-fei-tzu,* Chap. 7, cited in Fung Yu-lan, *A History of Chinese Philosophy,* Vol. I (Princeton, NJ: Princeton University Press, 1952), p. 326.
5. Legge, Analects XIII, 18, p. 270.
6. Alluded to by Wing-tsit Chan, "Chinese Theory and Practice, with Special Reference to Humanism," in Charles A. Moore, ed., *The Chinese Mind: Essentials of Chinese Philosophy and Culture* (Honolulu: University of Hawaii Press, East-West Center Press, 1967), p. 28.
7. This translation, though better than others such as "Noble person" or "Great person," still warrants caution since it may evoke a sense of arrogance. For this reason, it may be better to use the Chinese term *chün-tzu.*
8. Arthur Waley, trans., *The Analects of Confucius* (London: George Allen & Unwin, 1938), XV, 8, p. 195.
9. Legge, Analects, IV, 2, p. 165.
10. Ibid., VI, 21, p. 192.
11. Ibid., XII, 2, p. 251.
12. Ibid., XIV, 5, p. 276.
13. Waley, Analects, XVII, 6, p. 210.
14. Legge, Analects, XII, 22, p. 260.
15. Tu Wei-ming in his *Centrality and Commonality: An Essay on Confucian Religiousness,* rev. ed. (Albany: SUNY Press, 1989).
16. Waley, Analects, III, 3, p. 94.
17. Legge, Analects, I, 3, p. 139.
18. Anthony S. Cua, "An Excursion to Confucian Ethics," in *Dimensions of Moral Creativity: Paradigms, Principles, and Ideals* (University Park: Penn State University Press, 1978), p. 59.
19. Legge, Analects, VIII, 8, p. 211.

20. Ibid., XX, 3, p. 354.
21. Waley, Analects, II, 5, pp. 88–89.
22. Fung Yu-lan, *A History of Chinese Philosophy,* Vol. I, p. 67.
23. Ibid.
24. Waley, Analects, XIII, 24, pp. 177–78.
25. Legge, Analects, VIII, 2, 1, p. 208.
26. Ibid., VI, 17, p. 190.
27. From *Mencius* VIa, 6, cited in Fung Yu-lan, *A History of Chinese Philosophy,* Vol. I, p. 121.
28. From *Mencius* VII, A.4., cited in Wing-tsit Chan, "The Story of Chinese Philosophy," in Moore, *The Chinese Mind,* p. 36.
29. From *Mencius,* IVa.5, in Hsieh Yu-wei, "Filial Piety and Chinese Society," in Moore, *The Chinese Mind,* p. 175.
30. Ibid., IVa.27, p. 172.
31. *Hsiao ching (The Book of Filial Piety),* IX, in ibid., p. 171–72.
32. For this reason, bearing male descendants was of the utmost importance.
33. *Mencius,* Ia.7., in Moore, *The Chinese Mind,* p. 173.
34. Cited in Arthur Waley, *Three Ways of Thought in Ancient China,* (London: George Allen & Unwin, 1939) p. 161.
35. Hsun Tzu, "That the Nature Is Evil," in James Legge, trans., *The Chinese Classics,* Vol. II, rev. 2nd ed. (Oxford: The Clarendon Press, 1895), p. 81.
36. Ibid.
37. Fung Yu-lan, *A History of Chinese Philosophy,* Vol. I, p. 287.
38. Hsun Tzu, "That the Nature Is Evil," cited in Michael Brannigan, *The Pulse of Wisdom: The Philosophies of India, China, and Japan* (Belmont, CA: Wadsworth, 1995), p. 296.
39. Ibid., p. 293.
40. Antonio S. Cua, "The Concept of *Li* in Confucian Moral Theory," in Robert E. Allinson, *Understanding the Chinese Mind: The Philosophical Roots* (Hong Kong: Oxford University Press, 1989), p. 217.
41. Ibid., p. 218.
42. See ibid. where Cua offers his "completion thesis" that *li* is the concrete expression and realization of the virtues of *jen* and *i,* p. 223.
43. This is further manifested through the yin-yang confluence and the Five Elements, thus producing matter.
44. Chu Hsi, *Conversations,* 4.10, cited in Fung Yu-lan, *A History of Chinese Philosophy,* Vol. II, p. 551.
45. Ibid., p. 560.
46. Ibid.
47. Chu Hsi, "Moral Cultivation," cited in Brannigan, *The Pulse of Wisdom,* p. 306.
48. Ibid.
49. Ibid.
50. Ibid., pp. 304–305.

51. Wing-tsit Chan, trans., *Instructions for Practical Living and Other Neo-Confucian Writings by Wang Yang-ming* (New York: Columbia University Press, 1963), sec. 32, p. 33.

52. Cited in Fung Yu-lan, *A History of Chinese Philosophy,* Vol. II, p. 618.

53. The *Instructions* are recorded by one of Wang's students, Ts'u Ai.

54. Wing-tsit Chan, *Instructions,* pp. 10–11.

55. Ibid., p. 10. A.S. Cua has provided a rich analysis of Wang's position in his *The Unity of Knowledge and Action: A Study in Wang Yang-ming's Moral Psychology* (Honolulu: University of Hawaii Press, 1982).

56. Cited in Wing-tsit Chan, *Instructions,* p. xxxvi.

57. Donald Keene, trans., *Chūshingura (The Treasury of Loyal Retainers)* (Tokyo: Charles E. Tuttle, 1971), Act VII, p. 124.

58. *Chūshingura* was written in 1748 by Takeda Izumo, Miyoshi Shōraku, and Namiki Senryū. It was originally written as a puppet play (*jōruri*), and later staged for the classic Japanese theater, or *kabuki*. Since then, it has been written, staged, and eventually filmed in various versions. Each December, the month of the vendetta, it is annually performed for *kabuki*. It is also called the "Story of the *47 Ronin*" in other accounts. In fact, the official title of the original play, "Kanadehon Chūshingura," contains the term *kana,* which are *47* characters for Japanese syllables. Tradition tells us that *46* participated in the actual assassination and later committed *seppuku,* while the 47th relayed the news of the vindication to the widow and family of Asano. Upon his willing surrender later to the authorities, however, the 47th *ronin* was acquitted.

59. Nakae Toju, influenced by Wang Yang-ming's teachings, established the Oyomei school (Oyomeigaku), whereas Soko belonged to the Kogaku, and both schools opposed the prevailing Shushigaku, or school of Chu Hsi, which nevertheless reigned as the official philosophical school. In fact, most of the advisors to public officials were *jusha* who represented Chu Hsi's teachings.

60. From Nakae's *Okina mondō (Dialogue with an Old Man),* in Catharina Blomberg, *The Heart of the Warrior: Origins and Religious Background of the Samurai System in Feudal Japan* (Kent, England: Japan Library, 1994), p. 158.

61. Ibid., p. 160.

62. At an earlier time, *junshi* was acceptable as an honorable way to show one's ultimate loyalty to one's lord. Making this illegal allowed greater control by the military government, or Bakufu.

63. Cited in Blomberg, *The Heart of the Warrior,* p. 170.

64. Ibid., p. 172.

65. Sorai's student, Dazai Shundai, places much of the blame on Yamaga Soko for his association with the Asano clan as a teacher of Bushido principles, even though Yamaga was dead at the time of the vendetta and most likely did not have a direct association with any of the *ronin*.

For Dazai, accountability for the crime does not rest with the perpetrators but extends to those responsible for the perpetrators' actions.

66. See the discussion in Francis Fukuyama, *Trust: The Social Virtues and the Creation of Prosperity* (London: Hamish Hamilton, 1995), pp. 69–95.
67. Ibid., p. 91.
68. Ibid., p. 92.
69. Many family-run businesses failed *because* management was kept within the family and quite a number of sons and grandsons lacked the management skills to succeed. This was the lesson gleaned by the undoing of Wang Laboratories in Massachusetts, discussed in ibid., pp. 69f.
70. Roger Ames, "Rites as Rights: The Confucian Alternative," in Leroy S. Rouner, ed., *Human Rights and the World Religions* (Notre Dame, IN: University of Notre Dame Press, 1988), pp. 199–216.
71. Ibid., p. 203.
72. Ibid., p. 210.
73. Ibid.
74. Ibid., p. 199.
75. Ibid., p. 203.